THE ANONYMOUS GOD

THE ANONYMOUS GOD

The Church Confronts Civil Religion and American Society

Edited by
David L. Adams and Ken Schurb

CONCORDIA PUBLISHING HOUSE · SAINT LOUIS

Library of Congress Cataloging-in-Publication Data

The anonymous God : the church confronts civil religion and American society / edited by David L. Adams and Ken Schurb.
     p. cm.
   ISBN 0-7586-0819-5
   1. Civil religion—United States. 2. Christianity and culture—United States. 3. Lutheran Church—Doctrines. 4. Lutheran Church—Missouri Synod—Doctrines. I. Adams, David L., 1955– II. Schurb, Ken.
     BR517.A56 2005
     261'.0973—dc22   200423362

1 2 3 4 5 6 7 8 9 10   13 12 11 10 09 08 07 06 05 04

Contents

Contributors

DAVID L. ADAMS (Ph.D., Old Testament, Cambridge) is associate professor of exegetical theology at Concordia Seminary, St. Louis, Missouri.

RONALD R. FEUERHAHN (Ph.D., Historical Theology, Cambridge) is associate professor of historical theology at Concordia Seminary, St. Louis, Missouri.

DAVID R. LIEFELD (Th.M., Systematic Theology, Westminster Theological Seminary; M.A., History, Temple University) is a Lutheran Church—Missouri Synod clergyman currently on disability retirement.

CAMERON A. MACKENZIE (Ph.D., History, Notre Dame) is professor of historical theology at Concordia Theological Seminary, Ft. Wayne, Indiana.

JOEL P. OKAMOTO (Th.D., Systematic Theology, Concordia Seminary) is assistant professor of systematic theology at Concordia Seminary, St. Louis, Missouri.

ALVIN J. SCHMIDT (Ph.D., Sociology, Nebraska) is professor emeritus of sociology at Illinois College, Jacksonville, Illinois.

KEN SCHURB (Ph.D., History, Ohio State) is pastor of Zion Lutheran Church, Moberly, Missouri.

MARK E. SELL (S.T.M., New Testament Exegesis, Concordia Theological Seminary) is senior editor of Academic, Professional, and Consumer books at Concordia Publishing House.

Abbreviations

AC	Augsburg Confession
Ap.	Apology of the Augsburg Confession
K-W	Kolb, Robert, and Timothy J. Wengert, eds. *The Book of Concord*. Translated by Charles P. Arand et al. Minneapolis: Fortress, 2000.
LW	Luther, Martin. *Luther's Works*. American Edition. General editors Jaroslav Pelikan and Helmut T. Lehmann. 56 vols. St. Louis: Concordia; Philadelphia: Muhlenberg and Fortress, 1955–1986.
Tappert	Tappert, Theodore G., ed. *The Book of Concord*. Philadelphia: Fortress, 1959.
WA	Luther, Martin. *D. Martin Luthers Werke. Kritische Gesamtausgabe. Schriften*. 68 vols. Weimar: Hermann Böhlaus Nachfolger, 1930–1985.
WABr	Luther, Martin. *D. Martin Luthers Werke. Kritische Gesamtausgabe. Briefwechsel*. 18 vols. Hermann Böhlaus Nachfolger, 1930–85.

Introduction

KEN SCHURB

In 1973 Senator Mark Hatfield of Oregon, an outspoken evangelical Christian, perhaps surprised some people with remarks he made at a national prayer breakfast. He said:

> [L]et us beware of the real danger of misplaced allegiance, if not outright idolatry, to the extent we fail to distinguish between the god of an American civil religion and the God who reveals Himself in the Holy Scriptures and in Jesus Christ. If we as leaders appeal to the god of civil religion, our faith is in a small and exclusive deity, a loyal spiritual Advisor to power and prestige, a Defender of only the American nation, the object of a national folk religion devoid of moral content.[1]

Strong words! Senator Hatfield's remarks resulted from a discussion about civil religion—and, implicitly, also about the relationship between the Christian faith and American society—that had reached a significant peak in the years before he spoke.

DISCUSSION OF CIVIL RELIGION

Sociologist Robert Bellah is perhaps best known these days as the chief researcher on the project that resulted in the book *Habits of the Heart*. During the late 1960s and 1970s, however, his claim to fame centered upon a well-known 1967 article in which he observed that alongside the churches there was a significant civil religion in America. "Although matters of personal religious belief, worship, and association are considered to be strictly private affairs," Bellah wrote,

> there are, at the same time, certain common elements of religious orientation that the great majority of Americans share. These have played a crucial role in the development of American institutions and still provide a religious dimension for the whole fabric of American life, including the political sphere. This public religious dimension is expressed in a set of beliefs, symbols, and rituals that I am calling the American civil religion.[2]

Bellah went on to characterize this religion as elaborate and well-institutionalized. He thought it possessed such integrity as to demand of any prospective student the same sort of care required by other religions.

Bellah's article put "civil religion in America" on the map, as it were. By no means was he the first to have written about this phenomenon. In many ways, however, he established parameters within which it would be discussed for years to come, including the popularization of the very term "civil religion." Reminiscing later, Bellah observed that "[i]n 1967 I published an essay I have never been allowed to forget."[3] Many analysts greeted his "discovery" as the unmasking of a profound American cultural phenomenon. Quite a number of them found it quite disturbing. Others took issue with Bellah. They questioned, for example, whether American civil religion really was a differentiated system and to what degree it was truly institutionalized.[4] Similar questions might well be raised today. But what Bellah realized and described that appears undeniable, now as well as then, is the presence of a truly religious dimension in American civil life effectively transcending all of what might be called the traditional religions. Whatever "meaning" is offered by this civil religion, its chief function is to provide the glue that holds the national enterprise together. Bellah's thesis therefore rang true, whatever its flaws. It seemed to most people that he was on to something.

Still others heard Bellah's thesis and yawned. They had no particular quarrel with him. They simply took his article as yet another instance of a tedious academic tendency to state the obvious, only in fancier language. Their reaction points to a problem that commonly arises when civil religion is discussed. It all seems so self-evident once we have heard it. To say anything further can strike us not so much as helpfully elaborating on what is partially ambiguous but rather as haplessly belaboring what is perfectly apparent.

This may be a reason why few pastors in the United States, indeed few Christians here, have taken the time to consider American civil religion, its general impact on American culture, and its particular impact on the ministries of congregations confessing biblical Christianity. When we fail to pay attention, however, we pay a price. In this case, many historic Christian confessions in America have failed to recognize the force that civil religion exerts on our national religious consciousness. It is so close to us, so obvious, that time and again we fail to see it.

The present book aims to help us take notice. We should be devoting attention to American civil religion. Understanding its nature and function is crucial for correctly positioning the church and its proclamation in American society today and into the twenty-first century. That is, a working knowledge of American civil religion, its influence, and the whole subject of the church proclaiming its message in the public arena can help us both to keep the Gospel straight and to get it out.

DEFINITION OF CIVIL RELIGION

If anything, it would be surprising if the United States did *not* have a civil religion. As sociologist Robin Williams wrote half a century ago: "Every functioning society has to an important degree a *common* religion. The possession of a common set of ideas, rituals, and symbols can supply an overarching sense of unity even in a society riddled with conflicts."[5] America is no exception.

Over the course of U. S. history there have been several attempts to identify a common core of *religious* beliefs that lie at the heart of America (to say nothing for the moment about rituals, symbols, or political principles). For example, more than a century ago Josiah Strong wrote:

> The teaching of the three great fundamental doctrines which are common to all monotheistic religions is essential to the perpetuity of free institutions, while the inculcation of sectarian dogmas is not. These three doctrines are that of the existence of God, the immortality of man, and man's accountability. These doctrines are held in common by all Protestants, Catholics, and Jews.[6]

As Strong admitted, he was putting forth least-common-denominator doctrines. How can the church of Jesus Christ relate to a society that takes this listing, or a similar one, to be the "bottom line" set of tenets, the beliefs that are *truly* important? And what happens when the listing changes?

More recently, Ellis West put forth a general definition of civil religion. He writes: "*A civil religion is a set of beliefs and attitudes that explain the meaning and purpose of any given political society in terms of its relationship to a transcendent, spiritual reality, that are held by the people generally of that society, and that are expressed in public rituals, myths, and symbols.*"[7]

Several of the essays below have much more to say about the concept of civil religion and the form it has taken in America. The purpose of this introduction is not to "steal their thunder," so to speak. Yet a portion of one essay is pertinent here. Alvin Schmidt has formulated the definition of American civil religion as:

> the deeply held beliefs that unite Americans regarding their nation's values and practices pertaining to freedom, democracy, equality, progress, opportunity, toleration, and justice, which are portrayed by patriotic symbols in collective gatherings where they are publicly revered and honored as sacred because the values they symbolize are given by God, who is undefined, and who has chosen the United States to play a special, salutary role in human history.

STRATEGY FOR READING THIS BOOK

The present book is about American civil religion and the relationship of the church to the broader society. It contains two essays by David Adams, currently a professor of Old Testament but formerly (from 1996 until 2000) executive director of The Lutheran Church—Missouri Synod's Office of Government Information in Washington, D. C. One of his essays, "The Church in the Public Square in a Pluralistic Society," is largely informed by his experience in the nation's capital. It serves as a sort of "report from the front." It appeared previously, in a somewhat longer form, in the *Concordia Journal*.[8] Those who have never read this essay before would do well to start with it. If such is the case for you, please consider beginning your reading of this book toward the end (as this essay comes almost last in the present collection!) and working forward from there, taking the various essays in reverse order. Readers who require an orientation to Lutheran "two-kingdom" theology might wish to consult the appendix first, and read Mark Sell's essay before anything else.

If you are already familiar with the David Adams essay mentioned above, we advise you to start your reading at the beginning of this book, with his other essay. Originally a conference presentation, "The Anonymous God: American Civil Religion, the Scandal of Particularity, and the First Table of the Torah" contains additional background on the concept of civil religion going back to Jean-Jacques Rousseau.[9] Primarily, though, it expounds the first three commandments and applies them to the current situation shaped by American civil religion.

The next few essays, as they are arranged in this volume from front to back, unfold in more or less chronological order. Like other contributors, David Liefeld points out that the early church had to deal with civil religion, namely, that of Rome. He explains an attempt by the second-century church father Athenagoras to defend Christianity in the civic sphere. Then he discusses subsequent evaluations of Athenagoras's work down through the centuries, from a variety of theological standpoints. In view of the Lutheran distinction between God's two realms of governance, Liefeld concludes that we can draw from Athenagoras a model that is both interesting and potentially helpful today.

The next two contributions take us to the modern era. Cameron MacKenzie summarizes the subject of the church and the public square as it appeared in the writings of The Lutheran Church—Missouri Synod's first president, C. F. W. Walther (1811–1887). Walther had virtually nothing to say about civil religion as such. However, he did devote a great deal of reflection to the basic situation of the church in the United States. His comments are still worth contemplation.

The essay entitled "Historiography of American Civil Religion: The Cases of Martin E. Marty and Sidney E. Mead" fills in a bit of detail about the discussion of civil religion in this country immediately before and after Bellah's 1967 essay appeared. It contrasts two historians, one of whom trained the other. Both of these men not only told the story of societal religion in the United States but also, in his own way, made an impact on American civil religion.

Next, Joel Okamoto examines the religious situation in post-9/11 America. Sociologically, there has been a shift in American spirituality from "dwelling" to "seeking." This shift has had its impact on civil religion, as shown by the reaction to the terrorist attacks in New York City and Washington, D.C. Theologically, "seeking" turns out to be yet another breed of the theology of glory. As such, it must be confronted by the theology of the cross.

Historical theologian Ronald Feuerhahn offers a presentation that is both historical and theological. Historically, he surveys the church's interaction with the government, and government attempts to co-opt the church, from the early church to the reformers and down to America. Thus he summarizes eras treated in greater detail by the other essays. He proceeds to a theological evaluation of religious America in light of influences from the past.

Alvin Schmidt says much about the past in his essay, too, but his work is still more concerned with the present and the future. He points out that over the last 20 to 25 years (after the flurry of writing that followed Bellah's 1967 essay), American civil religion has changed its shape. It has moved from its former deistic posture to one that is more polytheistic. Polytheism, Schmidt notes, brings with it paganism.

ACKNOWLEDGMENTS

As general editors, David Adams and I owe our first word of gratitude to the contributors who have done so much to enrich this book's treatment of American civil religion and the relationship of the church to the broader society. It has been our privilege to help bring their contributions to a wider public.

One contributor must be singled out for special thanks, even though he wrote no essay. The Rev. Leroy E. Vogel, professor emeritus of historical theology and former dean of administration at Concordia Seminary, St. Louis, Missouri, advised us extensively on this project. Based on the expertise he showed for years in the classroom as he taught a seminary course on American civil religion, he gave us sound and welcome advice. He emphasized the way civil religion in effect tries to transcend all other religions while somehow including them, as duly noted above in words shamelessly cribbed by me from one of his e-mail messages. This book, including this introduction, has been improved by his work.

Notes

1. Robert D. Linder and Richard V. Pierard, *Twilight of the Saints: Biblical Christianity and Civil Religion in America* (Downers Grove: Inter-Varsity, 1978), 135.

2. Robert N. Bellah, "Civil Religion in America," reprinted in *American Civil Religion,* ed. Russell E. Richey and Donald G. Jones (New York: Harper & Row, 1974), 24.

3. Robert N. Bellah, "Religion and the Legitimation of the American Republic," in *Varieties of Civil Religion,* ed. Robert N. Bellah and Phillip E. Hammond (New York: Harper & Row, 1980), 3.

4. See John F. Wilson, "An Historian's Approach to Civil Religion," in Richey and Jones, *American Civil Religion,* 115–38. See also Wilson, *Public Religion in American Culture* (Philadelphia: Temple University Press, 1979).

5. Robin Williams, *American Society: A Sociological Interpretation*, 312, quoted in Will Herberg, *Protestant—Catholic—Jew: An Essay in American Religious Sociology* (New York: Doubleday, 1955), 87 (*Williams's emphasis*).

6. Josiah Strong, *Our Country: Its Possible Future and Its Present Crisis* (New York: Baker & Taylor, 1891), quoted in Sidney E. Mead, "The Post-Protestant Concept and America's Two Religions," in *The Nation with the Soul of a Church* (New York: Harper & Row, 1975), 24.

7. Ellis West, "A Proposed Neutral Definition of Civil Religion," *Journal of Church and State* 22 (Winter 1980): 39 (*West's emphasis*).

8. David L. Adams, "The Church in the Public Square in a Pluralistic Society," *Concordia Journal* (October 2002): 364–90.

9. Some of the above material on the discussion of civil religion was suggested by the original form of this essay.

1

The Anonymous God

American Civil Religion, the Scandal of Particularity, and the First Table of the Torah

DAVID L. ADAMS[1]

Introduction

The god of American civil religion has no name. This has not always been the case, and it may be that there will come a time in the future when it is not the case again. But for the present and for the foreseeable future, the god of American civil religion remains anonymous. In this essay we will examine the background for the anonymous god in American civil religion. We will also consider the challenges that the worship of this anonymous god presents for biblical Christianity in the light of the scandal of particularity and the First Table of the Torah (i.e., the First, Second, and Third Commandments).

THE ANONYMOUS GOD
IN AMERICAN CIVIL RELIGION

Even if the academic study of American civil religion may be said to begin with Robert Bellah in the 1960s,[2] civil religion itself surely did not. Indeed, if the sociologist Emile Durkheim is to be believed, every community, every definable group of people, has a religious dimension. Before him, the French political philosopher Jean-Jacques Rousseau (1712–1778) declared that at the head of every political society there stands a god. From Plato onward, political philosophers have recognized the importance of religion as a factor in national—today we might say cultural—formation. The reason for such observations is clear: Human communities are assemblies of beings seeking meaning. It is only natural that beings seeking meaning should seek it not only for themselves individually but also for the communities they form. Thus it is nearly inevitable that every culture has some kind of civil religion, at least a civil religion in the broad sense of a religious ideology that is both shaped by and helps in turn to shape the culture's collective consciousness.

The term *civil religion* occurs for the first time in book 4, chapter 8 of Rousseau's *The Social Contract* (1762). There Rousseau argues that Jesus, by teaching that the spiritual kingdom was separate from the political kingdom, instigated "those intestine dissensions which have never ceased to agitate the Christian peoples." It was to undo the mischief that the teaching of Jesus supposedly introduced into the body politic that Rousseau posited the modern state's need for a *civil religion*, a minimalist religion that would meet the needs of the state. Rousseau describes these needs in the following words:

> It is of consequence to the State that each of its citizens should have a religion which will dispose him to love his duties; but the dogmas of that religion interest neither the State nor its members except as far as they affect morality and those duties which he who professes them is required

to discharge toward others. . . . There is therefore a purely civil profession of faith, the articles of which it is the business of the Sovereign to arrange, not precisely as the dogmas of religion, but as sentiments of sociability without which it is impossible to be either a good citizen or a faithful subject.[3]

The Doctrines of Civil Religion

Rousseau proceeds to define the four necessary dogmas of this civil religion:

1. the existence of a powerful, wise, and benevolent Divinity, who foresees and provides for the life to come;
2. the happiness of the just;
3. the punishment of the wicked; and
4. the sanctity of the social contract and the laws.[4]

These "dogmas" serve the needs of the state in three ways. First, while Rousseau held that the modern state is grounded in a social contract between free and equal citizens rather than in the divine right of kings, he nonetheless understood that such a social contract needed (at least in the eyes of the common man) to be rooted in some transcendent reality. Thus one function of civil religion, for Rousseau, was to provide legitimacy to the state itself and for its laws. Second, the hope of a life to come, coupled with the happiness of the good and the punishment of the wicked, served the state by encouraging citizens to perform their duties rather than seeking their own individual will. Rousseau thought that enlightened citizens would do so by nature, but the less enlightened were likely to need some additional motivation. Third, the existence of a god who hands out rewards and punishments based on behavior provides a similar motivation toward moral goodness, thus serving the interest of the state to preserve a moral order.

To this list of civil religion's positive teachings, Rousseau adds one false doctrine that civil religion must unequivocally damn:

intolerance. As noted in Rousseau's words quoted above, the state's only religious interest is in requiring those "dogmas" that serve its other interests. Beyond these, no other dogmas should be allowed to be imposed by the state or its members upon others within the state. Thus intolerance is the great (and only) heresy of Rousseau's civil religion.[5]

The Development of an *American* Civil Religion

Although civil religion in America has not developed in *precisely* the form Rousseau envisioned, it has very nearly done so. American civil religion is the interpretation of the uniquely American experience in light of this specific culture's quest for transcendent meaning. Its exact form is a reflection of that distinctly American experience. Thus the precise shape of American civil religion today results from the confluence of a variety of philosophical, religious, and historical streams. Among these are:

- the political and moral philosophies of the Enlightenment;
- Protestant Christianity;
- the national moral crises of slavery, the Civil War, and the legacy of racism;
- the quest to define an American agenda since World War II; and
- the exchange of "the melting pot" for "the rainbow" as the dominant self-conception of American society.

Under these influences, American civil religion has assumed its present form. Its public expression has been shaped by its three greatest theologians: Thomas Jefferson (the American Moses), Abraham Lincoln (the American Jesus), and Ronald Reagan (the American Paul).[6] It is perhaps not surprising that all three of these men share some significant similarities. All were quite religious, but two of the three were not active adherents of any particular church body.[7] Each had a strong moral sense and a strong sense of public duty. Also, each had a significant role in shaping and articulating

America's national direction during his era. They tended to employ religion in serving the ends of the state, much as Rousseau might have anticipated. However, the vagueness of their pronouncements about God and their association of God with the American destiny strongly reinforced two additional tenets in the specifically American brand of civil religion:

1. the notion of America's manifest destiny, and

2. the anonymity of God.

Together with Rousseau's doctrines, these constitute the chief teachings of American civil religion.

Manifest Destiny

From very early in our nation's history, people have cultivated a sense of the unique, divinely appointed role of America in the world. This quite common sentiment, often employing the biblical image of America as a "city set upon a hill," is found both in the sermons of early American preachers and in the pronouncements of American politicians and preachers today. In early America there were also more explicit allusions to the special place of America in the heart of God. One of the most common of these was frequent comparison of the American experience with that of Old Testament Israel, to the point that this nation was sometimes called the "American Israel." Lincoln expressed a similar idea when he referred to America as "an almost chosen nation." America, at least in the minds of a great many Americans past and present, is not quite Israel, but almost so.

The notions of America's chosen-ness, its special place in the heart of God, and its manifest destiny are quite significant, yet they do not constitute the focus of our present discussion. We turn instead to the last of the "doctrines" of American civil religion: the anonymity of God.

The Anonymity of God

God's anonymity in American civil religion is a more recent development. For most of U. S. history the common understanding of the Establishment Clause of the First Amendment was that the federal government (and later the states) could not favor one *Christian* church body over another by designating one the state church or granting to it special privileges under the law. Christianity in general, however, did undeniably occupy a *de facto* privileged position in the American consciousness and also in the American legal system.[8] Thus when the term *god* was used in public discourse, the vast majority of Americans construed that term to mean the God who revealed Himself in the Old and New Testaments (or at least the Old Testament in the case of American Jews). There have always been some who did not share this concept of god, but their interpretation was largely on the fringes of American civil life.

To understand how this has changed, one must first recognize an underlying general shift in American cultural attitudes. The American experience has always been rooted in the notion of *inclusion*. This notion of inclusion, however, underwent a dramatic change in the latter half of the twentieth century. For most of American history inclusion meant *integration*. The United States stretched out her arms to embrace those who would come to her shores with the understanding that becoming *American* meant giving up something old to become a part of something new and better. Immigrants were expected to give up their former national identity and become a part of this new nation, unencumbered by the prejudices and distinctions of the old world. Theodore Roosevelt (1858–1919) reflected the common sentiment of his age when he called upon "hyphenated Americans"[9] to shed their hyphens and become one new nation and one new people.[10] In response to this attitude, German-Americans, Italian-Americans, Japanese-Americans, Chinese-Americans, and Irish-Americans came together in this new land to become one hyphen-free people: Americans. This is the spirit captured so eloquently by the British playwright Israel Zangwill (1864–1926) in the words of his character David Quixano: "America is God's Crucible, the great Melting-Pot where all the races of Europe are melting and re-forming!"[11]

During the course of the last half-century this fundamental American self-understanding has changed. As Jesse Jackson (b. 1941) once said, "I hear that melting-pot stuff a lot, and all I can say is that we haven't melted."[12] So, as a society we rejected *integration* as the basis of inclusion in the American identity. We promoted *diversity* in its place. With this shift came the exchange of the melting pot for the rainbow as the dominant metaphor for expressing the self-conception of American society.

In practical terms this shift has meant not merely recognizing the equality of persons of different races and the value of non-European cultures but also encouraging the use of languages other than English, inventing new culture-affirming holidays such as Kwanzaa, and even actively promoting homosexuality as a legitimate, alternative "sexual lifestyle." More to the point, within the realm of religion it has meant that all religions and all gods—and in the term *gods* the devil himself is included today—are to be equally tolerated, if not honored and respected within American culture.

This active promotion of religious diversity has created an American pantheon. In the ancient world the various gods each had a name, one commonly related to some aspect of the god's supposed character or nature and often simply the common noun related to the particular aspect of creation that was thought to be connected to the god's nature and under his sphere of influence. Because there are many aspects to nature, there were many gods. The subsequent panoply of divinities was most commonly pictured in one (or often both) of two ways: either (1) as an extended family that generally included at least three generations, in which the high god was the patriarch, or (2) as a governmental council that the high god ruled as a king. As the common mythology of the ancient world spread westward and eastward from its Sumerian roots and encountered other gods, those gods were incorporated either by adding them to the pantheon, as Baal, Anat, and Astarte were added to the Egyptian pantheon at the time of the Hyksos, or by identifying them with an existing god, as in the case of the Roman Jupiter being identified with the Greek Zeus, who was earlier identified with the Canaanite El, who was earlier identified with the Sumerian Enlil. Both of these processes often happened at the same time.

All of this is easy enough within the framework of a true polytheistic religion. However, a problem arose when this process came to American shores. The common American public consciousness is still largely shaped by the Judeo-Christian concept of monotheism (though now there is evidence of change in this consciousness). Within the framework provided by a monotheistic conception of god, one cannot add gods. Thus in the new American pantheon all the various names by which men call gods are identified with a single spirit-being malleable (perhaps we should just be honest and say *vague*) enough to accommodate any and all religious conceptions.[13]

But what to call this spirit-being? Neither Jesus nor Allah nor Buddha nor Krishna will do, even though all of them may be identified with one another in the public consciousness. Indeed, to use any name for god would run the risk of alienating the religious faith of *someone*, for it would appear to show favoritism in one direction or another. So, American society seems to have concluded that the spirit of religious tolerance requires that god be anonymous. He (or she or it) has no name. God is simply *god*. Calling the spirit-being *god* offends no one, we think, for it allows each person to define *god* according to his own religious understanding. What could be more generous than that? It also seems to preserve the First Amendment by showing no favoritism.

The anonymity of god in current American civil religion fits Rousseau's conception of civil religion very well. His concern, as noted previously, was to encourage people to respect the social contract that binds them together, to live moral lives, and to inspire them to choose duty over self-interest when those two conflict. For those things a powerful and benevolent deity is useful, as Rousseau observed. But anything beyond that is likely to cause dissension and conflict and is, therefore, both unnecessary and undesirable. To give god a name, any name, is to be exclusionary and intolerant. And the one thing Rousseau's civil religion (and ours) cannot bear is intolerance.

THE SCANDAL OF PARTICULARITY AND THE FIRST TABLE OF THE TORAH

All of this suits American civil religion, and contemporary American society, very well. It stands in fundamental conflict, however, with the historic Christian faith.

The Scandal of Particularity

Historic Christianity affirms what we sometimes call the scandal of particularity. The term *scandal* in this case comes from the Bible. The Greek term *skandalon* basically refers to a trap or a snare. By extension it comes to mean anything that might ensnare one. Because a *skandalon* would cause people to fall, they would naturally be upset by it. Hence the term also comes to mean something that gives offense or arouses opposition in people.

In New Testament Greek the use of the term is colored by how the Greek translation of the Old Testament (the Septuagint) used the term. Therefore, the term *skandalon* in the New Testament comes to be used for something that would cause one to stumble and fall, especially to stumble in one's relationship with God (i.e., to sin). Or it could refer to something that would give offense to others. But often the term has a still more specific meaning. In his letter to the Romans, St. Paul cites Isaiah 28:16 and applies it to Jesus:

> Behold, I am laying in Zion a stone of stumbling, and a rock of offense; and whoever believes in Him will not be put to shame. (Romans 9:33)[14]

The apostle recognizes that the identity of Jesus as the Messiah whom God has sent to rescue all mankind and restore them to a right relationship with God is just this sort of stumbling block, both to Jews and non-Jews:

> [W]e preach Christ crucified, a stumbling block to Jews and folly to Gentiles. (1 Corinthians 1:23)

Elsewhere Paul identifies the stumbling block as not only the person of Jesus, but especially His death on the cross (Galatians 5:11).

The scandal of particularity is an even broader notion, for it includes the understanding that God is at work in very specific times and places and ways to accomplish His will. The Christian faith is not a religion of *spiritual truths*, that is, of moral or inner principles by which one ought to (or even may) live. It is instead the claim, radical in the ancient world and still more radical today, that God has reached into human history to do those things necessary to restore the relationship between Himself and us that our first ancestors shattered. This scandal of particularity is at the heart of the Bible's claims to historicity. It renders Christianity fundamentally different from the various world religions.

The scandal of particularity has its origin in God's self-revelation in the Old Testament, particularly in that portion of the Ten Commandments called the First Table of the Torah.

The First Table of the Torah[15]

Generally speaking, the five books of Moses are concerned with two broad questions:

1. Who is Yahweh?

2. What does it mean to be chosen by Yahweh to be His people?
A summary of God's answer to these two questions is found in His
revelation to Moses in Exodus 20, the section we commonly call the
Ten Commandments.[16] The intersection between biblical Christianity and American civil religion comes in the First Table of the
Torah, which identifies Yahweh as the Creator and Redeemer and
defines the relationship of His people to Him as expressed in worship.

Much of our problem in understanding the First Table of the
Torah comes from the fact that we are reading it in an English
translation. A close reading of the Hebrew text helps to clarify some
common misconceptions about the First Table and also about how
we interact with the anonymous god of American civil religion.

The Prologue

Exodus begins with a divine self-identification formula:

Then God spoke all these words (saying): "I am Yahweh[17]
your God, Who brought you from the land of Egypt, from a
house of slaves." (20:1–2)

This statement, which according to the Jewish tradition is the
first of the "ten sayings," does two things. First, it identifies the
speaker as the God Yahweh, not any of the gods of other nations.
The identity of the true God is a major issue in the Book of Exodus. In Exodus 3 Yahweh introduces Himself formally for the first
time in the Bible, identifying Himself as the God who had called,
led, and protected Israel's patriarchs, and had promised them
descendents and a land in which they might dwell in His presence.
The revelation of God's name Yahweh marks a turning point in His
relations with the descendents of Abraham, for it is only in the context of revealing His name that Yahweh for the first time calls the
Hebrews (or for that matter anyone else) "My people" (Exodus 3:7,
10). It is only when God reveals Himself to the Israelites by name

that they become the people of God. And it is by this name that He wishes to be known among them forever:

> God further said to Moses, "Thus you shall say to the sons of Israel, 'Yahweh, the God of your fathers, the God of Abraham, the God of Isaac, and the God of Jacob, has sent me to you.' This is My name forever, and this [is the way] I am to be remembered[18] to the last generation. (Exodus 3:15)

In Exodus 6 this self-revelation is repeated, this time with an emphasis on what Yahweh is going to do to rescue the Hebrews and constitute them as *His people*. In Exodus 7 Yahweh reveals that the plagues He is about to inflict upon Egypt will have as their result even that "[t]he Egyptians shall know that I am Yahweh ..."(Exodus 7:5). The song sung by Moses and the Israelites after their miraculous deliverance at Yam Suph begins with a paean in honor of the God who has revealed His name *Yahweh*. The recounting of His deliverance culminates in the rhetorical question, "Who is like You, O Yahweh, among the gods?" In this manner the whole first part of the Book of Exodus is shaped by the question, "Who is Yahweh?" as well as the acts and words by which Yahweh reveals the answer that He is both the only true God and the Redeemer of His people Israel.

The second thing that is done by the Exodus 20:1–2 prologue is to establish the authority Yahweh has for the instruction that He is about to give His people. He is entitled to give them His teaching, and they are obligated to receive it because of the redemption that Yahweh has accomplished in bringing them out of Egypt. There follows, then, a series of principles by which the people of Yahweh are to live.

The First Commandment (Exodus 20:3)

You must not have other gods in My presence.

Here our English translations often let us down. We are accustomed to hearing this text translated as, "You shall have no other gods *before* Me." The wording of the Hebrew text is rather more precise. God says that His people must not have other gods, *'al panay*, "before My [i.e., His] face" or "in My [i.e., His] presence." The Hebrew word *'al* is most commonly translated *upon* or *on top of*, but it can also mean *beside* or *next to*. In fact, it includes the general notion of one thing being in the vicinity of another thing. The word *paniym* (here with the suffix meaning *my*) literally means *face*, but *face* is commonly used as a synecdoche for the whole person. Hence it is commonly translated as *me* or, in the case of God as *presence*.

The issue here is whether we ought to understand the phrase "before Me" to imply a matter of sequence or proximity.[19] Even a casual reading of the rest of the Old Testament makes it clear that Yahweh will not tolerate His people worshiping any other gods. The idea that it is acceptable to worship other gods as long as Yahweh is put first is nowhere to be found in the Old Testament. A contextual reading of the First Commandment clearly suggests that the issue is *proximity* and not *sequence*. Yahweh is not claiming the right to be *first* in the affections of His people; He is prohibiting His people from allowing any other god anywhere around Him. Yahweh does not want to be our *first* god, or to be first in our life; He must be our *only* God, the only divine being that we have anything to do with. The First Commandment is a demand for a radical and absolute exclusivity in our relationship with the realm of divine beings. This radical exclusivity is an essential part of the relationship between Yahweh and His people. As the first duty of the believer is to worship—or, as Christians might prefer to say, worship is the first good work of faith—the radical nature of this relationship is expressed most clearly in how the people of Yahweh worship. This scandalous particularity to which Yahweh calls His people is so crucial to the relationship between Yahweh and His people in worship that God continues to expand upon what He means by it.

Commandment 1b (Exodus 20:4)

> You must not make for yourself an idol or the likeness of anything which is in heaven above or which is on the earth below or which is in the seas below the earth.

With these words Yahweh prohibits any kind of worship that might recall or be confused with the worship of other gods. This prohibition is rooted in the way in which Yahweh relates to creation. Generally in religions of the ancient Near East, the realm of the divine was thought to be at one end of the spectrum and the realm of nature at the other end of the same spectrum, so there was a kind of continuity between them. Thus the gods were understood to be connected to those aspects of nature that reflected their character, and the gods were thought to be present within the realm of nature in the form of images. These idols did not merely *symbolize* the god, they *were* the god as he revealed himself in that place.

In the creation account of Genesis, the relationship between Yahweh and nature is not presented in this way. There is no spectrum with God at one end and nature at the other. Yahweh stands outside of the realm of nature, which is entirely His creation. The presence of God in the realm of nature is not revealed in any thing, but in mankind, and not because mankind intrinsically shares God's nature but rather because Yahweh bestowed His spirit and character upon man and appointed him as steward over all that He had made (Genesis 1:26–28). Thus man, and nothing else, could represent Yahweh within the realm of nature. When in rebellion Adam and Eve rejected their role, humanity could no longer fully present the image of God in the world until God Himself became man in Jesus Christ, who alone could be all that God intended that humanity could be, and more.[20] But that is beyond the scope of this study. The point here is that no thing within the realm of nature can be thought to present Yahweh to the world. As a result, no idol or image can be used in the worship of Him. In this way, too, Yahweh emphasizes the difference between Himself and all other gods and makes it clear that the forms in which other gods are worshiped are not appropriate for the worship of Yahweh.

He continues by making it clear that the reason for this demand for radical exclusivity in our worship is rooted in God's own character.

Commandment 1c (Exodus 20:5–6)

> You must not worship them and you must not serve them
> because I, Yahweh your God, [am a] jealous god inflicting
> [the punishment for] the guilt of the fathers upon the sons
> to the third and fourth [generations] to those who hate Me
> but giving grace to thousands [of generations]to those who
> love Me and keep My commandments.

Here it is Yahweh's own passion for His people that motivates Him. His desire to be their God and to have them as His people moves Him. It forms the basis for His demand of radical exclusivity in their relationship. It is this same love that is the basis for His forgiveness. Note how small is His wrath, which lasts only for three or four generations, in contrast to His grace, which extends to a thousand generations.

The theme of how Yahweh is to be worshiped continues with the next saying.

The Second Commandment (Exodus 20:7)

> You must not lift up the name of Yahweh your God like the
> empty [thing] for Yahweh will not allow to go unpunished
> anyone who lifts up His name like the empty [thing].

As we have seen, Yahweh is not revealed in the world by any *thing* within nature. He is known only by the name that He has chosen to reveal and by the deeds associated with that name. It is the revelation of His name that makes the Hebrews into His people, and it is by His name that He is to be remembered among His people forever. The name, then, is the only thing that Yahweh's people have by which to know and to worship Him.[21] As a result, the way in which Yahweh's people use His name becomes a central issue in worship.

Here is another point at which our common English translations of the text lead us astray in our understanding of what Yahweh is teaching His people. The Hebrew verb *nasa'*, commonly translated *lift up*, may indeed mean to elevate something physically. It is, however, very commonly used as a term for worship in the Old Testament. Indeed, to *lift up the name*, like the parallel phrase *call upon the name*, is essentially a synonym for *worship*.

There is an even bigger problem with our common translation of the Hebrew word *lashaw'*, commonly translated *in vain* (here *like the empty* [thing]). The noun *shaw'* occurs 54 times in 48 verses in the Old Testament. It is frequently used in combination with another noun in an adjectival way, meaning *false* or *empty* or *worthless*, as in a "false report" (Exodus 23:1), "vain offerings" (Isaiah 1:13), or "empty pleas" (Isaiah 59:4). Like many Hebrew nouns, it can also be used adverbially: to do something in an empty or worthless way is to do it *to no avail* or, as in our common translation here, to do it *in vain*. For example, Jeremiah pronounces judgment upon the land using the imagery of a woman trying to dress herself up to flatter her lovers by saying, "It is to no avail [*lashaw'*] that you try to make yourself beautiful" (Jeremiah 4:30). In the context of worship, *shaw'* is sometimes used adjectivally, as in the example of the "vain offerings" in Isaiah 1:13, but it is also used in a more specific way to refer to false gods. Thus *shaw'* becomes a euphemism for *idol*.

In addition to this text and its parallel in Deuteronomy 5:11, we read Jeremiah's accusation:

> My people have forgotten me; they make an offering to a *shaw'*. (Jeremiah 18:15)

or Jonah's:

> Those who keep *their faithfulness in* worthless *shaw'*[22] forsake
> their hope of steadfast love. (Jonah 2:8; Masoretic Text 2:9)

which echoes the language of the psalmist's:

> I hate those who keep *their faithfulness in* worthless *shaw'*,
> but I trust in Yahweh. (Psalm 31:6; Masoretic Text 31:7)[23]

In each of the these cases, *shaw'* can only be understood as a
euphemism for *false god* or *idol*. The same use is reflected in the
Second Commandment.[24]

This text, like its surrounding passages in the First Table, is primarily about how the people of Yahweh are to worship Him. The
presence of Yahweh is not revealed in images because Yahweh is
distinct from the realm of nature. As a result, His people may not
invoke images in His worship. They have only His name to call
upon and lift up. So they must not worship the one revealed by
that name in the manner that people would worship other gods.
Yahweh says:

> You must not worship Me as if I were a false god, for I will
> not allow to go unpunished one who worships Me as if I
> were a false god.

But we need to be careful here. One might conclude, as the
Jewish tradition has concluded, that one can avoid the danger by
not using the name Yahweh at all. This is a mistake. Yahweh wants
His people to use His name in worship in the right and faithful
manner. Therefore, the people of God are taught: "Oh give thanks
to Yahweh; call upon His name; make known His deeds among the
peoples!" (Psalm 105:1).[25] For the prophets of the Old Testament,
calling upon Yahweh by name is key to our salvation: "And it shall
come to pass that everyone who calls on the name of Yahweh shall
be saved" (Joel 2:32). So God promises through the prophet
Zechariah:

> Then I will put this third into the fire, and refine them as
> one refines silver, and test them as gold is tested. They will
> call upon My name, and I will answer them. I will say,
> "They are My people"; and they will say, "Yahweh is My
> God." (Zechariah 13:9)

That God intends this to be understood and employed by
Christians is clear from the New Testament's appropriation of Joel's
prophecy in Acts 2:21 and Romans 10:13.

Israel clearly understood this. Yahweh, the name of the only
true God, occurs 5,343 times in the 23,213 verses of the Old Testament,[26] more than once every four-and-a-half verses. In the same
way, worshiping Yahweh by name, calling upon His name, and
being called by His name are central elements of the faith of Israel,
old and new. Only later did the Jewish tradition shy away from
using God's name.

Unfortunately, Christians have inherited from the synagogue a
certain shyness about using the name Yahweh. Our failure to heed
the teaching of God's Word on this point arises from our failure to
understand the Second Commandment properly. Traditional
Christian interpretation tends to limit the Second Commandment
to not cursing, an issue that is at best peripheral to the thrust of the
actual text in its original context. Luther was influenced by this
Christian tradition of *mis*interpretation, and put his emphasis in
the wrong place just like the rest of us. Yet he did get the main
point. He understood the importance of calling upon God by
name, as he notes in the Large Catechism:

> [C]hildren should be constantly urged and encouraged to
> honor God's name and keep it constantly upon their lips in
> all circumstances and experiences, *for true honor to God's
> name consists of looking to it for all consolation and therefore
> calling upon it.*[27]

The obvious question arises: If the people of Yahweh are not to
worship Him using images, or to invoke His name in the manner

that the names of other gods are invoked, how are they to worship Him? The answer comes immediately:

The Third Commandment (Exodus 20:8–11)

Remember the Rest[28] Day in order to set it apart. [For] six days you may serve and do all your work, but the seventh day is a [day of] rest [set apart] for Yahweh your God: You must not do any work, [neither] you, your son, your daughter, your servant, your maid-servant, nor even your beast of burden nor your foreigner who is within your gates. because [over the course of] six days Yahweh made the heavens and the earth, the sea and all that is in it, then on the seventh day He rested. Therefore Yahweh blessed the Rest Day and set it apart.

Here the discussion of how Yahweh is to be worshiped is concluded. One day each week is to be set aside to worship Yahweh. The day and its worship are connected to Yahweh's creative activity. This statement connects back to the prologue that focuses on the redemptive activity by which Yahweh creates His people and stakes His claim upon them. The First Table of the Torah begins by describing Yahweh as Redeemer and concludes by describing Him as Creator. Among those who study biblical texts this technique is called *bracketing*, and it is an important structure for communicating emphasis in Hebrew narratives. The text focuses the discussion of worship on the name of Yahweh and defines the substance of that name in terms of God's creative and redemptive acts. Yahweh the Creator and Yahweh the Redeemer: This is the way the true God teaches His people to worship Him. No other kind of worship is acceptable to Him. To attempt to worship Him in any other way is to incur His wrath.

CONCLUSION:
YAHWEH, JESUS, AND THE ANONYMOUS GOD

There is, of course, more to the story. To complete the work of redemption Yahweh became man in Jesus of Nazareth, the Messiah, the Christ in whom both the redemptive purpose of God and the scandal of particularity that is at the heart of the First Table of the Torah find their ultimate realization. So the apostle Peter makes it clear that not only *may* we be saved through the scandal of the cross of Jesus Christ, but the scandal of the Yahweh incarnate, crucified for us on the cross, is in fact the *only* way that mankind can be made right with God: "This Jesus is the stone that was rejected by you, the builders, which has become the cornerstone. And there is salvation in no one else, for there is no other name under heaven given among men by which we must be saved" (Acts 4:11–12). Thus it is in His incarnation as Jesus that we worship Yahweh the Creator and Redeemer.

This point brings us back to the anonymous god of American civil religion. When St. Paul spoke to the Greeks on the hill of the Areopagus, he noted their altar to an "unknown god" (Acts 17:22ff.). The unknown god of the Areopagus was not an anonymous god; the Greeks assumed the god had a name but that they simply did not know it. The altar was the ancient equivalent of Pascal's wager, an attempt to take care of the just-in-case scenario: "Here is an altar to some god whose name we don't know, just in case we have left him out from ignorance, because we don't want him to be angry with us." Paul used the occasion as an opportunity to make the unknown god known. His speech in Acts 17 is an attempt to define God in terms of what He has done, the God who created, and who is about to judge, and . . . Well, Paul never got to finish because just as he got to the scandal of particularity and mentioned the resurrection, he was interrupted as his hearers were distracted by a different concern.

Paul understood that the unknown god had to be known. And to be known, God had to be proclaimed in terms of what He has done. That is our challenge as well. Just as Paul understood that the proclamation of the Gospel necessitated making the unknown god known (Acts 17:23), we too must give the anonymous god a name, the only name of the only true God. American civil religion wants us to be happy with an anonymous god, at least in public. That is the one thing that we can never do. The whole of the biblical revelation requires us to name God: to make known the name of Yahweh, the name of Jesus, and His deeds, creation and redemption. We may call upon this God, and this God alone, by name. To compromise with American civil religion on this point is to deny all that is fundamental to biblical faith. To worship an anonymous god is to worship an empty worthless god. To deny Yahweh His name is to treat Him as a *shaw'*.

In closing, I would like to note three observations about the First Table of the Torah that underscore how important this whole matter is from God's perspective. First, these commandments related to how God is to be worshiped are the only commandments of the ten that are connected with the self-revelation of God. Second, they are the only commandments that have specific threats of punishment attached to them. And, finally, the First Table contains the only commandments that are expanded with explanations. Together, these three aspects of the First Table serve to illustrate how much care God has taken to ensure that His people understand the importance of the right use of His name in worship.

Surely something of such great importance to God must be important for us, no matter how much it might run contrary to the spirit of our age or the pressure of our culture. If our proclamation of the person and works of Yahweh in Jesus Christ is an offense to our culture, then it is the *skandalon* that Jesus said that it would be. If, in the minds of Rousseau and his modern-day intellectual heirs, it is intolerant to declare in the public square that Yahweh is the only true God, that His teaching is the only ground for morality, and that receiving His grace revealed in the death and resurrection of Jesus Christ is our only way to be made right with God, then we shall have to bear the cross of being thought intolerant. God has gone to great extremes to reveal His name and the deeds associated with it so we might know and worship Him properly. We cannot allow God to become anonymous. At the risk of being thought impious, our perspective is rather like that of a cartoon that I once saw, in which a voice speaking from heaven addressed the cartoon character below with the words, "It's Yahweh or the highway!"

Notes

1. The Rev. Dr. David L. Adams is associate professor of exegetical theology at Concordia Seminary, St. Louis, Missouri. He holds M.Div. and S.T.M. degrees from Concordia Seminary, and a Ph.D. in Old Testament theology from Cambridge University. This paper was originally prepared as a lecture to the Minnesota Lutheran Free Conference and was delivered in the fall of 2002.

2. As subsequent essays in this volume will show, the concept of civil religion was understood and discussed among American academics well before the essay in which Bellah popularized Rousseau's term.

3. Jean-Jacques Rousseau, *The Social Contract*, in *Hafner Library of Classics*, ed. Charles Frankel (New York: Hafner, 1949), 1:117.

   It is worth knowing that while Rousseau affirmed a general belief in God, he rejected the historic Christian concept of sin. He believed that man is born innately good and morally innocent and becomes otherwise only through the corrupting influence of civilization. In his classic *Émile* (1762), he argued that if the negative force of cultural education (as he knew it in his day) could be eliminated, a child would grow into a superior moral being, fully respecting the rights and welfare of others. Thus, he maintained, children should be taught to follow the guidance of their hearts and the nobler emotions and religious sentiments, and to express these higher sentiments in their actions toward one another. Children thus freed of the corrupting influence of civilization would lead the human ascent to a higher plane of morality and religious development. Rousseau's concept of civil religion takes this view of man for granted. His ideal state is a democracy in which all people would vote, not according to their own prejudices or desires, but for what fulfilled the common good. Rousseau had a significant impact on the development of political theory, at least among the educated elite, in the period leading up to the American Revolution.

4. Rousseau, *Social Contract*, 1:117.

5. Rousseau, *Social Contract*, 1:117.

6. Some would include in this group John F. Kennedy, perhaps as a sort of American Peter. Kennedy certainly reflected American civil religion prominently in some of his speeches, but the brevity of his presidency might be thought to argue against placing him on the level of Jefferson, Lincoln, and Reagan in respect to his influence on the development of American civil religion. It is worth noting the ongoing role of the president as a sort of *Pontifex Maximus* in American civil religion. For most of our nation's history it has been the president, whoever he is, who is the chief spokesman of our civil religious ideals and the chief liturgist of our national religious rituals.

7. Both Jefferson and Lincoln were consciously opposed to the organized religion of the churches, and said so. Kennedy was, of course, Roman Catholic, though the degree to which he faithfully practiced Catholicism is a matter of debate.

8. The bias toward a law shaped by and reflecting Christian moral principles has been well documented and is perhaps nowhere illustrated more clearly than in the experience of the Mormons in seeking statehood for Utah and in the Supreme Court case that upheld the federal government's right to ban polygamous marriages (*Reynolds v. United States*, 98 U. S. 145 [1879]).

9. "There is no room in this country for hyphenated Americanism. . . . The one absolutely certain way of bringing this nation to ruin, of preventing all possibility of its continuing to be a nation at all, would be to permit it to become a tangle of squabbling nationalities" (Theodore Roosevelt, speaking before the Knights of Columbus, New York, 12 October 1915, as cited in John Bartlet, *Familiar Quotations*, ed. Emily Morison Beck, 15th and 125th Anniversary Ed. [Boston: Little, Brown, & Co., 1980], 688).

10. "There can be no fifty-fifty Americanism in this country. There is room here for only 100% Americanism, only for those who are Americans and nothing else" (Theodore Roosevelt, speech to the State Republican Party Convention, Saratoga, New York, 19 July 1918). Roosevelt had earlier drawn attention to the problem of "hyphenated Americans" in a speech on 12 October 1915 (see n. 9 above). This view, common at the time, included the understanding that becoming American was not only an issue of political or patriotic attitude but also included such practical matters as learning the English language. Here again Roosevelt speaks for most Americans of the period:

"Every immigrant who comes here should be required within five years to learn English or leave the country" (*Kansas City Star*, 27 April 1918).

11. Israel Zangwill, *The Melting Pot*, Act I.

12. Jesse Jackson, in an interview with *Playboy*, November 1969.

13. One may argue whether popular American religion has become polytheistic, openly embracing the worship of many gods, or whether it has developed a kind of theistic monism, in which all the various names of the various gods are thought to be simply names of one god. Both these perspectives can be found in popular American culture, though the latter (theistic monism) seems to be the more prevalent. It may be that, except as a matter of academic debate, there is very little practical difference to choose between them. In either case the particular and exclusive claims of the God of the Bible and of the historic Christian faith are rejected, or at the least ignored.

14. Compare to the similar reference in 1 Peter 2:8 (ESV). Unless otherwise indicated, Scripture quotations in this essay are the author's own translation.

15. The term *torah* is used in a variety of senses. It sometimes means the five books of Moses. At other times it refers to the entire Old Testament. In other places, particularly in traditional Jewish circles, it refers both to the written revelation of God in the Hebrew Scriptures and the oral tradition that the rabbis teach was given by God to Moses and handed down orally to the present. In still other places it refers to the Ten Commandments and yet again to the whole of the instruction that God gives His people so they will know how to walk in His ways. In this paper the term is generally used specifically to refer to the Ten Commandments and occasionally, more broadly, to the whole of God's teachings.

16. There is a twofold problem with the term "the Ten Commandments" in reference to the Exodus 20 text. First, many of the sayings commonly described as the "Ten Commandments" are not, properly speaking, commandments in the grammatical sense. This is reflected in the fact that the term *ten commandments* does not occur in the Bible. The precepts of Exodus 20 are referred to as *the ten sayings* (עֲשֶׂרֶת הַדְּבָרִים, *ʿªsereth haddᵉvarim*) on three occasions (Exodus 34:28; Deuteronomy 4:13; 10:4), but the phrase *the ten commandments* (עֲשֶׂרֶת הַמִּצְוֹת, *ʿªsereth hammitswoth*) is never used. The second problem is one of enumeration and division. Despite the fact that the Bible itself refers to the number ten in the three places cited above, there are not ten of these sayings, but at least 13. Hence the problem of numbering that has led to three major numbering

schemes: the one reflected in the Hebrew Masoretic Text and used by Catholics and Lutherans, the one reflected in the Septuagint and used by most Protestants, and the one used by contemporary rabbinical Judaism. However one numbers the individual commandments, it is common in Christian circles to group the Ten Commandments into the Two Tables of the Law (Torah), loosely associating a division of the content of the sayings with the two tablets of stone upon which God wrote His instructions to Israel through Moses. In fact, though, if we were strictly describing the content of the teaching, we would be more inclined to divide these ten sayings into three tables, as follows: the *First Table*, Exodus 20:1–11 (sayings 1 to 3 in the traditional division), which identifies Yahweh as the Creator and Redeemer and focuses on the relationship of His people to Him as expressed in worship; the *Second Table*, Exodus 20:12–16 (sayings 4–8 in the traditional division), which focus on the relationship of His people to Him as expressed in how they treat one another; and the *Third Table*, Exodus 20:17 (sayings 9–10 in the traditional division), which focus on the fundamental problem that corrupts our relationships with Him and with one another: the state of the heart.

17. This phrase occurs 20 times in the Book of Exodus (after appearing only twice in Genesis), illustrating how significant the identification of Israel's God is for the book. The phrase occurs more often in only two other books, Leviticus (52x), in which it underscores the basis of Yahweh's teaching in His person and character, and Ezekiel (87x), where it emphasizes both the authority of God's judgment upon Israel and its result (that the people and the world will know that Yahweh is indeed God).

18. Literally: "This is my remembrance."

19. In English the word *before* can have either meaning. For example, "I saw John before I went to town" clearly implies a sequence. On the other hand, "I know that I will stand before God" implies proximity. In some cases the usage can be ambiguous. "I saw John before Mary" may mean "I saw John before (I saw) Mary" or "I saw John (standing) before Mary." Only the context can clarify the meaning.

20. Thus Jesus is the Last Adam (Romans 5:14–15; 1 Corinthians 15:22, 45), true God and true man. Indeed, in one sense Jesus is the first true man since the fall, the first who could do what God intended humanity to be able to do at creation, to represent Him within the realm of nature.

21. Indeed, the name becomes a virtual euphemism for Yahweh Himself, as in Psalm 20:1: "May Yahweh answer you in the day of trouble! May the name of the God of Jacob protect you!"

22. This passage (with Psalm 31:6) is particularly interesting because it contains the double euphemism הַבְלֵי־שָׁוְא. Like שָׁוְא, הֶבֶל (*chebel*) basically means an empty thing or something as inconsequential as a breath of air, and is sometimes used by itself as a euphemism for an idol (cf. Deuteronomy 32:21; 1 Kings 16:13 et al.).

23. Note here the especially strong contrast between the false god (שָׁוְא) and Yahweh. Such contrasts are one of the most prominent characteristics of Hebrew poetry and make it clear that the שָׁוְא is being understood as a false god.

24. Exodus 20:7 and Deuteronomy 5:11.

25. See also 1 Chronicles 16:8 and, similarly, Isaiah 12:4f.

26. According to the Masoretic Text. There are 23,261 verses according to the English text division. The total of 5,343 occurrences does not include the many occurrences of names that have compounds with the *Ya* theophoric element or its variants (as in Jeremiah [Yirm^e-*ya* or Yirm^e-*yahu* "Yahweh will raise up"] or Jehoshaphat [y^e*ho-shaphat* "Yahweh has judged"], etc.).

27. Large Catechism, I, 70 (Tappert, 374, *my emphasis*).

28. The term *sabbath* is a transliteration of the Hebrew שַׁבָּת, from the verb שָׁבַת, meaning to cease, desist, or rest.

2
=

Civil Religion
and the Early Church

Syncretism and Doctrinal Integrity in the
Apologetic of Athenagoras of Athens

DAVID R. LIEFELD[1]

A thenagoras of Athens became a major figure in the early church's encounter with the pluralistic culture of the Roman Empire through a conciliatory appeal to the Roman joint emperors Marcus Aurelius Antoninus and his son Lucius Aurelius Commodus. Unlike Tertullian, who asked, "What indeed has Athens to do with Jerusalem?"[2] Athenagoras skillfully blended Greek philosophy and rhetoric with Christian doctrine in his appeal. For this, Athenagoras has sometimes been accused of syncretism,[3] a charge that at times also has been applied to the early church as a whole.

ATHENAGORAS AND HIS CULTURE

Although described as the "most eloquent" of the second-century apologists for the Christian faith,[4] Athenagoras is veiled in obscurity. There is very little mention of him in most catalogs of ancient works. Eusebius, for instance, makes no mention of him in an otherwise rather comprehensive survey of second-century apologists. Neither does Jerome refer to him. However, Methodius of Olympus does mention Athenagoras in a writing against Origen produced in the late third or early fourth century, and he is referred to in a fragment attributed to Philip of Side, deacon of Chrysostom in the fifth century, though it is a much debated description:

> Athenagoras was the first head of the school at Alexandria, flourishing in the times of Hadrian and Antoninus, to whom also he addressed his *Legatio* for the Christians; a man who embraced Christianity while wearing the garb of a philosopher, and presiding over the academic school. He, before Celsus, was bent on writing against the Christians; and studying the divine scriptures in order to carry on the contest with the greater accuracy, was thus himself caught by the Holy Spirit, so that, like the great Paul, from a persecutor he became a teacher of the faith that he persecuted. Philip says that Clement, the writer of the *Stromata*, was his pupil, and Pantaenus the pupil of Clement. Pantaenus, too, was an Athenian, and was a Pythagorean in his philosophy.[5]

While a few scholars have doubted his existence or have assigned his imperial appeal to Justin Martyr, it is widely accepted that Athenagoras was a philosopher from Athens who presented an appeal to the Roman emperors between the years A.D. 168 and 179, probably in A.D. 176 or 177.

Two works are attributed to Athenagoras: "The *Legatio* (or Embassy) for the Christians," also known as "The Plea (or Supplication) for the Christians," and "On the Resurrection," also known as *De Resurrectione*. Both survive only in the Arethas Codex of A.D. 914. Of primary concern here is the *Legatio* (Plea), which is addressed to Marcus Aurelius and his son Lucius, though scholars debate whether the *Legatio* was ever delivered in person to the joint emperors or even made it to them in written form at all.

W. H. C. Frend describes the *Legatio* and the other apologies of this time as "open letters" and suggests "there was a real market for these works of popular Christian philosophy among Christians and their opponents."[6] The *Legatio* is also very similar to the ambassadorial speeches that were an everyday part of imperial life. Fergus Millar points out that the Roman emperor "was what the emperor did," by which he means that "the emperor's role in relation to his subjects was essentially that of listening to requests, and of hearing disputes." In fact, Millar argues, "[i]f we follow our evidence, we might almost come to believe that the primary role of the emperor was to listen to speeches in Greek." If so, then one can imagine a social system surrounding the emperor, what Millar calls "an immensely complex network of relationships which bound the emperor to the educated bourgeoisie of the cities." In such a network, Millar suggests, it would be "the rhetoricians, the poets, grammarians and philosophers of the provincial cities who, after his senatorial 'friends', had the easiest access to the emperor."[7]

Menander codified ancient rhetorical traditions in the third century and so provides us a glimpse at the discursive environment in which Athenagoras operated. Robert Grant thinks Menander's "crown speech" provides the "framework and special points" for Athenagoras.[8] William Schoedel is convinced that "Christian apologies of the type found in Athenagoras and Justin can best be described as apologetically grounded petitions (using the term apologetic in a broad sense)." He thinks it is a mixed form that emerged "in response to the peculiarities of the social and religious situation of [Judaism and Christianity] and against the background of an imperial system open to the reception of ambassadors and petitions from a wide variety of individuals and groups."[9] Although Roman emperors dispensed with a petition (or a legal case) quickly or resorted to asking questions when they were not particularly interested in it, they usually granted sufficient time for ambassadorial petitions. Therefore, Schoedel concludes, "the length of the Christian apologies would be appropriate if they were modeled on speeches designed to be delivered as defenses before the emperor" and "the length of his [Athenagoras's] speech (whether rewritten after its delivery or not) would not in itself be incompatible with such a use of it."[10]

This leads to the intriguing possibility that Athenagoras may have made his plea (*Legatio*), perhaps later amplified for publication, to the emperors when they were in Athens in A.D. 176. Robert Grant points out that, shortly after the revolt of Avidius Cassius in the year A.D. 175, the emperor took his family on a tour of the eastern empire. Grant thinks several early apologetic writings, including the *Legatio* of Athenagoras, are associated with this imperial tour.[11] Barnes also thinks Athenagoras may have delivered his *Legatio* in person when the touring emperors were in Athens in September of 176 for initiation into the mysteries.[12] While it is not widely accepted that Athenagoras made such a personal appearance, there are several instances where the text appears to be a transcript of an actual appearance (e.g., "Although what I have said has raised a loud clamor . . ."[13]). The presentation of the *Legatio* before the emperors in Athens in A.D. 176 would be consistent with the text and its title.

We do not know whether Christians were persecuted at the time of Athenagoras because of an imperial edict or because of the general police powers at work against Christians in the empire.[14] But there was persecution, and this persecution is the most important contextual factor for interpreting the *Legatio*. According to Athenagoras, Christians were hated "because of our name." The specific accusations often raised against Christians, he wrote, were "godlessness, Thyestean banquets [cannibalism], and intercourse such as Oedipus practiced," in short, atheism and gross immorality. These were not charges of mere personal corruption but of threats

48

to the stability of Greco-Roman civilization. They were accusations that force us to take note of Roman civil religion.[15]

In general, the Roman civil religion was tolerant and pluralistic. It relied upon philosophy both to give a rational basis upon which to engage in civil discourse as well as a foundation for individual and social ethics. This civil religion focused on the imperial ruler-cult, with some similarities to the way the presidency now functions as the unifying focus of the American civil religion.[16] While only deceased emperors usually were deified and Donald Winslow observes that their living successors "were content to be referred to as *Divi filius*,"[17] both sacrifices to the gods and sacrifices to the "genius" of the emperor were mandatory. Failure to offer these sacrifices, even more than flag desecration today in the United States, was extraordinarily offensive and considered politically subversive by most Romans. The purpose of the sacrifices, according to Winslow, was the unity of the empire, the loyalty of its citizens, and the control of subversive groups.[18] It was in this context that persecutions of Christians, often officially sanctioned, broke out within the empire.

For a long time modern scholars underestimated the role of ritual in culture. More often now there is recognition that, as Robert Wuthnow observes, in every culture the entire collection of shared meanings will find dramatized ritual expression:

> In ritual a bond is established between the person and the moral community on which he or she depends. It is in this sense that ritual reinforces the moral order. Modern society, no less than the tribal group, depends continually on this source of reinforcement.[19]

We simply cannot dismiss the Roman preoccupation with the imperial sacrifices as premodern. The problem of civil religion is pervasive. It is a postulate of culture.

For almost a century persecution of Christians was sporadic and usually little more than harassment. However, persecution intensified when Christianity was perceived as a serious threat to the established social order. Then Christian apologists argued publicly that Christians could coexist peacefully in the Roman Empire with adherents of other religions. One of the arguments used by the apologists was that Christianity as a philosophy could promote social stability. "In response to the prevailing opinion that Christianity was a depraved superstition capable of producing only *impiety*," Robert Wilken writes, "Justin claims that it is a school of philosophy with genuinely religious beliefs in God and with a way of life, at least equal to, if not better than, the other philosophies."[20]

In the twenty-first century any premodern accusation of "superstition" seems quaint. But what about the pluralistic Roman society with its numerous and diverse religions? And what about the apparent priority given to accusations of superstition, even atheism, in a culture where the primary concern was obedience to the emperor? The answers to these questions lie in the way that superstition and atheism functioned for Roman civil religion. According to Wilken, these charges always "signified a religious group whose practices were at odds with those of the Romans and did not promote genuine religion."[21] Yet the issue was not "private, foreign idiosyncratic practices and beliefs of specific groups and peoples" so much as the "acts of public devotion to the gods." The charges of superstition and atheism were directed specifically at threats to society. "Traditionally Romans had distinguished superstition from true religion," according to Wilken, "for true religion promoted and engendered virtue, justice, public morality, whereas superstition did not."[22]

Cicero had written that religion must be politically useful:

So in the very beginning we must persuade our citizens that the gods are the lords and rulers of all things, and that what is done is done by their will and authority; and that they are likewise great benefactors of man, observing the character of every individual, what he does, of what wrong he is guilty, and with what intentions and with what piety he fulfills his religious duties; and that they take note of the pious and the impious. For surely minds which are imbued with such ideas will not fail to form true and useful opinions.[23]

The purpose of philosophy also, therefore, was to promote social welfare. More was involved than intellectual edification, writes Wilken: "Philosophy helped men avoid superstition and live a life of *philanthropia* towards other men and *eusebeia* toward the gods."[24] Romans believed that genuine religion accepted the unifying principle of order, the public philosophy, of the Roman Empire. Whatever else one might believe about religious matters, one must be committed to the civil religion that bound all members of the empire together harmoniously. The symbol of that unity was the ritual sacrifices mandated by the emperor. Failure to offer those sacrifices was rejection of the divine order that bound Romans together in harmony. It was superstition versus the true knowledge of God. It was, in short, atheism.

Marcus Aurelius most likely did not persecute Christianity deliberately, just as Athenagoras suspected, because early Christian writers did not identify Marcus Aurelius as a persecutor of Christians. The notion of deliberate imperial persecution derives, in the opinion of Paul Keresztes, from a failure to distinguish "between events of popular violence and the actions of some provincial governors and other officials, and of the relevant decisions of the Emperor himself."[25] All that Marcus ever did was to order the traditional sacrifices to the state gods so that he might shore up support for the empire during two particular periods of crisis: A.D. 161–168 and around A.D. 177. Because these imperial edicts required what Christians could not do, they led to intense persecutions. This was local persecution with governors responding to crowds angered by the failure of Christians to sacrifice. In short, Christians were not persecuted because they were Christians *per se*; they were persecuted because they would not do what was required by Roman civil religion. Ethelbert Stauffer's conclusion is that, while Rome could tolerate any religion, the imperial sacrifices were obligatory for everyone because this "was not fundamentally a matter of belief, but one of public order and discipline."[26]

As philosophy was considered fundamental to society, it was highly plausible for the early apologists to describe Christianity in terms of a philosophical school. It was also prudent strategy. Ramsay MacMullen notes that in "facing the overwhelming power of the Roman state, its opponents had little choice of weapons. They were obliged to strike only through ideas and words, that is, through the philosopher. . . . "[27] However, because most early Christians had no interest or competence in philosophy, the presupposition of the apologists is not that philosophy as such is a major part of the practice of Christians in this period. The apologists are interested only in making a public argument that Christianity can compete with Greco-Roman philosophy on its own terms in the maintenance of a harmonious and virtuous society.[28]

Athenagoras knew that acceptable religions and philosophies were needed to promote civic welfare. As a result, he makes frequent references both to the harmlessness of Christians and the social beneficence of Christianity. For example, he tells the emperors:

> You, who are more intelligent than others, know that those who faithfully regulate their lives by reference to God, so that each of us stands before him blameless and irreproachable, will not entertain even the thought of the slightest sin.[29]

> With us, on the contrary, you will find unlettered people, tradesmen and old women, who, though unable to express in words the advantages of our teaching, demonstrate by acts the value of their principles. For they do not rehearse speeches, but evidence good deeds. When struck, they do not strike back; when robbed, they do not sue; to those who ask, they give, and they love their neighbors as themselves. . . . But since we are persuaded that we must give an account of all our life here to God who made us and the

world, we adopt a temperate, generous, and despised way of life.[30]

These it is who know that the life for which we look is far better than can be told, if we arrive at it pure from all wrongdoing. These it is whose charity extends to the point of loving not only their friends, for the Scripture says, "If you love those who love you, and lend to those who lend to you, what credit is it to you?" Since we are such and live this way to escape condemnation, can anyone doubt that we are religious?[31]

Now that I have disposed of the charges brought against us and shown that we are religious, kindly, and gentle in spirit, I beg you, grant your royal approval to my request. . . . And who, indeed, are more justified in getting what they ask than we? For we pray for your authority, asking that you may, as is most just, continue the royal succession, son from father, and receive just increase and extension of your realm that all men will eventually be your subjects. This is to our interest too, "so that we may lead a quiet and peaceable life," and be ready to do all we are commanded.[32]

Simply put, Athenagoras is confident that the emperors will judge Christians to be model Roman citizens because Christianity is the true philosophy that can provide social stability: "Although we do no wrong, but, as we shall show, are of all men most religiously and rightly disposed toward God and your Empire. . . ."[33]

Athenagoras asks the "illustrious Emperors" merely to "hear me impartially." He asks that Christians be judged as philosophers are judged:

It is in this way, we know, that philosophers are judged. None of them before the trial is viewed as good or bad because of his system or profession, but he is punished if he is found guilty. (No stigma attaches to philosophy on that account, for he is a bad man for not being a philosopher lawfully, and philosophy is not responsible.) On the other hand, he is acquitted if he disproves the charges. Let the same procedure be used in our case. Let the life of those who are accused be examined, and let the name be free from all reproach.[34]

Significantly, the intended recipients of this philosophical discourse were themselves philosophers, particularly Marcus Aurelius (Leslie Barnard is convinced that Athenagoras is well aware of Marcus Aurelius's *Meditations* "to which he appealed obliquely"[35]). The *Legatio* is addressed to the emperors as "conquerors of Armenia and Sarmatia and—what is more important—philosophers." In discussing what other poets and philosophers have taught, Athenagoras ingratiates himself: "For I know that as you excel all men in intelligence and imperial power, so you surpass all in your grasp of every branch of learning, mastering them all with more success than those who devote themselves exclusively to one." Even when it comes to Scripture, Athenagoras suggests that, "seeing how well informed you are, I suppose you are not unaware of Moses, Isaiah, Jeremiah, and the rest of the prophets." Throughout his *Legatio* it is clear that, as Athenagoras declares, "I am making my defense to emperors who are philosophers."[36]

Frend concludes that "Athenagoras represents the beginnings of new trends within orthodox Christianity." Whether delivered orally or only in writing, the *Legatio* of Athenagoras reveals a public process underway to accommodate Christianity within Roman civic culture, a process, for Frend, in which "Athenagoras set his face firmly towards the harmony of Christianity and the state."[37] We should not underestimate the significance of this process because it produced the sacred canopy under which the Constantinian revolution would take place. The transformation of Roman civil religion after A.D. 312 under Constantine and his successors was the fulfillment of a process that began long beforehand.

THE SEARCH FOR COMMON GROUND

D. W. Palmer writes that "the debt of the apologists to Hellenistic culture is manifold, woven from various strands of rhetoric and philosophy."[38] While Justin treated the Old Testament as a *praeparatio evangelica* and quoted it in detail, Barnard asserts that Athenagoras ignored it and concentrated instead "on Platonism as the preparation *par excellence*."[39] Douglas Powell disagrees, arguing that the paucity of Old Testament citations by Athenagoras is "no attempt to shrug off the heritage of Judaism"; yet he admits that "his aim is that of Justin—to show that Christianity is a *philosophia*, a rational way of life in the service of truth."[40] This did not mean that Christianity was treated as merely one philosophy among others or that it could be defended without regard to biblical revelation, but it did mean that there was a self-conscious apologetic attempt to accommodate the hostile culture into which Christianity was spreading.

Most scholars would agree with Joseph Hugh Crehan that Christianity was not merely "a veneer upon a Platonic habit of thought" for Athenagoras,[41] but they also would agree with Henry Lucks that Athenagoras attempted a "synthesis of pagan Greek thought and Christian revelation."[42] The key to this synthesis was the role of reason in both philosophy and theology. For Athenagoras, reason could build upon the foundation of biblical revelation. With Athenagoras begins a sophisticated move well beyond mere restatement of biblical truths into the philosophical recontextualization of those truths, with all of its difficulties and risks. Lucks writes:

> With his [Athenagoras's] age begins the development of a philosophy distinctly Christian in so far as it unfolded itself in the history of philosophical thought as a system which used the Scriptures as a negative norm and as a source of confirmation of its teachings and of material for further speculation. . . . He takes a tolerant and appreciative attitude towards the learning of the pagans, neither accusing

them of borrowing from the Scriptures of the Old Testament nor condemning their learning as dangerous or subversive of Christian faith.[43]

This conciliatory attitude toward the philosophical synthesis of reason and revelation, Lucks concludes, reaches "its point of highest perfection in the philosophy of Saint Thomas Aquinas."[44]

Critical to the argument of Athenagoras, as Barnard points out, was the way in which "Christian and pagan met on equal terms."[45] Athenagoras approached the non-Christian reader with tolerant respect for the Platonic philosophy and religious ideas then circulating throughout the Roman Empire. His presuppositions are both Platonic and Christian. The goal for Athenagoras, according to Barnard, was an appeal to philosophical common ground:

> Athenagoras is acutely aware of the challenge set by Graeco-Roman philosophy to understand their tradition in a philosophical way without recourse to scriptural arguments. So he appeals to a common ground shared with readers and propounds a *modus vivendi*.[46]

Barnard remains convinced that Athenagoras "uses Platonic themes only when there is no possibility of conflict with Christian thought."[47] Abraham Malherbe agrees, insisting that, while Athenagoras is a Platonist, he is still a *Christian* Platonist.[48]

Like other early apologists, Athenagoras emphasized God as Creator rather than Redeemer. When he rebuts the charge of atheism, Athenagoras first draws upon what the philosophers have taught and then asserts that Christianity fits comfortably within this theistic framework. He writes:

> If, then, Plato is not an atheist when he considers the one uncreated maker of the universe to be God, neither are we atheists when we recognize and affirm him to be God by whose Word all things were created and by whose Spirit they are held together.[49]

In fact, Athenagoras asserts that there is a philosophical consensus in Greco-Roman culture about the existence of God that Christianity shares:

> All philosophers, then, even if unwittingly, reach complete agreement about the unity of God when they come to inquire into the first principles of the universe. We too affirm that he who arranged this universe is God. Why, therefore, are they allowed to speak and write freely about God as they wish, while against us, who can adduce proofs and reasons for our idea and right conviction of the unity of God, a law is put in force?[50]

Athenagoras also proposes a rational basis for the Christian faith: "To grasp the rational basis of our faith, that from the beginning there was one God who made this universe, look at the matter thus." Athenagoras even gives what generally is considered one of the earliest explications of a doctrine of the Trinity to buttress his defense against the charge of atheism, concluding: "Who, then, would not be astonished to hear those called atheists who admit God the Father, God the Son, and the Holy Spirit, and who teach their unity in power and their distinction in rank?"[51]

Athenagoras supports his arguments with carefully chosen citations from Hellenistic philosophy. While Plato had an honored status,[52] Athenagoras used an eclectic approach to the philosophers:

> But first let me note that in going through what the philosophers have said about God, I do not intend to give a full review of their opinions. . . . I shall rely on collections of maxims.[53]

Yet even this eclecticism was characteristic of the philosophers of his age. Malherbe made a comparison of the *Legatio* and the *Didaskalikos* of Albinus ("a typical representative of second-century Middle Platonism"[54]) and concluded that Athenagoras "intended to present Christian doctrine within the framework provided by a Middle Platonic epitome of Plato's philosophy."[55]

Although there seems to be ample reason for emphasizing continuity rather than discontinuity between Athenagoras and the philosophers of his day, Barnard thinks that Athenagoras was a pioneer in using the analogy of being in both philosophical and theological argument.[56]

Operating with what Ignatius called "the divine answer to a question that had in fact been asked everywhere, the divine fulfillment of an aspiration that was universal,"[57] Athenagoras sought to give new meaning to Christianity for Greco-Roman culture. Although rooted in the Scriptures, the apologetic method of Athenagoras sought to present Christianity, Barnard writes, "as the crowning perfection of Greek thought and culture."[58] It was his confidence in the mediating power of reason that led Athenagoras to approach the emperors as philosophers. So great is Athenagoras's confidence in reason that, once having dispelled "the uncritical rumors of the crowd," he is sure that Christians "shall cease to be persecuted."[59]

The cultural impact of this apologetic was not on particular individuals, such as Marcus Aurelius or other Roman officials, but on the general acceptability of Christianity.[60] In the centuries following the death of Jesus, the church was gradually becoming more socially and intellectually diverse. By the time of Constantine, according to R. A. Markus, "the Christian communities had become effective cross-sections of Roman urban society. They had not only grown larger, but—more importantly—lost much of their social and cultural homogeneity." As a result, "the lines which marked the Christians off from the world around them were becomingly increasingly blurred as Christianity became more 'respectable' and as more and more Christians came to share the culture, the values, tastes and life-styles of their non-Christian contemporaries."[61] Once leaders in the church might have been content to attack the culture, now they increasingly sought to persuade. The goal, writes Harold O. J. Brown, was "to win understanding."[62]

In pursuit of such a goal, mastery of Greco-Roman philosophy became important. Around the time of the *Legatio*, Jill Harries points out, "the growing wish on the part of some Christians to make themselves intelligible and acceptable to contemporary intellectuals" led to "the founding of a school of Christian learning in Alexandria by Pantaenus in 180, that was to nurse the talents of Clement of Alexandria and Origen."[63] By the time of Clement, the theologians of the church were not only well-versed in Hellenism but also persuasive in their use of it. In the great cities of the empire, Robin Lane Fox declares, Greco-Roman culture "was finding fluent expression in Christian books."[64] MacMullen assesses the cultural impact of these writers:

> Purely in terms of numbers, no doubt the contribution made by such types to the church's growth was insignificant. Yes, but on the other hand it was important that the new teachings should not be found ill-equipped in intellectual terms, or incomplete, vulnerable to tests commonly used in the evaluation of any school of philosophy.[65]

Fox agrees:

> In the Antonine age, a shared literary and philosophical education united senatorial Romans and prominent figures in the Greek-speaking cities. It helped the wide and disparate upper class to communicate on common ground and to maintain a sense of personal contact. Respect for this common culture was shared by Emperors and their households. By presenting Christianity in similar terms, Christians of varying education attempted to join the high culture which distinguished the period and gave cohesion to its governing classes.[66]

There was, in short, common ground in the common culture. Then, as now, that also meant civil engagement with the shared values of the civil religion. Ultimately, MacMullen concludes, "[t]he triumph of the church was not one of obliteration but of widening embrace and assimilation."[67]

There were, of course, limits. Eusebius cites Christians about the time of Athenagoras who were close to the philosopher Galen in Rome. Although Eusebius gives few details, it is clear that the philosophical assimilation of this group violated the integrity of Scripture:

> They have not hesitated to corrupt the word of God; they have treated the standard of the primitive faith with contempt; they have not known Christ. Instead of asking what Holy Scripture says, they strain every nerve to find a syllogistic figure to bolster up their godlessness. If anyone examines them with a text from Divine Scripture, they examine it to see whether it can be turned into a conjunctive or disjunctive syllogistic figure. They put aside the sacred word of God, and devote themselves to geometry—earth-measurement—because they are from the earth and speak from the earth, and do not know the One who comes from above. Some of them give all their energies to the study of Euclidean geometry, and treat Aristotle and Theophrastus with reverent awe; to some of them Galen is almost an object of worship. When people avail themselves of the arts of unbelievers to lend colour to their heretical views, and with godless rascality corrupt the simple Faith of Holy Writ, it is obvious that they are nowhere near the Faith. So it was that they laid hands unblushingly on the Holy Scriptures, claiming to have corrected them.[68]

However anxious the early church was to adapt Hellenistic philosophy for its mission outreach, it was also sensitive to the danger of doctrinal distortion. The standard of truth remained the Scriptures.

DOES THE MIX MAKE A MUDDLE?

The most sympathetic interpreters of Athenagoras are Roman Catholic scholars (such as Lucks and Barnard). This is consistent with Roman Catholic scholasticism, in which reason and revelation function in complementary fashion, as they did for Athenagoras. Yet many Protestants also adopt a positive attitude toward the work of Athenagoras and other second-century apologists, despite their more critical attitude toward scholasticism. They do this primarily by observing that these early apologists referred often to Scripture. Bruce Shelley, for instance, summarizes the use of Scripture in Athenagoras: "As do the other Apologists, he resorts to an inspired Scripture for his ethical and doctrinal teaching. And, though he gives no hint of a rule independent of the Bible, he does consider scriptural teaching a system."[69] Then, writing with regard to all of the apologists, Shelley concludes: "Perhaps the outstanding feature of this group of writings is their persistent appeal to the Scriptures."[70]

Other Protestants, however, have been more critical. Coming primarily from strict Calvinistic Reformed traditions, their criticism has been that Athenagoras (and all like him who integrate Christianity with philosophy) is guilty of a syncretism that violates biblical standards of truth. One such critic was the Dutch Calvinist Herman Dooyeweerd, who wrote:

> Thus theologians resorted to adapting or accommodating heathen thought to the doctrine of the Christian church. . . . [T]his led of necessity to an uncritical reception of a large amount of heathen conceptual matter into Christian philosophy. In turn, theology was infected at more than one point by the uncritical adoption of Greek philosophical doctrines.[71]

Addressing the synthesis of non-Christian philosophy and biblical revelation in particular, Dooyeweerd wrote:

> Accordingly, the Christian starting point stands in a real antithesis to the non-Christian ones. It annihilates them as religious starting points. Of themselves they have nothing to offer the Christian starting point by way of complementation. They have no inherent, positive truthfulness to set over and against that of the Christian starting point. The

> Christian ground motive, therefore, may not be conceived
> of as the higher synthesis of all the non-Christian ones; for
> a synthesis is unable to stand in absolute antithesis to the
> mutually antithetical elements which it itself has brought to
> a higher unity.[72]

Dooyeweerd thus attacked the fundamental presupposition of the *Legatio*, namely, that there is a point of contact in philosophy by which to defend Christianity in a hostile civic culture.

Another critic of the search for common ground was Cornelius Van Til, a founder and late professor of apologetics at Westminster Theological Seminary in Philadelphia. In virtually every work he produced, Van Til attacked the presupposition that Christian apologetics can use the best of non-Christian thought as a means for bringing the non-Christian to an appreciation of Christian truth. The problem in any synthesis of apostate philosophy and Christianity, for Van Til, is the problem of human autonomy: "The philosophy of the Greeks is a philosophy thought out by apostate or would-be autonomous man."[73] For Van Til, the non-Christian thinker is not a truth-seeker, but a rebel. As far as Van Til was concerned, the use of Greek philosophy by the early apologists only indicated "their inability to see and properly evaluate the destructive purposes of the enemy as it camouflaged itself under the flag of theism."[74]

In *A Christian Theory of Knowledge*, Van Til attempted a comprehensive critique of the church's attempt to synthesize Greek philosophy and biblical revelation. Van Til differentiated between philosophies of knowledge that do, and those that do not, presuppose divine self-sufficiency and man's complete dependence upon God. Arguing against a distinction between content and method, Van Til wrote: "Christians cannot allow the legitimacy of the assumptions that underlie the non-Christian *methodology*."[75] Any attempt to characterize non-Christian thought as neutral ignores the problem of autonomy that is inherent in the biblical definition of sin: "For sin is that by which men seek to interpret facts apart from the revelation of God. The sinner seeks a criterion of truth and knowledge independent of the revelation of God."[76] As a result, Van Til concluded that there is no common ground between the Christian and the non-Christian because "fallen man cannot by his own adopted criteria make a true analysis of his own condition."[77]

When Van Til applied this uncompromising epistemology to the early church, he acknowledged that its apologists and theologians were sincere in their desire to be faithful to the Scriptures. Where he faulted them is in what they actually did to achieve what they desired. Unlike Shelley and many other Protestants, Van Til carefully distinguished between reference to scriptural truths and use of Scripture alone as the criterion of truth. Van Til simply did not think that the early church clearly understood the implications of the Christian commitment to biblical revelation and authority because "a completely Biblical doctrine of man would have implied the complete rejection of all Platonism."[78] Putting it bluntly, Van Til declared "it is one of the great blunders of Christian apologetics that it has sought to answer lower forms of non-Christian thought by higher forms of non-Christian thought."[79]

Van Til's epistemological critique of Athenagoras's apology has its parallel in Schoedel's critique of Athenagoras's grasp of the social and political issues. In an article entitled "Christian 'Atheism' and the Peace of the Roman Empire," Schoedel argues that Athenagoras was naive to think he could approach the emperors philosophically. Schoedel acknowledges Athenagoras was representative of a growing elite in Christian circles that was seeking to interpret Christianity for their culture. Yet Schoedel thinks that in this attempt "even the elite which was well disposed to Rome did not in fact understand Roman religious attitudes and misconstrued the significance of Roman tolerance."[80] Critical to this misconception was the different understanding of custom and law in the political discourse of Greece and Rome.

An important part of Schoedel's argument is reflected in the opening lines of the *Legatio*:

> In your Empire, Your Most Excellent Majesties, different
> peoples observe different laws and customs; and no one is
> hindered by law or fear of punishment from devotion to
> his ancestral ways, even if they are ridiculous.[81]

Schoedel thinks Athenagoras failed to realize how custom was not
of any legal significance for Rome. Furthermore, law was only significant in the formation of citizens for the Greeks, while its
Roman role as a regulating instrument of social policy was foreign
to Greek thought. In short, Schoedel is convinced Athenagoras
tried to use Greek standards of tolerance and civility to influence
Roman public policy and did not grasp that Roman "respect for
local custom was overshadowed by the requirements of good social
order."[82] Schoedel thinks Athenagoras discussed the accusations of
atheism on purely theoretical grounds without grasping the social
(civil religious) impulses that compelled those accusations:

> Athenagoras is not unaware of the social sources of the per-
> secution of Christians, but he does not take seriously the
> problems posed by practical atheism. . . . Consequently
> Athenagoras' discussion of the practical atheism of the
> Christians confines itself to theological and philosophical
> considerations which render the worship of the popular gods
> irrational. The social issue is pushed to the periphery.[83]

Schoedel also thinks Athenagoras treats the practical atheism
of Diagoras on a purely theoretical level when, in fact, the situation
was rooted in social antagonisms. And Schoedel musters support
from those who gave speeches opposed to the unlicensed rites of
Dionysus: "Here was tolerance, but a tolerance limited by the
demand to preserve the traditional virtues of Roman society."[84]
Thus, for Schoedel, Athenagoras may have been correct when he
distinguished between Roman law and local customs. He may also
have been correct when he argued that Christians often were guilty
only of violating local customs. What Athenagoras failed to realize
was the seriousness of the social unrest that resulted from the violation of those local customs. The Roman governors, acting with

wide discretionary powers and in full accord with Roman law, moved forcefully to resolve social unrest. Local traditions had a place in Roman public life, but they also were well regulated by Roman law to produce a harmonious civil organism. Preservation of that well-regulated civil organism was Rome's highest priority. This priority not only affected Christians, Schoedel points out, for Rome often interfered "even in regularly established religious affairs of the cities in the interest of public order."[85]

Just as Van Til argued there was no epistemological common ground, Schoedel's arguments suggest there also may not have been any political common ground either. However seemingly tolerant the Roman state may have been, it was not neutral. Its overriding commitment to the maintenance of civil order would force it to intervene in any serious social disorder. Athenagoras seems not to have understood this as, Schoedel concludes, "he credits the emperors with a lofty intelligence and a breadth of spirit that had little direct relevance to the political requirements of the day."[86] Athenagoras also evades the imperial cult sacrifices. While his silence may have been strategic (in that addressing them would have put him into direct conflict with the emperors), these sacrifices were fundamental to Roman civil religion and the crux of the church's conscientious objection to it.

Rejection of "common ground" is the basis for the public philosophy promoted by the Christian reconstruction movement in the United States today. Rousas Rushdoony, a self-described disciple of Van Til,[87] argues that American Christians also should not settle for "statist" political theory any more than the early church could have. Rushdoony offers the following assessment of Roman civil religion:

> The empire was ready to grant "religious freedom" to the church *provided* the church recognized the right of the state to grant that freedom, which meant a recognition of the state as the principle of order. . . . All religions and all gods could have their place in Rome, as long as the Roman state

and its emperor were recognized as the link between the human and the divine orders, the link by whom all others held their continuity and linkage.[88]

Rushdoony thinks that this seemingly innocuous recognition of the state as the principle of order is, in fact, a deification of the state and therefore a violation of the First Commandment. Rushdoony also thinks that the modern state presents Christians with the same problem:

> In the modern state, a new form of royal divinity is exhaustively present. For the modern state, there is no reality beyond the material; theological order is on every hand increasingly limited or denied. A new theology of the state is instead in evidence. The state is that order in which man is truly human, in terms of this new view. In the state and its cradle-to-grave security man will find his salvation. The state has unlimited jurisdiction, because it is that order in which man realizes himself, the order in which man expresses his collective divinity: *vox populi, vox dei*, the voice of the people is the voice of God in this collective or democratic consensus.[89]

Rushdoony hopes that modern Christians will be as highly motivated for political resistance as he thinks that the early church was.

The crucial principle, for Rushdoony as for Van Til, is the absence of neutrality: "The state cannot be religiously neutral, because it is the religious organization of society in terms of law." As a result, for Rushdoony, "the state can either be messianic or ministerial, either a savior or a ministry of justice. For Biblical religion, the state is a ministry of justice; for non-Christian religions, for political religions, the state is man's savior." In Rushdoony's hermeneutic, "the two concepts are mutually exclusive, and there can be no compromise between them."[90] With this total rejection of syncretism Rushdoony also prescribes a culture committed to biblical presuppositions:

> Man, created in the image of God, has a cultural mandate, i.e., to exercise the implications of that image, to be God's king, priest, and prophet in, to, and over all creation, *subduing* it, i.e., bringing it under his dominion in knowledge, righteousness, and holiness.[91]

And within that culture, of course, must exist a Christian state: "In Christian society, church and state are both religious orders, the church as a ministry of grace and the state as a ministry of justice."[92]

This theocratic approach to civil government can be traced to Zwingli, who once wrote "no man is capable of administering a magistracy properly unless he is a Christian,"[93] and, even more important, to John Calvin whose magisterial *Institutes of the Christian Religion* systematically developed the cooperative relationship between civil and ecclesiastical authorities. While Calvin did not attempt a synthesis of church and state that characterized the thought of Aquinas, Ronald Wallace argues, he nevertheless "accepted the view which had prevailed since the Roman Empire professed Christianity, that the Church and State were one and the same people."[94] The result, according to Peter Ivan Kaufman, was that Calvin "persistently identified the city's political order with God's purpose and . . . demanded that Genevans accept clerical leadership in public life as part of their ministers' management of (and responsibility for) the community's corporate redemption." Calvin also was uncompromising in pursuing this task because, as Kaufman observes, "compromise was the course that led away from the reign of Christ."[95]

We need to understand, therefore, that some approaches to syncretism may lead us to an essentially Reformed hermeneutic. While rejection of syncretism in a Reformed hermeneutic has the advantage of being both rigorously systematic and logically consistent, it also clearly raises serious problems for confessional Lutherans.[96] One might also observe that, at least in Rushdoony's work, the hermeneutic does not do justice to the self-evident civility with which so many early Christians (such as Athenagoras in his *Legatio*) approached Roman civic culture.[97]

BEYOND IDEOLOGY TO CULTURAL REVOLUTION

There is a danger in Athenagoras's attempt to synthesize Greek philosophy and biblical revelation. It is the dangerous presupposition that there is some sort of philosophical, social, or political common ground from which Christian faith can be given a neutral and, presumably, positive evaluation. Not only that, but the *Legatio* seemingly failed to persuade the Roman authorities and so provide immediate relief from persecution.

However, we should not be too quick to condemn Athenagoras as a weakly Christianized Greek philosopher. As David Balas writes: "It would be entirely insufficient simply to register in the writings of the Fathers the expressions from Greek philosophical language, taking for granted that the meaning of these expressions remained the same." The essential question, Balas notes, "is precisely how these elements thus assimilated have been used, what their function is in the whole structure of thought in which they have been inserted, and how the meaning of technical terms has gradually been transformed." In most cases, Balas argues, the early church fathers have "deeply transformed" Hellenistic philosophy to defend "an authentic Christian faith."[98] In his treatment of similar issues in the writing of the New Testament, Ronald Nash argues that too much is made of philosophical parallels. Parallels, he argues, do not prove dependence.[99] While there is a critical issue to debate about the synthesis of reason and revelation (keeping in mind that Lutherans have accepted a *ministerial* use of reason), it is not at all self-evident that such a synthesis always compromised biblical doctrine. The use of Hellenistic philosophy by the early church may or may not have been consistent with biblical teaching. That most likely will have to be determined case by case.[100]

Athenagoras explicitly defended the trinitarian God of the Bible, however much he used Hellenistic philosophy in that defense. While an exposition of Christian soteriology is lacking, his was not an evangelistic tract but a public defense of Christianity against the charge of atheism, a defense against the charge that Christianity subverted Greco-Roman society. He was aware that his purpose was limited, for he wrote at the end: "[W]e do not want to seem to introduce matters beyond the scope of our present task," after he had observed that Christians "are not alone in believing bodies will rise again."[101] Nor was Athenagoras guilty of basing his argument on philosophy alone. While his point of contact may have been Hellenistic, he made clear to the emperors where his own faith was based: "At the outset I assured you, Your Majesties, that our teaching came from God." And again: "Were we satisfied with such reasoning, one would think our doctrine was human. But prophetic voices confirm our arguments."[102]

One should note also that throughout his philosophical reasoning Athenagoras undermined the basis upon which non-Christian thinking can stand, what Palmer calls negative theology:

> The Greek apologists of the second century make significant use of negative theology, which they take over from other sources. The main source is no doubt contemporary Middle Platonism. But the influence of Middle Platonism itself has sometimes been mediated by Hellenistic Judaism. Moreover, the apologists' use of negative theology is selective. Particular terms are chosen in order to oppose pagan concepts of deity. This polemic-apologetic function of negative theology recalls its origins in Greek philosophy as far back as Presocratics. On the other hand, the choice of negative theological terms is also determined by the Christian concept of God which the apologists wish to convey.[103]

In his argument about traditional gods, Athenagoras pointed out that "the very ones who accuse us of atheism for not acknowledging the same gods that they believe in are not agreed among themselves about the gods."[104] In his discussion of mythology, he observed that "those who make real gods out of the myths do everything rather than form a true theology. For they fail to realize that by the very defense they make of their gods, they only confirm the reproaches brought against them."[105] He also challenged the validity of gods that have been "created":

> Thus, if the myths about the gods, which the populace and the poets repeat, are false, to reverence them is superfluous. For these gods do not exist if the tales about them are untrue. If on the other hand, all these stories about the gods are true . . . then they no longer exist, since they have ceased to be, just as they originally had no being before they were created. And what good reason is there to believe some of the tales and to disbelieve others, since the poets told them in order to idealize their heroes? For surely those who so magnified them by their stories that they were taken for gods would not have invented their sufferings.

> That, therefore, we are not atheists, since we worship God the creator of this universe, and his Word, I have proved as best I can, even if I have not done the subject justice.[106]

Such pugnacious arguments surely demonstrate the vitality of Athenagoras's Christian monotheism.

Yet even so, the charge of syncretism remains. Was the method of Athenagoras always consistent with biblical standards of truth, given his incorporation of Hellenism? While syncretism may be defined simply as the attempted combination of different systems of philosophical or religious belief or practice, historians and cultural theorists sometimes view syncretism as accommodation, assimilation, and institutionalization. In practical terms, it can mean something as simple as the imperial church moving the celebration of Jesus' birth to December 25 (a feast day for Sol, the sun god) for reasons having to do with Roman culture rather than the exegesis of sacred Scripture.[107] (A mosaic beneath St. Peter's in Rome also depicts Christ riding in a chariot like the sun god and

Jesus as *Sol Invictus* was inscribed on a coin dating from about A.D. 350.) This could be described as syncretistic from both an historical and sociological perspective. Does this mean that Christians who sincerely desire to renounce syncretism of every description must disavow the observance of Christmas on December 25? Or would it not be more helpful if the church developed doctrinal rather than historical and sociological definitions of syncretism? What historians and cultural theorists mean by syncretism may produce more confusion than enlightenment in ecclesiastical usage. The Lutheran "two-kingdom" distinction also impels us to consider carefully a use of terminology appropriate to each sphere.

Perhaps, therefore, we might find a more satisfactory approach to the *Legatio* as public discourse. Its audience, after all, was civil and not ecclesiastical. Schoedel's judgment that "Athenagoras' apology was lost sight of in antiquity, in all likelihood, because it contributed so little to theology"[108] is both unduly harsh and illuminating. Athenagoras never intended his *Legatio* as Christian theology. We, too, should pay close attention to its purpose.[109] Wilken thinks "the apologists have been interpreted for the most part as the first Christian theologians," resulting in a "preoccupation with theological and philosophical ideas." While this can be justified because they were, after all, "engaged in an intellectual task," Wilken also thinks "something has been missing in the account of early Christian apologetics." What is missing, Wilken argues, is "the social 'reality' that they, as members of the Christian communities, were experiencing" within the larger historical picture of the Roman Empire.[110] For all of its philosophical language, we should not only read the *Legatio* ideologically but also culturally.[111]

We may begin by observing that it was not only what the text *said* that was significant but also what it *did*. More important, it was how the text did what it did *through* what it said. What is at issue here, according to James Boyd White, is "how we create community and reconstitute our culture in language," a process in which "language is not stable but changing and . . . is perpetually remade by its speakers, who are themselves remade, both as individuals and as communities, in what they say."[112] This need not mean a reduction of the text to something less than what it claims to be, as if cultural analysis always implies depriving the text of its truth claims.[113] It does mean, however, that the text takes on even greater cultural significance than the ideas because the text functions within the culture as a thing in itself. Luther's Ninety-five Theses, for instance, had more impact on Germany than as mere propositions about repentance. They literally were equivalent to the "shot heard around the world" of the American Revolution.[114] White points out that "whenever we speak or write we define ourselves and another and a relation between us, and we do so in words that are necessarily made by others and modified by our use of them." That is, "we are in part products of our language, but each time we speak we remake it." Therefore, however deeply embedded an author may be within a cultural matrix, there is always the potential for profound cultural change with the production of a text. "For while the text is necessarily made out of the resources found within the culture—its words, expectations, values, conventions," according to White, "it can nonetheless . . . be deeply critical of those materials and that culture. *It may even propose a new world*" (*my emphasis*). The written text can be so revolutionary because it has a capacity for permanence and widespread distribution that oral speech lacks. "The written 'text' has a unique place in the history of culture," declares White, "for it reduces to permanence a process that is otherwise ephemeral and renders public, through the multiplication of readings, what is in the first instance, essentially private."[115]

This hermeneutic gains significance when joined with the metaphor of society as text. That metaphor illuminates human polity with the rules of grammar and, according to Richard Brown, also portrays revolution in terms of rhetorical reconstitution:

> Just as practice within a specialized institution is conducted
> through its reigning grammar, so public action within a

political community is made possible by the grammars—constitutions, common laws, or traditions—through which political thought and conduct may be expressed. By this way of thinking, transformation of the grammars of a polity is a definition of revolution. Thus the political rhetor seeking to create a revolution must shift the fundamental assumptions by which the presently given world is defined. He must proffer an alternative notion of the nature of reality and the ways we can seize it—that is, must offer an alternative public language, an alternative way of encoding and decoding the world.[116]

What distinguishes all of this from ideological analysis, the search for meaning in a text, is the emphasis on what texts *do*. "The new vision is not convincing because it describes the world more precisely," Richard Brown declares. "The vision is compelling because it *creates* a world that is more existentially adequate."[117]

From this perspective, civil religion is the narrative that both identifies and legitimizes a society. In any society, some people have more power and authority than others to modify or maintain the narrative, but anyone who is capable of creating a text is also capable of engaging that narrative critically. If we construe this narrative as merely containing ideas, we will overlook its even more basic role in the ongoing social construction of reality. Writes Peter Berger:

> Worlds are socially constructed and socially maintained. Their continuing reality, both objective (as common, taken-for-granted facticity) and subjective (as facticity imposing itself on individual consciousness), depends upon *specific* social processes, namely those processes that ongoingly reconstruct and maintain the particular worlds in question. Conversely, the interruption of these social processes threatens the (objective and subjective) reality of the worlds in question. Thus each world requires a social "base" for its continuing existence as a world that is real to actual human beings. This "base" may be called its plausibility structure.[118]

The civil religion narrative also depends on a plausibility structure, and it, too, must be ongoingly reconstructed and maintained. Thus for Christians to evade substantive dialogue with civil religion is to avoid deliberative interaction with the cultural narrative that sustains us, the thought-world that engages us all. Athenagoras seems to have understood this.

The *Legatio* is part of a discursive field that reshaped Roman civic culture. Although texts do not reshape a culture in and of themselves, they do have considerable power in combination with what in hindsight turn out to be favorable circumstances, such as the conversion and military victories of Constantine.[119] What we often overlook in the so-called Constantinian revolution is that there had to have been a culturally powerful Christianity in place to convert and receive him. There had to have been an alternative thought-world, already well developed in civic culture, rivaling the one to which he was previously committed. Cultural changes of this magnitude do not take place overnight. Yet much of the focus often has been on the cultural changes after the conversion of Constantine, rather than on the development of Christianity's cultural plausibility before Constantine. The *Legatio* of Athenagoras forces us to think about the discursive field that made the Constantinian revolution possible.

As we conceptualize this cultural process, we might benefit from some insights gleaned by Robert Wuthnow after studying the Reformation, Enlightenment, and European socialism, all periods of intense cultural ferment:

> In each historical episode the leading contributors to the new cultural motifs recognized the extent to which the institutional conditions of their day were flawed, constraining, oppressive, arbitrary. Their criticism of these conditions was often extreme and unrelenting. It was sharpened by an alternative vision, a vision constructed discursively, a vision that was pitted authoritatively against the established order, not as its replacement but as a conceptual space in

which new modes of behavior could be considered. The strength of their discourse lay in going beyond negative criticism and beyond idealism to identify working models of individual and social action for the future.[120]

Wuthnow writes here of public discourse about the established order with an alternative vision, not for its replacement, but in which new modes of behavior could be considered. Perhaps this can be a description also of the early church and not only of three modern cultural revolutions.

The *Legatio* of Athenagoras was both the continuation of a pattern and groundbreaking. Through his skillful adaptation of traditional civic discourse, Athenagoras created a significant precedent for the relationship of church and state. In his 1979 study "In Praise of the King: A Rhetorical Pattern in Athenagoras," Schoedel sees this precedent and argues that it has been overlooked previously because "panegyrics have been dismissed as bad literature and interesting only for the historical facts buried in them."[121] One might add that the precedent also has been overlooked because the *Legatio* is dismissed for limited theological value!

The best parallel for Athenagoras's apology, according to Schoedel, is in Menander's (or Pseudo-Menander's) third-century handbook for the writing of panegyrics, in which there is a chapter "Concerning a Speech on the King." While Athenagoras does not follow this traditional pattern closely, except in his conclusion, Schoedel argues that what he does write betrays unmistakable awareness of the tradition. Particularly interesting, for Schoedel, is the way that Athenagoras adapts those traditional guidelines to suit his own rhetorical purposes. He moves away from the traditional emphasis on the king's courageous military exploits to an emphasis on the emperors' roles as peacemakers, a rhetorical strategy that becomes more popular after Athenagoras. Even more important, however, Athenagoras also structures his apology with an awareness of the advice (codified in Menander) that if a king "is a man of letters, you shall praise his philosophy and his knowledge of letters." In other words, the rather extravagant language in the apology need not always reflect specific knowledge about the emperors, particularly Marcus Aurelius, as philosophers. Rather, "his view of the emperor is drawn from the stock themes of rhetoric," observes Schoedel. Here, too, Athenagoras anticipates later emphases of the rhetorical tradition.[122]

Of particular interest to Schoedel is the "daring analogy" Athenagoras proposed between the co-emperors and the "one God and the Word that issues from him." Athenagoras seems familiar with the rhetorical tradition (again codified in Menander) to portray kings as emanations of divinity. That, of course, would violate Christian faith. What Athenagoras anticipates is later Christian teaching about the divine right of kings. He proposes that the emperors, who like Jesus and His Father are also a father and a son, have received their kingdom from above, from God. Here Athenagoras cites Scripture: "for the king's life is in God's hands (Proverbs 21:1)." To Schoedel, "it is remarkable how Athenagoras' analogy, *ad hoc* as it seems to be, anticipates later developments. Particularly important is Eusebius' application of Binatarian theology to the politics of the Christian court."[123]

The overall shape and purpose of the *Legatio*, for Schoedel, goes far beyond mere public statement of Christian faith in Hellenistic dress. The *Legatio* is a skillful adaptation of ambassadorial speech to serve a new rhetorical purpose. Within the familiar structure of a traditional panegyric to the king, Athenagoras introduced the limits of imperial power prescribed by biblical Christianity. Schoedel concludes: "In the end, Athenagoras' view, derived from the Bible, that the king is in God's hands checks the most extravagant claims of the rhetoricians and sets a limit to imperial power. The emperors' task is to provide a framework within which all men, including Christians, can pursue their lives in peace and quiet." However, that Athenagoras adopted so much of the "pagan imperial ideology," Schoedel admits, "explains why after the conversion of Constantine, Christian emperors could continue to function in ways appropriate to divine beings." Nevertheless, in Schoedel's opinion, the *Legatio* "may be seen as a sensitive response to an important strand in ancient political thought and a remarkable anticipation of the flowering of these ideas in the fourth century."[124]

When Athenagoras produced his *Legatio*, it may not have convinced anyone in particular, but as Marshall McLuhan wrote, his medium was the message.[125] By skillfully articulating Christian concerns in the language of Roman civic culture, Athenagoras communicated implicitly that Christianity was no superstition, no threat to Greco-Roman civilization. With that foot in the door (or camel's nose under the tent!), Athenagoras hoped that Christianity could increasingly gain a hearing within a culture that generally had dismissed it. While no substitute for the work of the Holy Spirit, Athenagoras hoped that his apology would help the church's evangelistic discourse proceed unhindered both by political restraints and by cultural prejudices.

One hundred years later, the church had made remarkable progress. Eusebius describes with enthusiasm the freedom and respect given the preaching of the Gospel by the end of the third century:

> How great, how unique were the honour, and liberty too, which before the persecution of my time were granted by all men, Greeks and non-Greeks alike, to the message given through Christ to the world, of true reverence for the God of the universe! It is beyond me to describe it as it deserves. Witness the goodwill so often shown by potentates to our people; they even put into their hands the government of the provinces, releasing them from the agonizing question of sacrificing, in view of the friendliness with which they regarded their teaching.[126]

And so the *Legatio* and other works of early theologians contributed to the *eventual* resolution of persecution through the process of cultural change. "The general social changes of the later second century coincided with a crucial inner change in the faith's public image," observes Fox.[127]

It is no accident that the progress Eusebius noted followed and overlapped with the efforts of thinking Christians to relate their faith to existing philosophies and ethics. Even if the Christian apologists' books were not widely read, their existence was proof that Christianity was now respectable.

Ironically, the official Roman civil religion undermined itself by prodding the church to become more cohesive than it might have been absent the persecution. It prompted the church to both produce and distribute widely the texts that shaped ecclesiastical orthodoxy and reshaped Roman civic culture. Harold O. J. Brown writes:

> In a sense, it was the government's policy of persecution and repression that made the early church truly catholic and ecumenical. Because the persecution was empire-wide, the apologies were read all over the Roman empire, as other theological texts would not have been. Thus the hostility of the government helped to popularize the first works of Christian theology. Long before Christianity was officially established, it had become an empire-wide institution.[128]

While the *immediate* persecution did not end, and the *Legatio* may never even have been read by the emperors to whom it was addressed, the process of interpreting Christianity to the cultural elites of the Roman Empire did have the salutary effect over time of making Christianity plausible.

The purpose of the *Legatio* was not evangelistic but civic. It is the distinction between Christianity as doctrine of the church and Christianity as public philosophy, what Lutherans articulate regarding the two different governments or kingdoms of God. Lutherans do not denigrate civil righteousness, in which Christians and non-Christians alike engage in works of compassion and justice. While the normative principles of the church may be the Gospel and faith, the normative principles of the civil order are law (including natural law) and reason. Robert Kolb writes that, regardless of Luther's contempt for reason when it came to spiritual righteousness, "Luther was quite confident that human rationality could and often would find a good set of positive laws and upright customs to serve a society—no matter how many or few Christians lived in it."[129] Therefore, instead of evaluating the *Legatio* by encyclopedic ecclesiastical standards (that is, how comprehensively did it present the Christian faith?), we may need to view it in terms of the rhetorical task that it assumed. This task was public defense of the rationality and social beneficence of Christianity, a task that became commonplace after Athenagoras, according to Wilken:

> Pagan thinkers had no franchise on rationality. The existence of a serious dialogue between Christian and Roman philosophers, conducted at the highest level for over three centuries (the mid-second century to the mid-fifth), is evidence that Christian thinkers did not supplant reason by faith and authority. The assertion that the gospel had a "proof peculiar to itself" was not a confession of unreasoning faith but an argument that commended itself to thoughtful men and women.[130]

Insofar as civil religion deals with the natural knowledge of God, what Athenagoras was trying to do in his *Legatio* may fit within Lutheran teaching on appropriate civic discourse. When Athenagoras engaged the Roman civil religion with critical respect rather than intolerant hostility, he provided an alternate vision of civic culture and a foundation for its eventual transformation.

The *Legatio* of Athenagoras helped to create what Athenagoras could only envision when he wrote it: a Roman civic culture in which Christianity was accepted as the true philosophy. The watershed was Constantine. "The Caesars too would have believed in Christ," Tertullian wrote, "if Christians could have been Caesars."[131] But, of course, they could and would! Furthermore, with respect for Rome grounded in the teachings of Jesus and Paul, the early church eventually developed what Stauffer called a *"Philosophia Imperii,"* by which he meant "a historical and theological picture of the universal mission of the Roman empire."[132] While Constantine was undoubtedly sincere in his Christian faith, he was convinced that religion remained essential to the unity of the empire. Constantine believed that the Christian church "should be brought in as the ally and close component of the government, and should be amalgamated with it," writes Michael Grant, "so as to achieve the *national unity* which the persecution had so conspicuously failed to supply."[133] Furthermore, as revolutionary as Constantine's conversion to Christianity sometimes may seem, Glanville Downey notes that the "new theory of the imperial power involved no radical departure. Constantine and his successors continued to keep most of the traditional forms of the imperial office."[134] The Roman civil religion had not been replaced but transformed.

It may have been during the reign of Constantine that Roman emperors actually lost their status as a god, according to Richard Pierard and Robert Linder, while retaining their positions as religio-political figures "under the Highest God, who now presided over Rome's fortunes."[135] But, for Eusebius, the great historian of what Kaufman calls the "redeeming politics of the Christian empire," the conversion and reign of Constantine was "the culmination of a historical process governed by the Logos from the very start."[136] Christians had discussed and debated the Roman civil religion over more than a century before Constantine and, as every great river flows from many sources, so the *Legatio* contributed to that "historical process" of which Eusebius wrote. "Athenagoras' *Legatio* is a valuable witness to the manner in which the Christian elite was unconsciously preparing the church for its role as the major vehicle of religious values in the Roman state," observes Schoedel.[137] Through civil engagement of the Roman civil religion in its own language and on its own turf, Athenagoras 'proposed a new world' of thought, and through this discourse helped, eventually, to create a new civic culture.

Notes

1. The Rev. David R. Liefeld, St. Peters, Missouri, is a Lutheran Church—Missouri Synod English District pastor currently on disability. He has an M.Div. from Luther Theological Seminary, St. Paul, Minnesota, a Th.M. in systematic theology from Westminster Theological Seminary, and an M.A. specializing in modern cultural history from Temple University.

2. Tertullian's famous comment clearly addresses Hellenistic syncretism:

   What indeed has Athens to do with Jerusalem? What concord is there between the Academy and the Church? What between heretics and Christians? Our instruction comes from the porch of Solomon, who himself taught that the Lord should be sought in simplicity of heart. Away with all attempts to produce a mottled Christianity of Stoic, Platonic and dialectic composition. We want no curious disputation after possessing Christ Jesus, no research after enjoying the gospel! With our faith we desire no further belief. (As quoted in Johannes Quasten, *Patrology,* Vol. 2: *The Ante-Nicene Literature after Irenaeus* [Westminster, Md.: Newman Press, 1962], 320.)

3. For purposes of this article, the term *syncretism* is here defined as the attempted combination of different systems of philosophical or religious belief or practice.

4. Walter J. Burghardt, "Book Review: *Athenagoras, Embassy for the Christians and the Resurrection of the Dead,*" *Theological Studies* 18 (1957): 448. Henry A. Lucks calls the writings of Athenagoras "artistic gems of early Christian literature" in which "his method of defense of the Christian belief and practice is persuasive and studiously inoffensive, yet accurate and arresting" ("The Philosophy of Athenagoras: Its Sources and Value," Ph.D. diss., The Catholic University of America, 1936, 22f.). Joseph Hugh Crehan considers the quality of these writings to be "higher than that of the other 2nd-century apologists" and calls Athenagoras "in many ways . . . the ablest of the Greek apologists" (*Athenagoras: Embassy for the Christians and the Resurrection of the Dead,* Vol. 23 of the *Ancient Christian Writers,* ed. J. Quasten and J. Plumpe [Westminster, Md.: Newman Press, 1956], 1005). See also Cyril C. Richardson, *Early Christian Fathers* (New York: Macmillan, [1953] 1970), 292; and Johannes Quasten, *Patrology,* Vol. 1: *The Beginnings of Patristic Literature* (Westminster, Md.: Newman Press, 1962), 229.

5. Leslie W. Barnard, *Athenagoras: A Study in Second Century Christian Apologetic* (Paris: Beauchesne, 1972), 13ff.

6. W. H. C. Frend, *The Rise of Christianity* (Philadelphia: Fortress, 1984), 234.

7. Fergus Millar, *The Emperor in the Roman World (31 BC–AD 337)* (Ithaca, N.Y.: Cornell University Press, 1977), 6f. and 9.

8. Robert M. Grant, "Forms and Occasions of the Greek Apologists," *Studia e materiali di storia delle religioni* 52 (1986): 219.

9. William R. Schoedel, "Apologetic Literature and Ambassadorial Activities," *Harvard Theological Review* 82, no. 1 (1989): 78.

10. Schoedel, "Apologetic Literature and Ambassadorial Activities," 59.

11. Robert M. Grant, "Five Apologists and Marcus Aurelius," *Vigiliae christianae* 42 (1988): 1–17.

12. T. D. Barnes, "The Embassy of Athenagoras," *Journal of Theological Studies* 26 (1975): 114. Schoedel concludes that "there is good reason to think that Athenagoras's *Embassy* was written to be presented to the emperor or delivered before him and that its author would have served as ambassador for the embattled Christian community." Of course, Schoedel admits, "[w]hether the emperor would in fact have read the address or listened to it is another matter. For he was a busy man, and it could take a long time for an ambassador to get an audience with him (Philo *Leg.* 182). And to judge from the models we have examined, the emperor may then have asked a few questions and gone on to other things. It is also conceivable that the ambassador presented an abbreviated version of his address or that the writing we now have was considerably reworked for publication" ("Apologetic Literature and Ambassadorial Activities," 74ff.).

13. Richardson, *Early Christian Fathers*, 310.

14. Paul Keresztes writes that "there is today an almost general agreement that the Christians, under normal circumstances, were not tried on the basis of either the *ius coercitionis or* the general criminal law, but on the basis of a special law introduced during Nero's rule, proscribing Christians as such" ("Law and Arbitrariness in the Persecution of the Christians and Justin's First Apology," *Vigiliae christianae* 18 [1964]: 204). However, Gerhard Krodel disagrees: "Uncertainty exists concerning the legal basis of their condemnation, but the notion that Nero issued a special edict proscribing Christianity lacks sufficient evidence" ("Persecution and Toleration of Christianity until Hadrian," in *The Catacombs and the Colosseum: The Roman Empire as the Setting of Primitive Christianity,* ed. Stephen Benko and John J. O'Rourke [Valley Forge, Penn.: Judson Press, 1971], 260). John J. O'Rourke agrees with Krodel: "Exactly when Christians came to be generally regarded as adherents of a new, illegal religion is difficult to determine" ("Roman Law and the Early Church," in *Catacombs and the Colosseum*, 179).

15. One can endlessly debate the definition of *civil religion*, but all societies create a frame of reference to provide order and give meaning or purpose to political life. In the premodern world that frame of reference was explicitly, even institutionally, religious. With modernity, the civil religion is a common core of values and beliefs that transcend institutional or formalized religious systems. Many scholars, therefore, prefer to label it *public philosophy*. Yet, even in the modern world, public philosophy continues to relate the state to ultimate meaning and so continues to qualify in the broad sense as *religious*.

16. A good survey of this stimulating topic is Richard V. Pierard and Robert D. Linder, *Civil Religion and the Presidency* (Grand Rapids: Zondervan, 1988). They write:

> In any event, scholars generally agree that whether he is religiously active or passive, the foremost representative of civil religion in America is the president. He not only serves as head of state and chief executive, but he also functions as the symbolic representative of the whole of the American people. He affirms that God exists and that America's destiny and the nation's policies must be interpreted in the light of the Almighty's will. The rituals that the president celebrates and the speeches he makes reflect the basic themes of American civil religion. (20)

17. Donald Winslow, "Religion and the Early Roman Empire," in *Catacombs and the Colosseum*, 247. Daniel N. Schowalter has demonstrated that "the relationship between the Emperor and the gods was not a static thing" and that "the portrayal of that relationship changed from emperor to emperor, and even within the reign of a single emperor." Therefore, it is not possible to describe all emperors in terms of one generalized "imperial cult." Nevertheless, it is still possible to say, as Schowalter does, that "the relationship between the emperor and the gods had a definite impact on the socio-political order in Rome" (*The Emperor and the Gods: Images from the Time of Trajan* [Minneapolis: Fortress, 1993], 126, 128).

18. Winslow, "Religion and the Early Roman Empire," 247.

19. Robert Wuthnow, *Meaning and Moral Order: Explorations in Cultural Analysis* (Berkeley: University of California Press, 1987), 123.

20. Robert L. Wilken, "Toward a Social Interpretation of Early Christian Apologetics," *Church History* 39 (1970): 447.

21. Robert L. Wilken, "The Christians as the Romans (and Greeks) Saw Them," in *Jewish and Christian Self-Definition*, Vol. 1: *The Shaping of Christianity in the Second and Third Centuries*, ed. E. P. Sanders (Philadelphia: Fortress, 1980), 106.

22. Wilken, "Christians as the Romans (and Greeks) Saw Them," 106.

23. Cicero: *Laws*, II, 15, in *De Republica, De Legibus*, trans. C. W. Keyes (London: Heinemann, [1928] 1959), 389.

24. Wilken, "Christians as the Romans (and Greeks) Saw Them," 107.

25. Paul Keresztes, "Marcus Aurelius a Persecutor?" *Harvard Theological Review* 61 (1968): 321ff.

26. Ethelbert Stauffer, *Christ and the Caesars* (London: SCM, [1952] 1955), 210.

27. Ramsay MacMullen, *Enemies of the Roman Order: Treason, Unrest and Alienation in the Empire* (Cambridge: Harvard University Press [1966] 1975), 93.

28. Writes Wilken: "Christianity was able to engender in men the same virtue, the same nobility, the same *philanthropia*, in short, the same piety which the other philosophers claimed to produce" ("Toward a Social Interpretation of Early Christian Apologetics," 447).

29. Richardson, *Early Church Fathers*, 335.

30. Richardson, *Early Church Fathers*, 310. Athenagoras also provides an unequivocal condemnation of abortion and infanticide (338f.):

    What reason would we have to commit murder when we say that women who induce abortions are murderers, and will have to give account of it to God? For the same person would not regard the fetus in the womb as a living thing and therefore an object of God's care, and at the same time slay it, once it had come to life. Nor would he refuse to expose infants, on the ground that those who expose them are murderers of children, and at the same time do away with the child he has reared. But we are altogether consistent in our conduct. We obey reason and do not override it.

31. Richardson, *Early Church Fathers*, 311.

32. Richardson, *Early Church Fathers*, 340.

33. Richardson, *Early Church Fathers*, 301.

34. Richardson, *Early Church Fathers*, 302.

35. Leslie W. Barnard, "Athenagoras, Galen, Marcus Aurelius and Celsus," *Church Quarterly Review* 168 (1967): 175. Barnard elaborates: "He [Athenagoras] knew the philosophical beliefs which the Emperor held and appealed, when occasion arose, to those beliefs—although also opposing them on fundamental matters such as the transcendence of God" (176).

36. Richardson, *Early Christian Fathers*, 300, 305, 308, and 310.

37. Frend, *Rise of Christianity*, 242.

38. D. W. Palmer, "Atheism, Apologetic, and Negative Theology in the Greek Apologists of the Second Century," *Vigiliae christianae* 37 (1983): 237.

39. Barnard, "Athenagoras, Galen, Marcus Aurelius, and Celsus," 169.

40. Douglas Powell, "Athenagoras and the Philosophers," *Church Quarterly Review* 168 (1967): 284f.

41. Crehan, *Athenagoras*, 15.

42. Lucks, "Philosophy of Athenagoras," 81.

43. Lucks, "Philosophy of Athenagoras," 81.

44. Lucks, "Philosophy of Athenagoras," 86.

45. Barnard, *Athenagoras*, 51.

46. Leslie W. Barnard, "Athenagoras: *De Resurrectione*," *Studia Theologica* 30 (1976): 5.

47. Barnard, "Athenagoras: *De Resurrectione*," 5.

48. Abraham J. Malherbe, "The Structure of Athenagoras' *Supplicatio Pro Christianis*," *Vigiliae christianae* 23 (1969): 20.

49. Richardson, *Early Christian Fathers*, 306.

50. Richardson, *Early Christian Fathers*, 306.

51. Richardson, *Early Christian Fathers*, 307 and 309.

52. Abraham J. Malherbe points out that "except for a short quotation from Empedocles in chapter 22, Plato is the only philosopher quoted *verbatim*, and this always with approval" ("Athenagoras on the Pagan Poets and Philosophers," in *Kyriakon*, ed. Granfield and Jungmann [Münster Westfalen: Verlag Aschedorff, 1970], 223).

53. Richardson, *Early Christian Fathers*, 305.

54. Barnard, *Athenagoras*, 38.

55. Malherbe, "Structure of Athenagoras' *Supplicatio Pro Christianis*," 20.

56. Barnard writes: "Athenagoras implies that God, the cause of man is Being and that Being is related by analogy to the being that man has. It is doubtful if the Middle Platonist philosophers by Athenagoras' day had evolved this idea of the analogy of being from the hints Plato gave. Athenagoras, in fact, may well be a pioneer in this connexion" (*Athenagoras*, 45).

57. Quoted in Jaroslav Pelikan, *Jesus through the Centuries: His Place in the History of Culture* (New Haven: Yale University Press, 1985), 34. David L. Balas also writes: "Christianity had to be announced to cultivated pagans as the fulfillment of their deepest longings, including their intellectual yearnings" ("The Encounter between Christianity

and Contemporary Philosophy in the Second Century," *Anglican Theological Review* 50 [1968]: 138).

58. Barnard, *Athenagoras*, 47.

59. Richardson, *Early Christian Fathers*, 303.

60. Harold O. J. Brown provides the consensus assessment of the official impact of the *Legatio* and other apologies: "Did the apologists succeed in their goal of changing the minds of emperors and government officials? There is no record that they did." However, Brown immediately proceeds to surface the cultural impact of these works: "What they did accomplish was to launch the intellectual discipline of theology, which eventually made Christianity the most thoroughly analyzed and academic of the world's great religions" (*Heresies: The Image of Christ in the Mirror of Heresy and Orthodoxy from the Apostles to the Present* [Garden City, N. Y.: Doubleday, 1984], 77).

61. R. A. Markus, "The Problem of Self-Definition: From Sect to Church," in *Jewish and Christian Self-Definition,* Vol. 1: *The Shaping of Christianity in the Second and Third Centuries,* ed. E. P. Sanders (Philadelphia: Fortress, 1980), 12.

62. Brown, *Heresies*, 77.

63. Jill Harries, "The Rise of Christianity," in *The Roman World,* ed. John Wacher (London: Routledge & Kegan Paul, 1987), 2:802.

64. Robin Lane Fox, *Pagans and Christians* (San Francisco: Harper & Row, 1986), 307. R. H. Barrow agrees: "It [Christianity] was now the religion of some of the ablest and best-educated men of the day" (*The Romans* [Baltimore: Penguin, (1949) 1964], 180).

65. Ramsay MacMullen, *Christianizing the Roman Empire (A.D. 100–400)* (New Haven: Yale University Press, 1984), 106.

66. Fox, *Pagans and Christians*, 305.

67. Ramsay MacMullen, *Christianity and Paganism in the Fourth to Eighth Centuries* (New Haven: Yale University Press, 1997), 159.

68. Eusebius, *The History of the Church from Christ to Constantine* trans. with an intro. by G. A. Williamson (Baltimore: Penguin, 1965), 237. See also R. Walzer, *Galen on Jews and Christians* (London: Oxford University Press, 1949), 77ff.

69. Bruce Shelley, *By What Authority* (Grand Rapids: Eerdmans, 1965), 78.

70. Shelley, *By What Authority*, 81.

71. Herman Dooyeweerd, "Reformation and Scholasticism in Philosophy," prepublication manuscript (1984), 1:38.

72. Dooyeweerd, "Reformation and Scholasticism in Philosophy," 1:66.

73. Cornelius Van Til, "Christianity in Conflict," unpublished syllabus (Philadelphia: Westminster Theological Seminary, n.d.), 1.1.79.

74. Van Til, "Christianity in Conflict," 1.1.27.

75. Van Til, *A Christian Theory of Knowledge* (Nutley, N.J.: Presbyterian and Reformed Publishing Co., 1969), 18.

76. Van Til, *Christian Theory of Knowledge*, 33.

77. Van Til, *Christian Theory of Knowledge*, 43.

78. Van Til, *Christian Theory of Knowledge*, 104. Van Til praises Tertullian for his uncompromising rejection of Hellenism (see *Christian Theory of Knowledge*, 104 n. 1). However, even Tertullian does not escape Van Til's scathing critique of the early church fathers: "Would that he had himself always been fully true to it. . . . It is because he was not fully true to his own principles of Scripture that Tertullian did not offer a good defense of the truth of Christianity" (*Christian Theory of Knowledge*, 109).

79. Van Til, *Christian Theory of Knowledge*, 134. Augustine also is a target of Van Til's criticism. While Van Til thinks that Augustine makes real strides toward the development of a thoroughly Christian theology, Augustine nevertheless continues to believe (in Van Til's opinion) "that a true theism is found among the Greeks and that therefore he can use the arguments given for the defense of theism as these have been worked out by the philosophers" (*Christian Theory of Knowledge*, 119).

80. William R. Schoedel, "Christian 'Atheism' and the Peace of the Roman Empire," *Church History* 42 (1973): 309.

81. Richardson, *Early Christian Fathers*, 300.

82. Schoedel, "Christian 'Atheism' and the Peace of the Roman Empire," 312ff.

83. Schoedel, "Christian 'Atheism' and the Peace of the Roman Empire," 311.

84. Schoedel, "Christian 'Atheism' and the Peace of the Roman Empire," 314.

85. Schoedel, "Christian 'Atheism' and the Peace of the Roman Empire," 315.

86. Schoedel, "Christian 'Atheism' and the Peace of the Roman Empire," 317.

87. Rushdoony concluded the foreword of his 1958 book on Van Til's philosophy with this endorsement: "This work, therefore, is thus both an exposition of a philosophy, and an exposition as well of Van Til's

development of that philosophy, a school of thought to which this writer subscribes" (*By What Standard? An Analysis of the Philosophy of Cornelius Van Til* [Fairfax, Va.: Thoburn Press, (1958) 1974], vii). Echoing Van Til, Rushdoony elsewhere writes: "Apart from Biblical faith, there is no theistic religion, and Biblical religion is unique in its affirmation of a totally personal and sovereign God" (*The Biblical Philosophy of History* [Phillipsburg, N.J.: Presbyterian and Reformed Publishing Co., (1969) 1979], 87).

88. Rousas John Rushdoony, *Politics of Guilt and Pity* (Fairfax, Va.: Thoburn Press, [1970] 1978), 304ff.

89. Rushdoony, *Politics of Guilt and Pity*, 309.

90. Rousas John Rushdoony, *The Foundations of Social Order: Studies in the Creeds and Councils of the Early Church* (Fairfax, Va.: Thoburn Press, [1968] 1978), 220ff.

91. Rousas John Rushdoony, *The One and the Many: Studies in the Philosophy of Order and Ultimacy* (Fairfax, Va.: Thoburn Press, [1971] 1978), 33.

92. Rushdoony, *Foundations of Social Order*, 221.

93. Ulrich Zwingli, *The Latin Works of Huldreich Zwingli*, ed. Clarence Nevin Heller (Philadelphia: Heidelberg Press, 1929), 3:294.

94. Ronald S. Wallace, *Calvin, Geneva and the Reformation: A Study of Calvin as Social Worker, Churchman, Pastor and Theologian* (Grand Rapids: Baker [1988] 1990), 120, 122. Wallace elaborates on the notion, sometimes claimed, "that Calvin aimed to produce in Geneva what can be called a 'Christian culture.' " Wallace says that "such a phrase is confusing" and that however much Calvin expected Geneva to be transformed by its role in the Christian order, "it always remained a 'secular' city. Calvin did not believe we could blend the Christian with the human" (120).

95. Peter Iver Kaufman, *Redeeming Politics* (Princeton, N.J.: Princeton University Press, 1990), 120ff. Kaufman also writes regarding Calvinism: "If magistrates were to formulate policy that corresponded to God's law, pastors must instruct them. If citizens were to nominate and support able, pious magistrates, pastors must counsel and direct them." Therefore, in Calvin's Geneva, "the clergy never relinquished their roles as chief monitors and guarantors of God's new order *and . . . lay gubernatores in the consistory. . . were part of the ministry of the church*—part of its scriptural and properly reformed administration" (124).

96. Kaufman presents Calvin's view of Luther's deficiencies in this area, which serves also as a warning about fundamental hermeneutical differences between Lutheran and Reformed:

From Calvin's perspective, Luther and other reformers of the so-called first generation were partly to blame for the second generation's difficulties with the radicals. The early reformers had underscored the centrality of Christ's atonement and the liberty granted Christians who truly believed that Christ died to liberate them. Luther and his associates, however, left no directions for the management of communities filled with liberated Christians. Calvin insinuated that the first reformers left the reform of government to chance and circumstance. He believed that government must be carefully monitored, although he was aware that deductions of this kind could hardly be verified from the evidence in the New Testament, where the few magistrates mentioned were hostile to the gospel. His efforts to redeem politics and his generalizations about redeeming politics could be illustrated best with anecdotes from the Hebrew scriptures. Calvin was a tireless and prolific student of the Old Testament, where collaboration between magistrates and ministers appeared to be a critical part of God's providential direction of history. Calvin concluded that God had appointed two ministries to assist the elect in shaping and policing a civil order that reflected the importance and influence of their election. (*Redeeming Politics*, 114ff.)

97. It is hard to tell sometimes, as in the following comment, whether Rushdoony is simply glossing over those (such as Athenagoras) who don't fit his pattern or whether he means to exclude them from the true Christian church: "The orthodox Christians, before and after Constantine the Great, insisted on the supremacy of Christ and His infallible Word over state and church, and emperors and bishops were alike rebuked in terms of it" (*Politics of Guilt and Pity*, 305).

98. Balas, "Encounter between Christianity and Contemporary Philosophy," 141f.

99. Ronald H. Nash, *Christianity and the Hellenistic World* (Grand Rapids: Zondervan, 1984). Malherbe also argues that Paul was only conversant with Hellenistic philosophy throughout most of his Epistles: "When he first formed churches, therefore, Paul made use of elements from the Greco-Roman philosophical moral tradition, but adapted them to express his theological understanding of his enterprise and to form communities of believers" (Abraham J. Malherbe, *Paul and the Popular Philosophers* [Minneapolis: Fortress, 1989], 71).

100. The most glaring abusers of Hellenism in the early church were Gnostics. Powell actually thinks Athenagoras may have cast his apology in philosophical, rather than biblical, language precisely to combat Gnostics; see "Athenagoras and the Philosophers," 288.

101. Richardson, *Early Christian Fathers*, 339.

102. Richardson, *Early Christian Fathers*, 336, 308.

103. Palmer, "Atheism, Apologetic, and Negative Theology," 251.

104. Athenagoras, *Legatio*, XIV.

105. Athenagoras, *Legatio*, XXII.

106. Richardson, *Early Christian Fathers*, 334ff.

107. Marianka S. Fousek writes: "The traditions and folklore of the baptized peoples were also 'baptized' in the process. A most striking example of this is the introduction of Christmas into the church's calendar. It was typical of the fusion of formerly pagan customs with Christian celebrations" (*The Church in a Changing World: Events and Trends from 250 to 600* [St. Louis: Concordia, 1971], 16). MacMullen also describes the influence of pagan culture on the ritual life of the church through hymnody. Whereas creed and doctrine remained inviolable, the church often made concessions to the desires of the newly converted for familiar music in their worship life. Rather than merely ban pagan music-making practices, "music could still be Christianized. And that process produced Christian hymns. The church, considering how the boundaries around itself were defined, and to set it off from rival cults without too much reducing the rewards of life for those who were converted, had to take account of such practical considerations" (*Christianizing the Roman Empire*, 75).

108. Schoedel, "Christian 'Atheism' and the Peace of the Roman Empire," 309.

109. Palmer opposes the tendency to read the apologists with doctrinal lenses, noting that this frequently forces them "into a systematic framework which is not in keeping with the method and purpose of the apologists themselves." Whenever this happens, argues Palmer, "later doctrinal categories are imposed upon the material of the apologists" ("Atheism, Apologetic and Negative Theology," 236).

110. Wilken, "Toward a Social Interpretation of Early Christian Apologetics," 438.

111. Wilken offers a similar assessment: "In his analysis of the contemporary Christian church Gustafson examined the church as, among other things, a community of language, a political community, an ethnic community. He wished to show that it was possible to speak about the Christian community in language other than the community's own characteristic language, such as the Biblical, liturgical, and theological concepts derived from Christian tradition. . . ." Wilken's point is that "concepts from sociology illuminate aspects of the church's life that the Biblical concepts do not" ("Toward a Social Interpretation of Early Christian Apologetics," 437).

112. James Boyd White, *When Words Lose Their Meaning: Constitutions and Reconstitutions of Language, Character, and Community* (Chicago: University of Chicago Press, 1984), x.

113. This is not the place to weigh the pluses and minuses of the "linguistic turn" of recent historiography. I reject the ethical and epistemological relativism often associated with this method, though I do think that there are many useful insights we can glean from it. An incarnational Lutheran theology works well within a social construction of reality where even divinely revealed truth is enacted by a believing community amid nonbelieving communities.

114. "Luther wrote his Ninety-five Theses in Latin. Several copies were printed in folio by Johann Gruenenberg of Wittenberg and were translated almost immediately into German. Within two weeks they were known and read all over Europe, and within a month they had reached England" (William R. Estep, *Renaissance and Reformation* [Grand Rapids: Eerdmans, (1986) 1989], 119).

115. White, *When Words Lose Their Meaning*, 276, 278, 280.

116. Richard Harvey Brown, *Society as Text: Essays on Rhetoric, Reason, and Reality* (Chicago: University of Chicago Press, 1987), 128f.

117. Brown, *Society as Text*, 129.

118. Peter L. Berger, *The Sacred Canopy: Elements of a Sociological Theory of Religion* (Garden City, N.Y.: Anchor Books, [1967] 1969), 45. The social construction of reality also is supported by recent brain research that has identified our left hemisphere as an "interpreter." Writes Michael S. Gazzaniga: "The interpreter constantly establishes a running narrative of our actions, emotions, thoughts, and dreams. It is the glue that unifies our story and creates our sense of being a whole, rational agent. . . . It builds our theories about our own life, and these narratives of our past behavior pervade our awareness" (*The Mind's Past* [Berkeley: University of California Press, 1998], 174).

119. Mary Fulbrook made a similar argument at the conclusion of her *Piety and Politics: Religion and the Rise of Absolutism in England, Wuertemberg and Prussia* (Cambridge, England: Cambridge University Press, 1983), 188ff.:

It may be that cultural factors will not take us very far in explaining different political developments. The "course of German history" has less to do with the Lutheran doctrine of obedience to authority than with specific social, economic, and political developments. It is on the latter that the direction of obedience postulated in Lutheran doctrines depends; the substantive content given to the emotions evoked by religious ideas is formulated in specific political circumstances. . . . It is on the circumstances that the specific content and power of religious orientations depends.

But in "favourable" circumstances, such orientations may have considerable power to influence the course of events in one direction or another.

120. Robert Wuthnow, *Communities of Discourse: Ideology and Social Structure in the Reformation, the Enlightenment, and European Socialism* (Cambridge: Harvard University Press, 1989), 582ff.

121. William R. Schoedel, "In Praise of the King: A Rhetorical Pattern in Athenagoras," in *Disciplina Nostra: Essays in Memory of Robert F. Evans*, ed. Donald F. Winslow (Cambridge, Mass.: Philadelphia Patristic Foundation, 1979), 89.

122. Schoedel, "In Praise of the King," 75–81, 82f.

123. Schoedel, "In Praise of the King," 86.

124. Schoedel, "In Praise of the King," 88, 90.

125. "This is merely to say that the personal and social consequences of any medium—any extension of ourselves—result from the new scale that is introduced into our affairs by each extension of ourselves, or by any new technology" (Marshall McLuhan, *Understanding Media: The Extensions of Man* [New York: New American Library, 1964], 23).

126. Eusebius, *History of the Church*, 327.

127. Fox, *Pagans and Christians*, 334.

128. Brown, *Heresies*, 77.

129. Robert Kolb, "Christian Civic Responsibility in an Age of Judgment," *Concordia Journal* 19, no. 1 (January 1993): 20.

130. Robert L. Wilken, "No Other Gods," *First Things* 37 (November 1993): 15.

131. As quoted in Pelikan, *Jesus through the Centuries*, 50.

132. Stauffer, *Christ and the Caesars*, 213.

133. Michael Grant, *Constantine the Great* (New York: Scribner's, 1994), 222.

134. Glanville Downey, *The Late Roman Empire* (New York: Holt, Rinehart & Winston, 1969), 31.

135. Pierard and Linder, *Civil Religion and the Presidency*, 40.

136. Kaufman, *Redeeming Politics*, 22, 21.

137. Schoedel, "In Praise of the King," 90.

3
=

The Lutheran Church—
Missouri Synod
and the Public Square
in the Era of C. F. W. Walther

CAMERON A. MACKENZIE[1]

To discuss The Lutheran Church—Missouri Synod and the "public square" in any kind of comprehensive way would require a book, maybe more than one.[2] However, by investigating what the founders of the Synod thought about issues of church and state, we may discover in part why the Synod is so troubled today about appropriate ways of participating in the public life of the community. The synodical forefathers expressed their convictions as the clear teachings of the permanent and unchanging Word of God. In so doing, they imposed a theological imprint upon the LCMS that continues to shape the thinking and behavior of many in the Synod today, but not everyone, as many believe that new situations require new answers. Nevertheless, because the synodical founders articulated their positions on the basis of the Scriptures and the Lutheran Confessions, it may be possible to discern the outline of an answer to the Synod's problems today in their writings *if* the LCMS maintains the same commitments as its founding generation.

Of course, it will not do simply to assert that Walther and his synodical contemporaries were always correct and that one can solve everything simply by quoting them. No, one needs to test their statements by God's Word just like any statement written today. Still, the synodical fathers are worth listening to. Contemporary theologians do not possess a monopoly on wisdom and insight. Therefore, it is the height of arrogance to ignore the voices of those who shared our Lutheran convictions and dealt with issues similar to our own, simply because they lived a long time ago.

In the early years of the LCMS, issues concerning church and state arose frequently because immigrant Lutherans had no prior experience with a country in which there was no state-supported Lutheran ecclesiastical establishment. Thus there are abundant sources for investigating the question of how the church participates in the public square or if it ought to participate at all.[3] C. F. W. Walther addressed church/state questions often during his long career,[4] and he was certainly not the only Missourian to do so;[5] but a good starting place for considering the views of the Synod's founding generation on such matters is an essay Walther delivered on the subject in 1885 as a part of a long series devoted to the theme "The doctrine of the Lutheran Church alone gives all glory to God, an irrefutable proof that its doctrine alone is true."[6]

Walther's 1885 installment is particularly significant for at least two reasons. First, in preparing his convention essays Walther was always careful to elicit proof for his statements not only from the Scriptures but also from the Lutheran tradition, preeminently the confessions and Luther himself. Therefore, the entire series of essays presents us with direct evidence of how Walther understood and *applied* his Lutheranism to the situation of the church in America. The applications are especially interesting because the church faced a different situation in Walther's day than it did in Luther's. Second, in this essay Walther was reflecting upon church/state questions after living in the United States for more than 45 years. For a long time he had experienced firsthand what it meant for the Lutheran Church to lack the status and support it had in the land of its birth but to enjoy religious liberty instead.

On one hand, the main thesis of the 1885 essay is entirely unsurprising, for it reflects clear biblical theology: "The Lutheran church believes, teaches, and confesses according to God's Word that *secular authorities* do not have the right or the power to rule over their subjects in matters of faith and conscience" (270, *emphasis original*).[7] As St. Peter put it: "We ought to obey God rather than men" (Acts 5:29).[8]

On the other hand, Walther's development of this thesis is quite interesting in that he treats not only the question of whether the state can exercise authority over faith and conscience but also more broadly the relationship of church and state, including the obligations of Christians toward their government. In so doing, Walther interprets the Lutheran tradition in a way that is most congenial to his American context while actually dismissing the views of some of the orthodox Lutheran fathers.

With respect to relationships between church and state, Walther makes three basic points in his 1885 essay: (1) the fundamental obligation of the Christian to obey his government whatever the form; (2) the duty of the state to protect the church; and (3) the necessity of separating church and state. Regarding the first point, Walther is simply a biblical theologian. Relying upon Romans 13, which he identifies as the *sedes doctrinae (der Sitz der Lehre)* on the subject of government, Walther points out that the obligation of obedience does not depend on the form of government but on the scriptural teaching that every form of government, *including tyranny*, exercises its authority only on account of the will of God.[9]

The United States, of course, owed its existence to a rebellion against constituted authority; and on more than one occasion during Walther's lifetime, Europe, including the German states, experienced uprisings on the part of those who espoused the same ideals of freedom and equality that animated Americans. But Walther will have none of it. In this essay, he insists that "one never hears of truly Lutheran citizens and countries being involved in revolution—except in countries where Lutheran churches no longer exist—even when Lutherans suffered extreme persecutions" (271).[10]

But if Lutherans reject revolution, how could Lutherans in America be loyal to a government that first came to power through rebellion against lawful authority? Walther's answer is simple: "As soon as an invader establishes his power, a citizen is obliged to obey that government, because [the invader] has the power which, in the final analysis, makes it a valid government" (272).[11] Governments rise and fall only because God so wills it. The government that exists, therefore, is the one that God would have us obey.

But even so, attaining power does not legitimate the act of revolution that preceded it; and Walther is very careful to distinguish the exercise of political power (which God has sanctioned) from the means employed to obtain power (which God may or may not sanction). In particular, Walther does not endorse the liberal, democratic revolutions of his day as a Christian way of replacing one political arrangement by another. In fact, in a sermon preached in 1854 but published only a few years before his 1885 convention essay, Walther repudiates such rebellions as thoroughly unchristian. Commenting on 2 Peter 2:10, 19 ("[they] despise government. Presumptuous are they, self-willed, they are not afraid to speak evil of dignities. . . . While they promise them liberty, they themselves are the servants of corruption"), Walther characterizes the revolutionary era of his day as a sign of the last times:

> If we compare the state of affairs in our day with this pic-
> ture, we can see that also this prediction is being literally
> fulfilled before our very eyes. Now that the great apostasy
> has taken place, . . . the world wide battle against civil laws
> has begun. . . . . That the government is God's servant and
> substitute on earth, that those who resist the government
> resist God's ordinance and fight against God, is now almost
> universally ridiculed as a teaching of the age of ignorance
> . . . . they are not afraid to revile heads of government; yes
> they pour upon them the vilest mockery and ridicule in
> words and writing. . . . To exterminate all kings and privi-
> leged groups and grant democratic freedom to all people
> has been called the goal toward which the world is mov-
> ing.[12]

All this Walther finds abhorrent. Unlike the revolutionaries, he
believes that what makes a government legitimate is not the will of
the people but God's establishment, no matter what the form of
government. According to his 1885 essay, any rebellion against the
"powers that be," whether traditional forms of authority (kings or
aristocrats still prevailing in Europe) or republican forms (elected
officials, as in the United States), is a rebellion against God (271).[13]
Thus the form of the state does not matter and no one form is
more Christian than any other.

So Walther acknowledges the legitimacy of a democratic
republic like his own, but he has little use for the rhetoric of popular sovereignty that undergirds it. In his 1854 sermon he describes
the goal of liberal revolutionaries and mocks it: "The government
should not be the government but the voters' stooge without a will
of its own; it should ask only what the people want, give free rein to
all who hate honor, chastity, and order, and even place the seal of
approval upon their lawless deeds."[14] Clearly, for Walther, democracy *per se* has no intrinsic merit as a form of government.

It is no surprise then that Walther denounces especially those
who identify political freedom with Christian liberty:

But the most frightening thing about all this is that many Christians have themselves drunk from the intoxicating cup of false thoughts of freedom. Even Scripture is not seldom misused to justify this bogus freedom. The reading of atheistic literature which preaches the overthrow of all divine and human laws is gradually bearing bitter, ruinous fruit even among Christians.[15]

As Walther understood it, contemporary advocates of political, social, and economic freedom who used the Gospel to justify their claims were actually corrupting the Gospel. In a lengthy foreword to the 1863 volume of *Lehre und Wehre*, which Walther as editor presumably wrote, he explores the nature of this theological aberration and summarizes the fundamental issue for orthodox believers with these words:

> The question is whether the old rule, *Evangelium non abolet politias*, i.e., the Gospel does not abolish political arrangements, is false or whether instead the Gospel requires equality of political rights; whether freedom, i.e., the freedom with which Christ has made us free, makes us free in a bodily and civil way; whether therefore Christ was the sort of messiah that the Jews were waiting for, a liberator of his people from earthly oppression; *and whether therefore the Gospel brings with it a revolutionary element that overturns the outward arrangements in the world.* [emphasis original][16]

Walther's answer to all this is a resounding no because the Scriptures sanction all sorts of human inequalities and require those who are in subordinate positions to obey. Thus the Christian *qua* Christian has no real interest in the distributions of temporal power that characterize the public square.

However, despite his affirmations of traditional political and social arrangements (including slavery) in this 1863 essay, Walther indicates that a Christian should be concerned that within any particular economic and political system relationships be carried out in ways that are Christian, just, and in conformity with love. With slavery especially in mind, Walther points to several scriptural passages that show how masters are to treat their slaves. He then prescribes as "the true duty of every Christian" to see to it that "in a legal way through all possible means it should be brought about that masters observe those godly rules [regarding slaves] and that the government sees to it that they do."[17] Not *who* has the power but *how* power is exercised is the question to which the Scriptures speak.

So at this point (1863) and regarding this particular issue (slavery), Walther opens the door for Christian participation in politics, working within the system to reform it but not overthrow it. However, by the time he writes his 1885 essay, this idea is missing, and his emphasis is entirely on obedience.[18] In particular, he does not treat the obligations of citizenship in a free state, for example, voting or running for public office. Perhaps one can understand this reticence as evidence of Walther's remaining as close as possible to the literal meaning of his sources: the Scriptures, the confessions, and the orthodox Lutheran theologians, none of which, for obvious reasons, discuss participation in democratic processes. It is also true that Walther's theme in this essay is more directed to what the government should do than it is to what citizens should do. Still, it is striking that after 45 years, he has virtually nothing to say about the Christian's obligations when living in a republic except, "Obey the law!"

However, we should also note that in passing Walther does mention Christian prayer on behalf of the state in his 1885 essay.[19] His published sermons include some preached on "national days of humiliation and prayer" in which he strongly stresses the obligation of prayer.[20] Prayer, along with repentance, is Walther's prescription to the Christian community when the country is in trouble.[21] What did Walther say about prayer in such circumstances?

First, in a sermon delivered in the midst of the American Civil War with all its horrors, Walther maintains that the first cause of everything, including the war, is God. Walther writes:

> Surely it is easier to recognize that pestilence and famine
> resulting from crop failure come from God, since in the
> case of these calamities men are not the intermediate cause.
> Ungodly men may indeed always be the mediate cause of
> all wars; still, their ultimate cause is always God, who uses
> war as His chastening and punishing rod.

God is in charge, not man: "God is not only the Creator, but also the Ruler of the world. . . . He is no idle spectator who allows the world to do what it pleases." And God's sway extends even to the wicked. Like Luther in *The Bondage of the Will*, Walther insists that

> God is never the cause of sin, but without God's will no
> sinner can move and direct his heart, tongue, hand or foot.
> . . . Everything must finally fall in line with His [God's]
> ways, and everything must lead to His goal.[22]

But what is God's goal in permitting war? Simply to move men to repentance. And of what sins should they repent? Walther has plenty to say about the sins of America, but basic to them all is pride. In the wake of many temporal blessings from God, including civil and religious liberty, Americans were not grateful but became proud. They "ascribed to themselves the glory that out of pure grace God has bestowed on them, robbed God of His glory, [and] assumed honor for themselves." Such pride led to a host of other sins, and Walther enumerates a long list, but the worst of all is that "thousands upon thousands have lost the last spark of faith and love that had been kindled in their hearts." For Walther, this means that God is punishing sin with sin, so the love of many has grown cold.[23]

Moreover, Walther indicts especially his hearers, presumably the people of his own church, for not repenting of their sins. Instead of learning from the Civil War to return to the Lord, they have placed their trust in man while nourishing "hatred of the enemy and partisan frenzy" ("*Feindeshass und Parteiwuth*"). They have derived their view of the war from "ungodly, atheistic newspapers" ("*gottlosen atheistischen Zeitungen*"), which portrayed it as ushering in a "new age of complete freedom and equality" ("*eines neuen Zeitalters vollkommener Freiheit und Gleichheit*") instead of listening to God's Word about what war really means as a call to repentance. Rather than following a different way from the world, they have fallen right in with the world and so will embrace its fate unless they repent![24]

According to Walther, then, repentance is the basis of prayer for the nation in times of calamity. Because God is in charge of what happens to a nation and because His purposes are good, the believer can know for sure that misfortunes come as divine warnings. Certainly, they are a form of punishment, but more important, God sends them to wake people from their sins and turn them back to God so they do not lose their eternal salvation as well as their temporal well-being.

Besides the content of prayer when the nation is at risk, there is also the question of context. With whom do we pray when our country is in trouble? Although Walther himself does not address this question directly in materials regarding church and state, the topic does come up elsewhere in his writings. It is reasonable to conclude that Walther would not join in public prayer with representatives of heterodox churches or non-Christian religions.

For example, in his 1882 convention essay on prayer, Walther attacks Catholics for praying to saints, the Reformed for making prayer a means of grace, and *both* of them for teaching that "in prayer to Christ one must completely turn away from the person of our Redeemer and turn to His divinity." Instead, Walther insists that in true prayer "Christ is to be called upon and worshiped as God and man in one person, not alone in respect to His divinity."[25] He is hardly laying the groundwork for joint prayer.

In his *Pastoral Theology*, Walther offers a long quotation from the orthodox theologian J. K. Dannhauer to answer the question about what sins subject a person to church discipline. The fourth item in Dannhauer's list is "syncretism," identified as "communion with the heterodox [*Irrglauben*]," and as an example of syncretism he mentions prayer with heretics or schismatics.[26]

Finally, in this connection there is an interesting set of theses that J. H. Fick presented to the 1870 and 1871 conventions of the Western District (at which Walther was also listed as present) on the relationship of evangelical Lutherans to the public schools of America. One of the dangers these theses list for Lutheran children attending public school is the prayers found there, almost always involving heterodox or nonbelievers. In the first case, prayer with the heterodox, the explanation to the theses argues that those who pray with one another should be one in the faith. However, Lutherans and Reformed are not one in faith and therefore not one in prayer. Each prays for the conversion of the other, so it is impossible for them to pray together! Moreover, prayers and songs that are not orthodox are dangerous to salvation.

Of course, in some schools the prayers might not be Christian at all but based on "natural religion." This is the second case. But such prayers are not real prayers because true prayer must be directed to the triune God and expressed in the name of Jesus. Participation in nontrinitarian prayer amounts to a denial of the true God.[27] Because of such prayers, parents should not send their children to public schools.

Given this kind of thinking, it is virtually impossible to imagine the first generation of synodical leadership participating in prayer services with non-Lutherans and non-Christians, even at times of national emergency. Instead, Walther's principles would lead true Lutherans to pray with one another and call upon God in a spirit of repentance for forgiveness and help in their time of trial.

As mentioned previously, in Walther's 1885 essay on church and state the emphasis falls on Christian obedience. However, Walther does open the way for some very limited participation in the public square when he discusses the government's responsibilities toward the church. Walther maintains that "the secular government does have the responsibility of providing for the church protection against injustice, and insofar as 'government' is made up of individuals who are members of the church, the government must use its power to serve the church" (277).[28] Earlier in the essay, Walther had delineated the limitations of lawful government, that it "has no right to command its subjects to do what God has forbidden, or to prohibit what God has commanded" (270).[29] But now he turns to the obligations of government and insists that it take care of the church.

On the one hand, this has nothing to do with the nature of the church *per se*. Instead, Walther writes, "[the government] does . . . have a general duty to be concerned about the Church as *a social unit within the state*. Without demanding any special privileges for the church, we do want government to provide us with the same freedoms and rights which all other social units within the state enjoy" (277, *emphasis original*).[30] For Walther, God has established the state "for the purpose of protecting life and property" (273),[31] a purpose equally applicable to the church as to any other entity in society. Therefore, the government should carry out its duties as they apply to the church.

Potentially, these duties could include taking action "against those who err in the faith and establish or practice principles *that pose a danger to the state*" (284, *emphasis added*).[32] It is the danger to the state that justifies such action, not false religion. Again relying on his Reformation-era sources, Walther mentions as examples the pope and the Anabaptists, but he also refers to a contemporary group, the Mormons: "Having been driven out of Missouri and Illinois on account of their thievery, they settled in Utah. If they refuse to give up their immoral polygamy, they will have to expect being chased out of there too" (285).[33] But to go against a group such as the Mormons does not mean that the government applies the Scriptures in the interests of orthodoxy. Walther teaches that government "rules on the basis of reason," not the Bible (273).[34] Here Walther is discussing beliefs and practices that are subversive of the social order. For him, a state that does not protect property and marriage is cultivating self-destruction. So the state must take measures against any groups, including religious ones, that threaten its existence or the well-being of its people.

So Walther's first point has to do with the general obligation of the government to protect its people, including the church. On the other hand, he also insists that "government representatives . . . *when they are members of the church*" (*my emphasis*) have a special interest in protecting the church, for "every Christian should use his gifts in the service of Christ and His kingdom" (277).[35] To be sure, Walther is *not* suggesting that Christian politicians work to change the system in America by establishing confessional Lutheranism as the state religion. But what Walther *is* suggesting is that Christians in government use their positions to make sure that government carries out its duties with respect to the church. Walther writes:

> At 1 Tim. 2:1–2, Christians are admonished to pray for the government for this reason: "that we may live peaceful and quiet lives in all godliness and holiness." That points up beautifully the responsibility government has over against the church, and that when government officials are themselves members of the church, they have a double duty in this regard. (277)[36]

Along with all Christians these government officials are to pray for the state, but because they are officials they also need to establish and maintain the temporal conditions under which Christians may indeed lead "peaceful and quiet lives."

It is at this point that one could make a case for Christian politics in a limited sort of way. Although it is somewhat disappointing that Walther makes no note of it, his reasoning can apply not only to elected government officials but also to those who do the electing. An obvious corollary of his argument, then, is that the Christian *voter* should cast his ballot in such a way as to ensure the government is carrying out its role with respect to the church. The church does not demand special privileges, but it should enjoy the same privileges as others, and Christians who participate in government should protect those privileges.

The third and final point from Walther's analysis in his 1885 essay with relevance for the contemporary situation is that he affirms American separation of church and state. Although Walther rejects any notion of "natural rights" and virtually ignores the obligations of citizenship in a free republic, he is enthusiastic about at least one feature of American life: freedom of religion.

> We Lutherans in America can never sufficiently thank God that the federal Constitution [of the United States] makes it impossible for the government to favor one religion over another.... Although in Germany people fear the fall of the church into sects, if the church would no longer be maintained by the use of governmental power, here [in America] such fears are put to shame by a freedom of religion that continues to benefit both state and church with the choicest and most precious blessings. [288–89][37]

This is hardly the first time that Walther had expressed himself this way regarding the American system. In 1862 in his well-known essay *The Right Form of an Evangelical Lutheran Local Congregation Independent of the State*, he had contended that

> the church's independence of the state is not a defect or an abnormal condition, but the right and natural relation which ought always to obtain between church and state. According to God's Word, church and state are two distinct kingdoms.[38]

At the same convention in which Walther gave that essay, G. Schaller delivered an address in which he made the same point: "State and church simply are two completely different kingdoms at the same time. One [kingdom] is spiritual, the other secular. One is maintained and ruled by the sword and force, the other without sword and force, through God's Word alone. Every alliance between the two is unnatural and can only result in damage to the church."[39]

Nine years earlier (1853), in a Fourth of July address to a young men's society, Walther talked extensively about the blessings of religious liberty in comparison to old-world arrangements, again proceeding from the axiom that church and state have two different functions and two different means for carrying them out. "The State," he argues, "is certainly not an institution of God by which its citizens are to be led to *eternal* life. The State . . . is rather an arrangement for *this* life, for order in the world, . . . that justice and righteousness be meted out" (*emphasis original*).[40] But while the state must resort to force to carry out its mission, the church relies upon immaterial means: "Her power is the faith that overcomes the world, her weapon the Word of the Almighty."[41]

Therefore, the only positive thing that the state can actually do for the church is to permit the church to do her work. The United States provided what the church needed most from the state:

Not privileges, but *liberty*; not government regulations which enforce beliefs of religion but *freedom* of religion to proclaim these doctrines to the whole world; not the protections and spreading of religion with temporal power, but freedom of religion to defend itself and to reach out with the weapon of the persuasive Word; not control of the State, but *freedom* to live in the State, to have a hospitable reception, a place of refuge, a lodging-place. (*emphasis original*)[42]

More than 30 years later, in his 1885 convention essay, Walther was still making the same point: "Government has neither the right nor the power to arrogate to itself control over church government, nor to force people to conform to the true faith, or what it may consider to be true faith" (277).[43] In support of this, Walther argues first from the Scriptures. From Acts 18:12–16 (the apostle Paul before Gallio), he concludes that "the Holy Spirit . . . wanted us to know that the secular government as such has no business making decisions in matters of doctrine," and from John 18:36–37 (Christ before Pilate) he concludes that "Christ, the King of Truth, has a kingdom that is not of this world, and for that reason He does not allow His kingdom to be defended with secular power and weapons. . . . It is contrary to the kingdom and spirit of Christ to try to force people to conform to 'true faith' " (278).[44] Walther also cites the parable of the wheat and the tares to show that the government "has neither the right nor the power to employ force in opposing heretical faith and worship" (285).[45]

In short, both institutions, church and government, have God-given responsibilities, but they are radically different responsibilities and employ radically different means to carry them out. Therefore, neither should attempt to discharge the tasks of the other. In particular, the church should *not* rely on the coercive powers of the state to maintain true Christianity. The church and the public square are two different things.

Interestingly, Walther's insistence on separation of church and state does not mean that the state must be atheistic or even agnostic. According to Walther's reading of American history, the founders of the United States meant for it to be Christian.[46] He had no problem with the government's requesting (not commanding) the churches to observe special days of thanksgiving or humiliation,[47] with Bible-reading in the public schools,[48] or even with the state's denying citizenship rights to atheists and other non-Christians.[49] For Walther, freedom of religion meant freedom for the church to carry out its God-given tasks free from state interference. It did not mean state hostility or even neutrality with respect to Christianity.[50]

Besides his reading of U. S. history, Walther was very much influenced in his position by his understanding of church history. In his 1885 essay, he deals with the history of church/state relationships especially in the era of the Reformation. Of course, he is fully aware of how important the Lutheran princes were to the success of the Reformation. He willingly acknowledges their contribution: "The value of the services which the Lutheran government officials rendered to the church at the time of the Reformation simply cannot be overestimated!" (278).[51]

But how does he square their involvement in the church with his insistence on the independence of the church from the state as the biblically correct position? He does this by presenting a nuanced interpretation of Lutheran church history supported by a careful, if selective, reading of the documents, even though this necessitated his repudiating the position of later Lutheran dogmaticians, especially J. W. Baier, whose dogmatics Walther edited and used as a textbook at Concordia Seminary.[52]

Of course, Walther can cite statements from the Lutheran Confessions in support of distinguishing church and state, and he does: from the Augsburg Confession[53] and the Apology.[54] But he also has to deal with Luther's "Treatise on the Power and Primacy of the Pope," which says: "Especially does it behoove the chief members of the church, the kings and the princes, to have regard for the interests of the church and to see to it that errors are removed and consciences are healed."[55]

On the face of it, one could understand this statement as saying that government should use its power to suppress heresy and promote the Gospel; but Walther insists that Melanchthon is not addressing the responsibilities of government *per se* but those of all Christians, "especially" ("*fürnehmlich*"), as the text itself indicates, those who can do something about them:

> We are here speaking of a general Christian duty, a duty which Christian government officials are in a better position to discharge, simply because of their influential position. For that reason this passage speaks of them not as rulers but as members of the church. (277–78)[56]

Similarly, when Walther reviews the activities of the princes on behalf of the Lutheran Church in the sixteenth century, he insists either that they were carrying out the "general duty [of the government] to be concerned about the Church as *a social unit within the*

state" (*emphasis original*) (277)[57] or that they were acting as concerned members of the church, not as government officials. So, for
example, when John the Constant authorized a visitation of the
churches in Saxony and then later established a consistory for the
church in his realm, Walther maintains that "the Elector was not
acting in this matter in his capacity as a government official; rather,
he was merely fulfilling his duty of love as the man best qualified
for the job" (280).[58]

In view of the rather rapid development of Lutheran state
churches at the time of the Reformation, it is not self-evident that
the princes at any rate understood that they were acting simply as
church members and not as government officials. Nevertheless, in
support of his argument, Walther finds passages in Luther's writings that seem to make this distinction. For example, one passage
describes the elector's decision to authorize the visitation as an
exercise of Christian love, but a later one complains that the civil
authorities were becoming too powerful in the church (280).[59]
However, Walther does not cite the orthodox Lutheran theologians
of the seventeenth century to support his thesis that the authentic
position of Lutheranism is "the doctrine that the government has
neither the right nor the power to assume control of the church."
Instead, he contends that in this case, the "later Lutheran dogmaticians strayed far afield from the original Lutheran position" (281).[60]

In other words, Walther's commitment to religious liberty is so
great that he is willing to part company with some of those whom
he otherwise routinely quotes as the best representatives of true
Christianity. On the one hand, this demonstrates the intensity of
his conviction that the Scriptures and confessions teach the separation of church and state. But on the other hand, it also shows the
depth of his appreciation for the American system. For Walther,
freedom of religion, as he experienced it in the United States, was
an inestimable blessing from God to His church.

As we have seen, in most other respects, Walther displays little
use for American democracy. He rejects its political rhetoric, has

virtually nothing to say about voting, and thinks that the Civil War is punishment for sin. He urges his people to repent and pray to rescue their country from its troubles but otherwise simply to obey, not because the United States is a good country, but because it exercises political power under the authority of God, just like any other state regardless of its political form. Indeed, for Walther, there is no specifically Christian form of government.

Accordingly, when we look to Walther and our synodical forebears for advice on the question of the church and the public square, we find little encouragement for political activism on the part of the church. Although there is room in Walther's theology for such activism on the part of government officials and perhaps even voters who are Christian, there is none at all for the church *per se*, for God has established two separate institutions, church and state, each with its own purpose and role. The task of government is to look after man's temporal well-being; the task of the church is to preach the Word of God in its truth and purity for the salvation of souls. Clearly, each has more than enough to do without entering into the work of the other.

Notes

1. The Rev. Dr. Cameron A. MacKenzie is professor of historical theology at Concordia Theological Seminary, Ft. Wayne, Indiana. He holds an M.A. in history from the University of Chicago, an M.A. in classics from Wayne State University, an S.T.M. in New Testament from Concordia Theological Seminary, and a Ph.D. in history from the University of Notre Dame. This essay is a revised version of a presentation given as part of the annual theological symposium at Concordia Seminary, St. Louis, Missouri, in fall 2002.

2. For example, Wayne W. Wilke, "Changing Understanding of the Church-State Relationship: The Lutheran Church—Missouri Synod, 1914–1969," Ph.D. diss., University of Michigan, 1990; and Robert Nichols, "Views on Church and State in The Lutheran Church—Missouri Synod, 1885 to 1919," M.Div. thesis, Concordia Theological Seminary, 1972.

3. Needless to say, others have already treated this topic. Particularly useful are Angelika Dörfler-Dierken, *Luthertum und Demokratie: Deutsche*

und amerikanische Theologen des 19. Jahrhunderts zu Staat, Gesellschaft und Kirche (Göttingen: Vandenhoeck & Ruprecht, 2001), 259–333; and August R. Suelflow, *Servant of the Word: The Life and Ministry of C. F. W. Walther* (St. Louis: Concordia, 2000). But see also Suelflow, "Walther the American," in *C. F. W. Walther: The American Luther,* ed. Arthur H. Drevlow, John M. Drickamer, and Glenn E. Reichwald (Mankato, Minn.: Walther Press, 1987), 13–35; and "The Two Kingdom Concept in 18th- and 19th-century Lutheranism in America," in *God and Caesar Revisited,* ed. John R. Stephenson (St. Catharines, Ontario: Luther Academy, 1995), 69–86. Also see James Heiser, "The Church-State Relationship and Augustana XVI in the Writings of C. F. W. Walther and S. S. Schmucker," *Logia* 5 (1996): 5–13.

4. See Dörfler-Dierken, *Luthertum und Demokratie,* 278–301, for a thorough treatment of Walther's attitude toward church and state. For primary sources, see C. F. W. Walther, "3rd Sunday after Easter (2): 1 Peter 2, 11–20," in C. F. W. Walther, *Standard Epistles,* trans. Donald E. Heck (Livermore, Iowa: n.p.), 239–45. For the original, see C. F. W. Walther, *Amerikanisch-Lutherische Epistel Postille Predigten,* 2d ed. (St. Louis: Lutherischer Concordia Verlag, n.d.), 232–38. As far as publication date is concerned, the foreword is dated 1882 (p. iv), but a footnote in the text (p. 233) gives 1854 as the year Walther preached this sermon. Also, C. F. W. Walther, "23rd Sunday after Trinity: Matthew 22:15–22," in C. F. W. Walther, *Old Standard Gospels,* trans. Donald E. Heck (Livermore, Iowa: n.p.), 343–49. For the original, see C. F. W. Walther, *Amerikanisch-Lutherische Evangelien Postille* (St. Louis: Druckerei und Stereotypie der Synode von Missouri, Ohio, u. a. St., 1875), 339–44. Also, C. F. W. Walther, "A Fourth of July Address Made before a Christian Young Men's Society (1853)," in *The Word of His Grace: Occasional and Festival Sermons* (Lake Mills, Iowa: Evangelical Lutheran Synod, 1978), 152–58. For original, see C. F. W. Walther, *Lutherische Brosamen* (St. Louis: Concordia, 1897), 362–69. See also C. F. W. Walther, "Zehnte Predigt zur Eröffnung der Synode," in *Lutherische Brosamen* (St. Louis: M. C. Barthel, 1876), 495–508.

5. See, for example, "Referat über die Lehre von der Obrigkeit," in *Verhandlungen der Siebenten Jahres-Versammlung des Westlichen Districts . . . 1861* (St. Louis: Synodal-Druckerei, 1861), 18–20; G. Schaller, "Synodalrede," in *Verhandlungen der achten Jahresversammlung des Westlichen Districts . . . 1862* (St. Louis: Synodal-Druckerei, 1862), 6–11; "Acht Thesen über das Verhältniss von Staat und Kirche in Rücksicht auf etliche Zeitfragen," in *Fünfzehnter Synodal-Bericht des Mittleren Districts . . . 1870* (St. Louis: Druckerei der Synode von Missouri, Ohio und anderen Staaten, 1870), 44–49; and F. C. D. Wyneken, "Besprechung der Thesen über das Recht, die Vorzüge und

Pflichten der Freikirche," in *Achtzehnter Synodal-Bericht des Mittleren Districts . . . 1874* (St. Louis: Druckerei der Synode von Missouri, Ohio u.a. Staaten, 1874), 16–58.

6. Walther delivered the entire series as convention essays before the Western District of the LCMS beginning in 1873 and concluding in 1886, less than a year before his death. Among the doctrines treated were, of course, the central topics of the Christian religion, such as justification, the means of grace, sanctification, and prayer. But at the end of the series he also presented eight theses devoted to the teaching of the Lutheran Church regarding *earthly* authorities; and in Thesis 7, he took up the topic of church and state and treated it at length in the convention essay of 1885. For an introduction to the entire series, see Suelflow, *Servant of the Word*, 155–60.

For the 1885 essay, see *Sechsundzwanzigster Synodal-Bericht des Westlichen Districts der deutschen evang.-luth. Synode von Missouri, Ohio und anderen Staaten 1885* (St. Louis: Luth. Concordia-Verlag, 1885), 13–51. An English translation has been printed in C. F. W. Walther, *Essays for the Church* (St. Louis: Concordia, 1992), 2:270–89. In this article, quotations in the text are from the English translation. Parenthetical page numbers likewise refer to the English. References to the German are in the footnotes.

7. "Die lutherische Kirche glaubt, lehrt und bekennt nach Gottes Wort, ferner, dass die *weltliche Obrigkeit* weder Recht noch Macht habe, über Glauben und Gewissen ihrer Unterthanen zu herrschen" (*Synodal-Bericht 1885*, 14).

8. Scripture quotations in this essay are from the KJV.

9. "Ob sie [die Obrigkeit] rechtmässig in's Amt gekommen, oder ob sie fromm, oder ob sie unseres Glaubens ist, kann also hier nicht massgebend sein. . . . Der Obrigkeit, die die Gewalt über uns hat, sollen wir unterthan sein; sonst versündigen wir uns nicht sowohl an einem Menschen, als an Gott selbst" (*Synodal-Bericht 1885*, 15–16).

10. "Man von wirklich lutherischen Staatsangehörigen und in wirklich lutherischen Ländern nie von Revolution gehört hat, es sei denn, dass die lutherische Kirche in denselben zu existeren aufgehört hatte, selbst in Zeiten der furchtbaren Bedrückungen" (*Synodal-Bericht 1885*, 16).

11. "Sobald sich aber ein solcher Eroberer festsetzt, so ist er die zum Gehorsam verbindende Obrigkeit, denn er hat die Gewalt, welche schliesslich zur gültigen Obrigkeit macht" (*Synodal-Bericht 1885*, 19).

12. "Vergleichen wir nun mit diesem Bilde den Stand der Dinge in unseren Tagen, so sehen wir nur zu deutlich, dass auch diese

Vorausverkündigungen von den letzten Zeiten jetzt vor aller Welt Augen buchstäblich in Erfüllung gehen. Nachdem fast überall in der ganzen Christenheit ein grosser Abfall vom Glauben erfolgt ist, . . . hat man nun den Kampf endlich auch gegen alle bürgerliche Ordnungen in der Welt begonnen. . . . Dass die Obrigkeit Gottes Dienerin und Stellvertreterin auf Erden ist und dass daher diejenigen, welche sich wider die Obrigkeit setzen, Gottes Ordnung widerstreben und wider Gott selbst streiten, dass verlacht man jetzt fast allgemein als eine Lehre aus dem Zeitalter der Unwissenheit und Unmündigkeit. . . . man . . . erzittert nicht, die Majestäten zu lästern, ja, übergiesst sie in Rede und Schrift mit dem gemeinsten Spott und Hohn. . . . Vertilgung aller Könige und Bevorzugten und republikanische Freiheit für all Völker erklärt man für das Ziel der Welt, mit dessen Erreichung endlich das Zeitalter kommen werde" (*Epistel Postille*, 232–33; English: *Standard Epistles*, 239–40).

13. "Es ist nicht etwa nur eine Störung der öffentlichen Ruhe, wenn man sich der weltlichen Obrigkeit widersetzt, sondern recht eigentlich ein Kämpfen gegen die göttliche Majestät." "In unserem Lande ist z. B. nicht der Präsident, Congress, sondern das Volk der Souverän. Aber widersetzen wir uns diesen vom Volk angestellten Beamten, so widersetzen wir uns der Souveränität des Volkes und damit Gott selbst" (*Synodal-Bericht 1885*, 16, 16–17). See also *Epistel Postille*, 235.

14. "Die Obrigkeit soll nicht mehr Obrigkeit sein, sondern eine willenlose Handlangerin ihrer Wähler, die nur fragt, was das Volk will, und die allen Gelüsten derjenigen, die Ehrbarkeit, Zucht und Ordnung hassen, Freiheit giebt und denselben noch das Siegel der Gesetzlichkeit aufdrückt" (*Epistel Postille*, 233; English: *Standard Epistles*, 240).

15. "Unter allem das Erschrecklichste in unserer Zeit ist aber, dass selbst viele, welche Christen sein wollen, von dem Taumelkelch der falschen Freiheitsgedanken getrunken haben. Selbst die heilige Schrift missbraucht man nicht selten dazu, um den Freiheitsschwindel, der jetzt über die Völker ausgegossen ist, zu rechtfertigen. Das Lesen atheistischer und den Umsturz aller göttlichen und menschlichen Ordnungen predigender Zeitungsblätter trägt mehr auch unter den Christen seine bitteren, verderblichen Früchte" (*Epistel Postille*, 233; English: *Standard Epistles*, 240).

16. "Es handelt sich um die Frage, ob der alte Kanon: *Evangelium non abolet politias* d.i. das Evangelium hebt die politischen Ordnungen nicht auf, ein lügenhafter sei und ob vielmehr das Evangelium auch bürgerliche Gleichberechtigung verlange; ob die christliche Freiheit, d.h., die Freiheit, damit uns Christus befreiet hat, uns leiblich, bürg-

erlich frei mache, ob also Christus ein Messias war, wie die Juden ihn erwarteten, ein Befreier seines Volkes von irdischem Drucke; *ob sonach das Evangelium ein revolutionäres, die äusserlichen Ordnungen in der Welt umstossendes Element in sich trage*" ("Vorwort," *Lehre und Wehre* 9 [1863]: 44).

17. "Dafür nun auf gesetzlichem Wege mit allen möglichen Mitteln zu wirken, dass jene göttlichen Regeln von den Herren beobachtet und dass die Beobachtung derselben auch von der Obrigkeit überwacht werde, das achten wir daher für die wahre Aufgabe eines jeden Christen. . . . Solche Bestrebungen, bei denen man zwar die Knechtschaft selbst stehen liesse, . . . aber für eine christliche, gerechte, *der Liebe gemässe Gestaltung dieses politischen und ökonomischen Verhältnisses Sorge trüge*, würden Gott zu Ehren and den Menschen zum Heil gereichen" ("Vorwort," 45).

18. Of course, one may not obey the government when it commands something clearly against God's Word, and Walther gives as an example an unjust war. In such a case, Walther believes that the Scriptures recognize a right to flee a tyrannical government, though one may not otherwise resist it. See *Synodal-Bericht 1885*, 17, 23 (English: "1885," 271, 274).

19. "1 Tim. 2,1. 2. werden die Christen ermahnt, für die Obrigkeit zu bitten, und zwar deshalb, 'dass wir ein ruhig und stilles Leben führen mögen in aller Gottseligkeit und Ehrbarkeit'" (*Synodal-Bericht 1885,* 28; English: "1885," 277).

20. See, for example, his sermons for a Day of Humiliation during the Civil War in *Evangelien Postille*, 398–404 (English: *Standard Gospels,* 391–97); in *Lutherische Brosamen*, 270–78 (English: *Word of His Grace,* 144–51); and in *Epistel Postille*, 491–96 (English: *Standard Epistles,* 240). There is also such a sermon from 1849 in his *Casual-Predigten und -Reden* (St. Louis: Concordia, 1892), 154–63.

21. See Dörfler-Dierken, *Luthertum und Demokratie,* 292–96, for a discussion of the Christian's obligation to pray for his government.

22. "Es ist wahr: dass Pestilenz und Hungersnoth infolge von Missernte von Gott kommen, sind leichter erkannt, da bei diesen Landplagen die Menschen nicht die Mittelursachen sind. Allein mögen immerhin gottlose Menschen Mittelursachen aller Kriege sein, die letzte Ursache derselben ist immer Gott, der dieselben zur Ruthe seiner Zucht und Strafe gebraucht. Gott is nicht nur der Schöpfer, sondern auch der Regierer der Welt. . . . Er ist kein müssiger Zuschauer, der die Welt thun lässt, was ihr beliebt. . . . Zwar ist Gott nie die Ursache der Sünde, aber ohne Gottes Willen kann kein Sünder Herz, Zunge, Hand noch Fuss regen und lenken. . . . In seine Wege muss endlich alles ein-

schlagen, zu seinem Endziel muss endlich alles führen" (*Lutherische Brosamen*, 273–74; English: *Word of His Grace*, 146–47).

23. "Unser Volk hat, was Gott ihm aus freier Gnade gegeben hatte, sich selbst zugeschrieben, Gott die Ehre genommen und sich die Ehre gegeben." "Und, was das Erschrecklichste ist, Tausende und aber Tausende haben das Fünklein des Glaubens und Liebe, das in ihrem Herzen angezündet war, in der reissenden Fluth der Kriegsleidenschaften verloren" (*Lutherische Brosamen*, 274–75; English: *Word of His Grace*, 147–48).

24. *Lutherische Brosamen*, 277 (English: *Word of His Grace*, 149–50).

25. "Reformierte und Papisten können sich also weder auf die Schrift, noch auf das christliche Altertum berufen, wenn sie sagen: beim Gebet zu Christo müsse man von der Person unseres Erlösers ganz absehen und nur zu seiner Gottheit sich wenden." "Hieraus folgt nun . . . dass Christus als Gott und Mensch in einer Person, also nicht nur nach seiner Gottheit, sondern auch nach seiner Menschheit anzurufen und anzubeten sei" (C.F.W. Walther, "Dass nur durch die Lehre der lutherischen Kirche Gott allein alle Ehre gegeben wird, dies erhellt zehntens aus ihrer Lehre von der Anrufung und Anbetung Gottes," in *Vierundzwanzigster Synodal–Bericht des Westlichen Distrikts . . . 1882* [St. Louis: Druckerei des Lutherischen Concordia–Verlags, 1882], 48, 45; English: C. F. W. Walther, "Prayer," in *Essays*, 2:233, 232).

26. "4. Synkretismus, bestehe er nun in Gemeinschaft mit Irrglauben (welchen Synkretismus das Concil von Laodicäa dem Bann übergibt: dass man mit Ketzern oder Schismatikern nicht beten solle, siehe Canon 32. und 33 . . .)" (C. F. W. Walther, *Americanisch–Lutherische Pastoraltheologie*, 5th ed. [St. Louis: Concordia, 1906], 342). For Dannhauer, see Erwin L. Lueker, ed., *Lutheran Cyclopedia*, rev. ed. (St. Louis: Concordia, 1975), s.v. "Dannhauer, Johann Konrad."

27. "Weit entfernt, dass das Beten, wenn es in den Freischulen gestattet ist, denselben einen Werth geben sollte, bringt gerade das Beten, da es zumeist von Falsch—und Ungläubigen geübt wird, grosse Gefahr für die Seelen der Kinder mit sich" (J. H. Fick, "Thesen über das rechte Verhältniss eines evangelisch–lutherischen Christen zu dem hiesigen Freischulwesen," in *Fünfzehnter Synodal–Bericht des Westlichen Districts . . .1870* [St. Louis: Druckerei der Synode von Missouri, Ohio, und anderen Staaten, 1870], 75; and *Sechzehnter Synodal–Bericht des Westlichen Districts . . . 1871* [St. Louis: Druckerei der Synode von Missouri, Ohio und anderen Staaten, 1871], 51–52).

28. "Zwar die weltliche Obrigkeit die Kirche in ihrer Freiheit gegen Unrecht zu schützen und, sofern sie (die Obrigkeit) aus Personen

besteht, welche Glieder der Kirche sind, derselben mit ihrer Macht zu dienen schuldig sei" (*Synodal–Bericht 1885,* 27).

29. "... dass ... die weltliche Obrigkeit kein Recht habe, ihren Unterthanen zu gebieten, was Gott verboten, oder zu verbieten, was Gott geboten hat" (*Synodal–Bericht 1885,* 15).

30. "Obwohl nämlich nach Gottes Wort die Obrigkeit in der Kirche nich regieren soll, so hat sie doch erstlich im Allgemeinen die Pflicht, sich der Kirche *als einer Gesellschaft im Staate* anzunehmen. Ohne von der Obrigkeit besondere Vorrechte für unsere Kirche zu beantspruchen, verlangen wir doch von derselben, dass sie unsern Freiheiten und Rechten denselben Schutz angedeihen lasse, den alle anderen Gesellschafte innerhalb des Staates geniessen" (*Synodal–Bericht 1885,* 27–28).

31. "... den Staat, der keine Anstalt zur Seligmachung der Seelen, sondern zum Schutz Leibes und Gutes ist" (*Synodal–Bericht 1885,* 21).

32. "... dass ... zwar die weltliche Obrigkeit das Recht habe, diejenigen Irrgläubigen, welche staatsgefährliche Grundsätze aufstellen oder doch befolgen, unschädlich zu machen und gegen dieselben einzuschreiten" (*Synodal–Bericht 1885,* 42).

33. "In Amerika gehören unter diese Rubrik die Mormonen, die, wegen ihrer Dieberei aus Missouri und Illinois vertrieben, in Utah sich niederliessen, aber auch da der Ausweisung gewärtig sein müssen, sie die unsittliche Vielweiberei nicht aufgeben wollen" (*Synodal–Bericht 1885,* 43).

34. "Die Obrigkeit ... soll auch den Staat ... nicht eigentlich nach Gottes Wort regieren, sondern nach der Vernunft" (*Synodal–Bericht 1885,* 21).

35. "Diese Verpflichtung [der Obrigkeit] haben aber nach unserer Ueberzeugung die obrigkeitlichen Personen in doppeltem Masse, wenn sie selbst Glieder der Kirche sind, weil ja jeder Christ seine Gaben in den Dienst Christi und seines Reiches stellen soll" (*Synodal–Bericht 1885,* 28).

36. "1 Tim. 2, 1. 2. werden die Christen ermahnt, für die Obrigkeit zu bitten, und zwar deshalb, 'dass wir ein ruhig und stilles Leben führen mögen in aller Gottseligkeit und Ehrbarkeit'; womit die Pflicht der Obrigkeit der Kirche gegenüber auf's herlichste angedeutet wird, zwar nicht allein dann, wenn die obrigkeitlichen zugleich Glieder der Kirche sind, aber sonderlich dann" (*Synodal–Bericht 1885,* 28).

37. "Wir Lutheraner in Amerika können daher Gott nicht genug danken, dass es unsrer Obrigkeit durch die Bundesconstitution unmöglich gemacht ist, einer Religion vor einer andern den Vorzug zu geben. ...

Während man in Deutschland den Zerfall der Kirche in lauter Secten
fürchtet, wenn die Kirche von der obrigkeitlichen Zwangsgewalt nicht
mehr zusammengehalten werden sollte, so bewährt sich hier zur
Beschämung jener Furcht die Religionsfreiheit zum höchsten und
reichsten Segen für Staat und Kirche" (*Synodal–Bericht 1885*, 50).

38. " . . . so ist doch Unabhängigkeit der Kirche vom Staat nicht ein Man-
gel oder ein regelwidriger Zustand, sondern das rechte, naturgemässe
Verhältniss, in welchem die Kirche immer zum Staate stehen sollte"
(C. F. W. Walther, *Die rechte Gestalt einer vom Staate unabhängigen
evangelisch–lutherischen Ortsgemeinde* [St. Louis: Aug. Wiebusch u.
Sohn, 1864], 6; English: *The Form of a Christian Congregation*, trans.
John T. Mueller [St. Louis: Concordia, 1963], 6).

39. "Staat und Kirche sind einmal zwei ganz verschiedene Reiche; das
eine ist geistlich, das andere weltlich; das eine wird durch das Schwert
und Gewalt, das andere ohne Schwert und Gewalt, allein durch
Gottes Wort erhalten und regiert, und jedes Bündniss zwischen bei-
den ist nicht naturgemäss und kann nur zum Schaden der Kirche
ausschlagen" (Schaller, 8 [see above, n. 5]; English: *Essays*, 1:66. This
essay was wrongly attributed to Walther in that collection. I thank
Robert E. Smith, who translated the essay, for pointing this out to
me.).

40. "Ein Staat ist ja nicht eine göttliche Anstalt, durch welche die Glieder
desselben zum *ewigen* Leben geführt werden sollen! Der Staat . . . ist
vielmehr eine Ordnung Gottes für *dieses* Leben, die nemlich darum
bestehen soll, damit es ordentlich in dieser Welt hergehe, . . . Recht
und Gerechtigkeit gehandhabt werde" (C. F. W. Walther, "Rede am 4.
Juli gehalten vor einem christlichen Jüng-lingsverein," *Lutherische
Brosamen*, 364; English: *Word of His Grace*, 154).

41. "Ihre Kraft ist der weltüberwindende Glaube, ihre Waffe das Wort des
Allmächtigen" (*Lutherische Brosamen*, 368, *my translation*; for another
English rendering, see *Word of His Grace*, 157).

42. "Nicht Privilegien, sondern *Freiheit*; nicht Staatsgesetze, welche den
Glauben an die Lehren der Religion gebieten, sondern *Freiheit* der
Religion, diese Lehren vor aller Welt zu predigen; nicht Vertheidigung
und Ausbreitung der Religion mit leiblicher Gewalt, sondern Freiheit
der Religion, sich mit den Waffen des überzeugenden Wortes selbst zu
vertheidigen und auszubreiten; nicht Herrschaft im Staate, sondern
Freiheit, darin zu wohnen, eine gastliche Aufnahme, ein Hospitium,
eine Herberge" (*Lutherische Brosamen*, 368–69; English: *Word of His
Grace*, 157).

43. " . . . dass [die weltliche Obrigkeit] weder Recht noch Macht habe, die
Regierung der Kirche an sich zu reissen und zum wahren Glauben,

oder was sie dafür hält, zwingen zu wollen" (*Synodal–Bericht 1885*, 27).

44. "Der Heilige Geist hat diese Geschichte ohne Zweifel unter Anderem auch darum aufzeichnen lassen, dass man wisse, in Sachen der Lehre habe die weltliche Obrigkeit als solche kein Urtheil zu fällen." "Christus, der König der Wahrheit, hat hiernach nicht ein Reich von dieser Welt und will daher sein Reich auch nicht mit weltlichen Waffen vertheidigt haben. . . . Es ist also gegen Christi Reich und Geist, Leute zum rechten Glauben mit äusserlicher Gewalt zwingen zu wollen" (*Synodal–Bericht 1885*, 30, 30–31).

45. " . . . gewiss ist es . . . dass die weltliche Obrigkeit . . . weder Recht noch Macht habe, gegen falschen Glauben und falschen Gottesdienst, oder was sie doch dafür hält, ihre Zwangsgewalt in Anwendung zu bringen" (*Synodal–Bericht 1885*, 44).

46. C. F. W. Walther, St. Louis, to J. C. W. Lindemann, Addison, Ill., 26 April 1870, in C. F. W. Walther, *Briefe von C.F.W. Walther* (St. Louis: Concordia, 1916), 2:193.

47. *Synodal–Bericht 1885*, 32 (English: "1885," 279); *Evangelien Postille*, 398 (English: *Standard Gospels*, 391).

48. Walther to Lindemann, 192–93.

49. Walther to Lindemann, 192; *Lutherische Brosamen*, 366.

50. See Dörfler–Dierken, *Luthertum und Demokratie*, 287–92, for Walther's conception of "*Christliche Obrigkeit*."

51. "Wie wichtig waren die Dienste, welche die lutherischen Fürsten der Reformationszeit der Kirche leisteten!" (*Synodal–Bericht 1885*, 30).

52. Suelflow, *Servant of the Word*, 106–7.

53. AC XXVIII (Tappert, 81).

54. Ap. XVI (Tappert, 222).

55. "Treatise on the Power and Primacy of the Pope," 54 (Tappert, 329). Walther quotes the German text with modernized spelling. For the original, see *Die Bekenntnisschriften der evangelisch–lutherischen Kirche*, 10th ed. (Göttingen: Vandenhoeck & Ruprecht, 1986), 488.

56. " . . . dass hier von einer allgemeinen Christenpflicht die Rede ist, welche christliche Fürsten in ihrer hohen Stellung auszuüben nur mehr befähigt sind. Darum wird hier von ihnen auch nicht geredet, insofern sie Fürsten, sondern insofern sie Glieder der Kirche sind" (*Synodal–Bericht 1885*, 29). See also Schaller, 8 (English: *Essays*, 1:66).

57. " . . . im Allgemeinen die Pflicht, sich der Kirche *als einer Gesellschaft im Staate anzunehmen*" (*Synodal–Bericht 1885*, 27).

58. "Der Kurfürst handelte hierbei aber nicht in seinem obrigkeit-lichen
Amte, sondern nach der Pflicht der Liebe als der dazu am besten
geeignete Mann" (*Synodal–Bericht 1885*, 33). For Luther's position on
this issue, see Lewis W. Spitz Jr., "Luther's Ecclesiology and His Concept of the Prince as *Notbischof*," *Church History* 22 (1953): 113–41.

59. *Unterricht der Visitatorn an die Pfarhern um Kurfurstenthum zu
Sachssen*, WA 26:197 (English: *Instruction to the Visitors*, LW 40:271);
*Auslegung des ersten und zweiten Kapitels Johannis in Predigten 1537
und 1538*, WA 46:737–38 (English: *Sermons on the Gospel of John*, LW
22:227–28).

Walther also cites the following relevant comment from Luther: "Die
Berufung und Wahl der rechtgläubigen Kirchendiener ist eigentlich
und ursprünglich nicht Sache der Obrigkeit, sondern der Kirche.
Wenn aber die Obrigkeit gläubig und ein Mitglied der Kirche ist, so
beruft sie, nicht weil sie Obrigkeit ist, sondern weil sie ein Mitglied
der Kirche ist." Walther identifies his source as the periodical
Unschuldige Nachrichten (1715): 383. However, the Weimar Edition of
Luther's Works does not include it because the editors concluded that
the document from which the quotation comes, *Bedenken Luthers,
Melanchthons, Bugenhagens, Jonas' und Myconius', ob in Erfurt die
wahre Kirche Christi sei*, was probably written by Fr. Myconius and
then later assented to by Luther. See WABr 7:509. However, E. L.
Enders included it in his edition of Luther's correspondence, *Dr. Martin Luther's Briefwechsel* (Calw & Stuttgart: Verlag der Vereinsbuch-
handlung, 1907), 11:40–49.

60. "Die lutherische Kirche der ersten Zeit . . . an der Lehre festhielt, dass
die Obrigkeit weder Recht noch Macht habe, die Regierung der
Kirche an sich zu reissen. . . . Aber leider! sind die späteren
lutherischen Dogmatiker in diesem Stücke von der Lehre unserer
Kirche weit abgewichen." Walther offers a long quotation from Baier,
to show at least one possible source of the error, the misapplication of
Old Testament passages to New Testament realities before concluding, "Aerger kann kaum das Welt—und Kirchenregiment wider das
klare Zeugniss unserer Kirche in ihrem Grundbekenntniss mit einan-
der vermengt und vermischt werden, als es hier unser lieber Baier
thut" (*Synodal–Bericht 1885*, 35, 37).

4

Historiography
of American Civil Religion

The Cases of Martin E. Marty
and Sidney E. Mead

KEN SCHURB[1]

After the appearance of Robert Bellah's landmark 1967 article,[2] the ensuing debate about civil religion in the United
States continued quite actively for a decade and more.
Would-be participants found the roundtable for this discussion
extraordinarily large, with plenty of seats. Here was a topic in the
field of American religion accessible to researchers other than theologians or church historians cut from the conventional cloth.
Preparation for the 1976 bicentennial celebration did not hurt the
growing interest in civil religion either, for this topic seemed rich
with potential both to illumine the "American character" and to
sell books.

In a sense, however, this discussion was hardly new. While the Bellah essay may have served as a "wake-up call" for some, at least within certain circles of religious scholarship, others had been laboring through the night on civil religion, albeit under other names. Most of these people were saying that the 1950s had indeed been a very dark night of culture religion in America.

The present essay is concerned with writing on American civil religion undertaken during the third quarter of the twentieth century. More precisely, it examines work done from about 1955 to about 1980. Thus it covers the dozen or so years before Bellah's 1967 essay and the dozen or so after. Instead of surveying contributions by many scholars, particularly those from the relative "newcomer" disciplines at the table, it focuses on the work of two prominent church historians: Martin Marty and Sidney Mead. To be sure, historical assessment is only one way to view the complex subject of American civil religion, yet there is no denying its importance. It should be noted, however, that these men went beyond their roles as chroniclers or analysts and became commentators and even advocates in the civil religion debate. Partly following their lead, this essay will critically assess the positions they took.

MARTIN E. MARTY

For 35 years (1963–1998) Martin Marty taught the history of modern Christianity, especially American Christianity, at the University of Chicago Divinity School. Before that, the theologically trained Marty served as pastor of a Lutheran Church—Missouri Synod congregation in the Chicago suburbs. In 1959 Pastor Marty wrote a book bemoaning the average American's beliefs amid the religious revival of the postwar years. Professor Marty again took up civil religion in the 1970s and early 1980s. We will examine both stages of his engagement with this topic.

Marty's "early" analysis targeted the postwar religious "kick" that depicted God as understandable, manageable, comforting in the extreme, and—above all, perhaps—one of us: "an American jolly good fellow."[3] Marty wrote that such a "packaged God" resulted from a "morally and intellectually debilitating relativism" that also gave rise to "the personless man and the blurred community."[4]

The first step toward the packaging of God had been taken in America when the Puritans opted for a "looser" version of Calvinism, which eventually gave way to Arminianism. As time went by, Marty noted, "more and more was laid upon man."[5] In the face of secular onslaughts, and lacking strong reinforcement for the Protestant tradition, the concept of redemption had grown shallow and illusory by the middle of the twentieth century. Many of the old forms remained but were divested of their former content. Instead there arose a new content, oriented to pluralism and social utility. In 1959 Marty called it "religion-in-general." At that time some were thinking that the "religion of democracy" should find a place within religion-in-general.[6] "Whatever else it includes," Marty cautioned, "the 'new shape' of American religion is not basically Protestant."[7]

"Religion-in-general" and the "religion of democracy" differed considerably from the Christian faith. Marty indicated that their advocates could be welcomed by Christians "as partners in support of the national consensus, but not as allies in witness to God the Father of Jesus Christ." He urged Christians to "resist their efforts to establish their version of the democratic creed as the official American faith."[8] Here Marty was putting his foot down hardest. Up to this point, he had been resisting "religion-in-general" and especially the "religion of democracy" for offering content different from and opposed to the Christian faith.

But without missing a beat, Marty now started tapping out a new rhythm. That is, he continued to press the case against "religion-in-general," but he began doing so on different grounds. Marty quoted Jacques Maritain, who had written that any temporalized religious inspiration runs the risk of terminating in a failure if religion in its own order does not victoriously resist any trend toward becoming itself temporalized, that is to say, if, in the inner realm of human souls, faith in supernatural Truth and obedience to the law of God, the fire of true love and the life of divine grace are not steadily growing.[9]

A shift in Marty's argument was in the making, away from content and toward function. He was starting to aim the spotlight at religious effect. Correspondingly, he began relegating to the background his earlier criticism about un-Christian content in emergent 1950s American culture religion. His newer complaints, as in the above quotation from Maritain, concerned "temporalization" and the like. Marty worried that asking "participants in the dialogue" to "desert their diversities and obscure their particularities" would "enhance the new establishment [of a common national faith] at the expense of the religious vitality of the individual conspiracies." Notably, "religious vitality" now established the all-important context for mentioning "commitment to truth."[10]

Marty's willingness to soft-pedal content became more explicit as he outlined his proposal concerning a "culture ethic" for American Protestants. While his stated object was that "clarity and distinctiveness of religious [!] definition . . . be restored to Christian witness lest it come at the last to resemble the man in the street's idea of God as a 'vague, oblong blur,' " Marty contended that the full-scale relativism of "religion-in-general" could be opposed without bringing back "arrogant absolutisms."[11] He suggested beginning with "the proclamation of what is truth *for us* and our community, presented as an option for the faith and hope of the world."[12]

Marty's espousal of the transcendent was crippled by his commitment to pluralism with unity in the ecumenical sphere. The worst thing he could bring himself to say about his most negative definition of syncretism (namely, a mixing together of religions to produce a "hybrid faith") was that it is "not creative" or that it was "unfaithful to man's higher visions and responses to the call for truth."[13] Syncretistic religion does not do what a good religion should, Marty insinuated. Thus his argument was in considerable measure based on religious function, even though he championed biblical content in places.[14] Some years later, Marty's former teacher Sidney Mead referred to *The New Shape of American Religion* and characterized its author as a "defender of an implicit but vaguely defined Protestant orthodoxy against 'religion in general.'"[15]

Actually, the "early" Marty's case arose at least as much from the linking of a vaguely defined allegiance to "religion" together with a strange partner, the *neo*orthodoxy that was enjoying some popularity in America and in the Missouri Synod during the 1950s.[16] "In place of dissipating relativism," he wrote confidently, "there can be witness to truth tempered by recognition of the incompleteness of all human vision."[17] Marty approvingly cited a line from a 1620 Puritan sermon that God has "more truth and light to break forth from His holy word."[18] Similarly, the leading neoorthodox theologian Karl Barth had called attention to the Reformed tradition's "timeless appeal to the open Bible and to the Spirit which from it speaks to our spirit." In fact, Barth had contrasted this Reformed approach with that of Lutheranism.

> Our fathers had good reason for leaving us *no* Augsburg Confession, authentically interpreting the word of God, *no* Formula of Concord, *no* "Symbolic Books" which might later, like the Lutheran, come to possess an odor of sanctity. They left us only *creeds*, more than one of which begin or end with a proviso which leaves them open to being improved upon in the future. The Reformed churches simply do *not* know the word dogma, in its rigid hierarchical sense.[19]

Building on neoorthodox and Reformed premises, Marty wanted to pursue an ecumenical dream while retaining theological particularity. But as we have come to appreciate still more in the postmodern atmosphere of the early twenty-first century, making claims about the truth "for us" can fail to communicate the fact that the biblical message remains true even when it is not received in faith. Hearing such relative claims will not necessarily lead people to realize, for example, that rejecting Christ's Gospel in unbelief leaves one eternally under the full weight and accusation of God's Law. Contenting oneself simply to assert the truth "for me" can evacuate the transcendent content of theology to the point where all that remains is a set of concerns about "religious vitality" or something similar. In 1959 Marty did not account for the prospect that the depletion of content he so deplored in generalized religion could occur in his own backyard, as it were, via customs and procedures intended to safeguard pluralism.

A preview of Marty's later analysis of civil religion can be found in a 1965 article where he affirmed that "vague elements of a religious consensus" existed down through the years in America.[20] Now distancing himself from the neoorthodoxy that could look upon societal religion only as a negative, Marty went on to distinguish between "integral" societal religion ("totalist, organic, dogmatic" in nature) and "nonintegral" societal religion (which he called "open-ended, tentative, historical"). Marty ventured that Christians could interact or "conspire" with the second sort. Of course, this brand of societal religion would affect them even as they tried to make an impact upon it. "Assent to societal values may take on a quasi-religious character, however, without becoming an ultimate threat to a particular faith," he determined.[21]

Marty went further along these lines in 1974 when he wrote a chapter for what became a well-known book of readings on civil religion.[22] At first glance, his essay presented a useful "map" with which to sort out various features of a civil religion terrain that had grown conceptually cluttered with the many reactions to Bellah's 1967 essay. Before sketching four distinct types of civil religion, though, Marty announced the purpose of his typology. He wanted to enable people to "judge civil religion in the context of what it sets out to do and not what scholars think it should do. On those terms Will Herberg need not have seen all forms of civil religion as potentially idolatrous. . . . "[23] While Marty himself had not gone so far in 1959, his own critique had been similar to Herberg's. Fifteen years later, he was again distancing himself from neoorthodox, existentialistic sorts of commentary upon American civil religion. But while Marty may no longer have wished to hold civil religion up to scrutiny based on a function *he* wanted to see it perform, he was not finished with functional assessments of American civil religion. Finally, almost at the end of an essay largely devoted to grappling with classifications of civil religion, Marty rather surprisingly advised "creative apathy," including good humor, "to prevent people from taking the claims and counterclaims of civil religion so seriously."[24]

In a chapter of a book published during the bicentennial year, Marty noted that civil religion had changed somewhat since Bellah's famous essay appeared and that it had to change with the shift in national mood from the late 1960s to the mid-1970s. (He did not explicitly mention Watergate, but it readily comes to mind.) Empirical studies of popular involvement in civil religion were sorely needed. Still, Marty judged the intellectual category of civil religion to be durable, and rightly so, he added in effect. Those discussing civil religion before and after 1967 were touching on two key aspects of national and religious life. The first was the challenge within a pluralistic milieu to relate various parts of society, including religious parts, to the national whole. The other was the extent to which civil religion "allows for the civil order and, most of all, the nation, to be transparent to a transcendent order of being."[25] Between pluralism and transcendence, we might add, there was little question about which was more likely to be recognized and "valued" in late twentieth-century America where societal processes promoting pluralism tended to evacuate transcendent messages from the public square.

While he followed the theoretical discussion about civil religion, Marty remained quite interested in the common sense of people who had never heard of the theory. In a 1979 essay[26] he argued that

> the American laity, often without benefit of clergy, as it were, came to differentiate sharply between what we may call ordering faith and saving faith. . . . The essentials of all religions served well enough to order government, but they did not save souls. . . . [27]

So while millions of Americans looked to the teachings of their churches for salvation, when it came to ordering society, they thought something like public religion as envisioned by Benjamin Franklin or Thomas Jefferson bore a striking similarity to their own convictions. This distinction between "ordering faith" and "saving faith," crude as it may have been in the minds of those millions, had remarkable staying power. "Even today," Marty wrote, "when groups overtly fuse their saving faith with ordering faith, they exclude themselves or are rebuffed by others."[28] This enduring *modus vivendi* enabled members of various denominations to continue feeling at ease at what Marty called "the republican banquet."[29]

A couple of years later, Marty wrote of a "communion of communions" especially sensitive to the public order. This clustering, which his book's title termed *The Public Church*, was "a partial Christian embodiment within public religion."[30] Marty borrowed the latter term from Franklin, finding it preferable to "civil religion." He characterized the public church as a sort of fulfillment of Franklin's vision. Marty anticipated that its contributions would fall more in the realm of "ordering faith" than "saving faith." "Saving faith calls for a particular story and a communal language," he wrote. "The ordering faith or ordering *logos* sees God active even where people are not in the process of being reconciled, only of being governed and governing."[31] Marty therefore admired the work of John Courtney Murray and others who held "some rudimentary version of natural law ... [namely,] that in the structure of the universe or the given world there are the bases for political values and society."[32] He directed the public church to theologians such as Augustine, Calvin, and Luther, all of whom taught about civil righteousness.[33]

Marty had moved from attacking a prominent form of civil religion to reporting on and attempting to encourage a Christian presence at the table of public religion. Although in 1959 he warned that "[t]he national religion thrives on plural belonging," his own enthusiasm for plural commitments grew over the years.[34] Accordingly, his later writings dulled the neoorthodox edge with which he had written earlier. Yet side by side with these changes, continuities can be traced in his thinking. Even in 1959 Marty thought a national consensus important; later he allowed that elements of this consensus might be "quasi-religious," tenets of an "ordering faith" based on works of God accessible to all regardless of anyone's "saving faith." Also, religious function stood out as decisive in Marty's evaluation, early and late. In 1959 he opposed a civil religious phenomenon that did not do what a good religion should do, presumably in the realm of "saving faith." But later he approved and encouraged public religion that proved quite effective in the realm of "ordering faith."[35]

Marty's mature thought should be held up to scrutiny. To be sure, Christians in America (or any other nation) may rightly regard their country and its symbols with an allegiance that can be called "quasi-religious." Even so, as Marty agreed in principle, we must constantly guard against idolatry of the nation itself, its form of government, or its mores. But, for instance, when astronauts killed in a space shuttle mishap or public servants who perish while helping victims of terrorist attacks are thought to have gone to heaven because they died in service to their country, ordering faith has exceeded its bounds and civil righteousness has pressed beyond the civil sphere. Is this transgression recognized by the millions

Marty counts upon to distinguish "saving faith" from "ordering faith"? Are they as adept at spotting such transgressions as Marty thought they were in pointing to places where saving faith encroaches upon ordering faith?[36]

Another example: When interreligious prayer services are held at times of national crisis, do Marty's millions regard these services strictly as "ordering faith" occasions? If so, they are ignoring the convictions of many participants in these services who come from religious traditions that observe no distinction between "ordering faith" and "saving faith." They are also ignoring the biblically based counsel of Luther, who insisted that human beings can have nothing to do with the hidden God and that God can only be approached as He has revealed Himself in Jesus Christ.[37]

SIDNEY E. MEAD

Sidney Mead had been Martin Marty's professor and mentor in doctoral study at the University of Chicago Divinity School. After Mead moved to the University of Iowa several years later, he offered a few criticisms of Marty's 1959 book. One of Mead's most important articles, "The Nation with the Soul of a Church," was initially published during 1967, like Robert Bellah's famous essay.[38] Perhaps it looked like Mead was trying to enter the civil religion discussion, but he reported that he always felt uncomfortable in those circles. He thought he had different and simpler points to make.[39] Whether Mead's points were truly simpler is debatable, but they were unquestionably different.

At least briefly, Mead followed American religion back to pre-revolutionary days. He noted the ideas of those times about a "democracy of the Saints." As democracy embraced the entire community over the years, biblical concepts were replaced more and more by Enlightenment parallels. "By the end of the eighteenth century," Mead announced, "for the first time in the history of

Christendom a genuinely *religious* alternative to Christianity surfaced; and it has persisted. . . ."[40]

Here Mead took exception to the views of his former student Marty. In Mead's terms, the "religion of the republic" was less a result of deterioration and secularization than it was the product of conscious determination by men like Benjamin Franklin. But it differed from the civil religious phenomenon that Marty, Will Herberg, and others had begun to sense in the 1950s and early 1960s. Mead later wrote in retrospect: "The egregious blunder of Will Herberg in his *Protestant—Catholic—Jew* was to equate the American faith or 'common religion' with the outward manifestations of 'the American Way of Life.'" Herberg and others like him had confused "specific notions" of the latter sort with the former "high generalities," Mead charged. Therefore, they ended up not even recognizing the religion of the republic, let alone appreciating it.[41]

In Mead's estimation, Henry Steele Commager had been correct to note that America was a Christian nation in everything but law by the start of the twentieth century. Yet the exception of law towered in importance to Mead, who wrote: "The United States was never Protestant in the sense that its constitutional and legal structure was rooted in or legitimated by particularistic Protestant theology."[42] Rather, the country and its law were given the stamp of legitimacy by the religion of the republic, that is, a religion compatible with religious freedom and pluralism within the nation.[43]

On occasion, Mead could go so far as to write that

This theology [of the religion of the republic] is not only *not* particularistic; it is designedly antiparticularistic, in this respect reflecting the predominant intellectual slant of the eighteenth century. These thinkers held that only what is common to all religions and all sects—[Benjamin] Franklin's "essentials of every religion"—is relevant to the being and well-being of the *common*wealth. This is the theology behind the legal structure of America, the theology on which the practice of religious freedom is based and its meaning interpreted. Under it, one might say, it is religious particularity, Protestant or otherwise, that is heretical and schismatic—even un-American![44]

Such outbursts against the churches came infrequently from Mead.[45] But as the religion of the republic commanded Mead's attention in his self-appointed role of apologist (in addition to historian), he consistently held that its content was more religiously significant than the teachings of any given denomination, or group of them. "As a layman I would have to admit that the particularities that form the foundation of sectarianism have become practically meaningless to me," he noted, "and I suspect that my counterparts on the campuses and in the pews are legion."[46]

Mead referred to the writings of G. K. Chesterton, who had commented that "America is the only nation in the world that is founded on a creed . . . set forth with dogmatic and even theological lucidity in the Declaration of Independence." This religion, Mead continued with Chesterton, taught that all men were equal and that government was a servant of the people. It condemned anarchism and (by implication) atheism.[47] Mead grew impatient with what he saw as Herberg's denial that this common religion was a religion at all.[48] On the contrary, he maintained that there was in the religion of the republic a prophetic voice and even, after a fashion, a testimony to transcendence.

If the early Martin Marty had shown himself a disciple of Barth to a great degree, Mead was avowedly taking his cue from Paul Tillich when he asserted that the founding fathers wanted to "plumb for the universal" that lies hidden in the idiosyncrasies of teaching and practice among the various churches.[49] Thus, Mead continued, "[w]e are not surprised to read that after attending the preaching of one minister on five successive Sundays, [Benjamin] Franklin gave up when he became convinced that the minister's motive was to make good Presbyterians rather than moral citizens."[50] Tillich, too, was after something quite beside confessional fidelity when he wrote:

> In the depth of every living religion there is a point at which the religion itself loses its importance, and that to which it points breaks through its particularity, elevating it to spiritual freedom and with it to a vision of the spiritual presence in other expressions of the ultimate meaning of man's existence.[51]

Precisely this kind of breakthrough formed the challenge for Christianity as posed by Tillich and seconded by Mead. By losing itself to gain the world in this way, Christianity could continue to bear to the human race the genuine religious answer.[52]

Mead seems to have been influenced by the view that "the truth is in the whole." Therefore, he was on the constant lookout for enduring natural communities that gathered people of common biological origin. The longer such a community lasted and the more territory it covered, the more truth Mead thought it had.[53] With such truth, it also had greater potential to give individuals a firm sense of their personal identity.[54]

While Mead could comment that the religion of the republic did not *necessarily* "undermine belief in the efficacy of sectarian forms or expressing the universal," that universal remained the important thing. Therefore, Mead wrote: "Church members in America have always been faced with the necessity to choose, implicitly at least, between the inclusive religion of democracy and the particularistic Christianity of their sect."[55] As a case study, he cited the then-recent *A Study of Generations*, which reported on research conducted among the three largest Lutheran church bodies in the United States. Three out of every four participants told the survey that all religions take a person to the same God, while three of four also said faith in Christ was absolutely necessary for salvation! Mead submitted that "these members polled are both Lutheran Christians and loyal citizens of the commonwealth in which they live." In other words, "the theology of their denominations is different from the theology that legitimatizes the constitutional and legal structures of their country." But these church members were trying to cling to both. The result was that even in what Mead called "the least theologically eroded of all the Protestant denominations," the religion of the republic held significant sway.[56]

Such republican religion may not have been identical with the civil religious phenomena criticized earlier by Herberg and Marty, but it certainly formed part of their background. Mead at one point called them "the popular triumph of the theology of the Declaration [of Independence] over the theology of the competing denominations."[57] As a partisan of the religion of the republic, Mead did not disapprove.

Still, he made no great effort to delineate the content of the religion of the republic. Writing a dogmatics on its behalf never found a place on Mead's "to-do" list. He cited Benjamin Franklin and Josiah Strong on the dogmas of republican religion, but he added that "these are specific notions respecting the content of the universal, which anyone may legitimately oppose and argue for another constellation of specific notions." For Mead it sufficed to know that "the universal, however latent, is encapsulated in the particular forms of the sects."[58] Going any further to describe the content of this universal was a task he approached quite cautiously. What he finally set down is therefore most revealing:

> I have my opinion of what "that" is to which "every living religion points"; namely, that no man is God. This is what I understand to be the functional meaning of "God" in human experience . . . a concept of the infinite seems to me necessary if we are to state the all-important fact about man: That he is finite. This is the premise of all democratic institutions. It is the essential dogma of the religion of the Republic. . . .[59]

Mead was scandalized by particularity, specifically the particular and conflicting teachings of various churches. In retrospect, he wrote: "[M]y study of religion in American history, whatever else it may be, becomes a quest to discover and delineate *the* religion of the pluralistic culture in which I have lived and moved and had my being."[60] Like the nineteenth-century American characterized by Alexis de Tocqueville, Mead apparently thought it reasonable that "the greater truth should go with the greater number."[61] But the "greater truth" of the American religion proved to be quite meager in content, amounting basically to the fact of human finitude. Yet Mead held to it, asking rhetorically: "[C]an we not recognize that our individual refusal to be God, and our cherishing and preserving a system that defends the right of each to tell the other 'that he is not God' is, perhaps, in Lincoln's words, 'the last, best hope of earth' which we may 'nobly save or meanly lose'?"[62]

Marty and Mead were each in a quandry with an aspect of the civil religion challenge identified by Marty himself in 1976, namely, allowing for the nation to be made "transparent to a transcendent order of being." Marty's problem arose from his commitment to respect pluralism and his corresponding hesitancy about making *too* strong a transcendent statement. Mead was less concerned about potentially offending the various churches. But the older he grew, the more difficulty he had asserting a transcendent order *of being*. Notice that in the last block quote above, from an essay originally published in 1970, he contented himself to say that a *concept* of the infinite was needed to teach the great lesson that people are finite. There, at least, Mead did not even find God Himself so necessary. His thinking had parted company with Chesterton's analysis of America.[63]

Once again, it can be noted, there were affinities between Mead and Tillich. According to Tillich, "absolute faith," the only faith that could give rise to courage, was to experience the power of being in the face of nonbeing. Tillich added that the content of absolute faith was not the God of traditional theism, but instead the "God above God." Absolute faith, then, "is the accepting of the acceptance without somebody or something that accepts," according to Tillich.[64]

But in some ways Mead was breaking with Tillich too. For all of his verbiage suggesting transcendence, Mead's ultimate emphasis fell on the functional. This was his preferred approach as an historian.[65] But he said as much also, for instance, when as commentator and advocate he wrote about "the functional meaning of 'God' in human experience."[66] Reduced to its essentials, the religion of the republic did what a good religion should. Like other religious expressions, it proclaimed what Mead deemed "the all-important fact about man: That he is finite."[67] Yet this fact of human finitude, apparently the last vestige of religious content that Mead cherished, not only stands far removed from the biblical message of the triune God and human salvation, it is not even specifically "religious"!

While Mead was uncomfortable with particularistic churches, and though he could growl at them on occasion, he by no means set out to abolish them. He conceded that they were necessary to the religion of the republic. For they acted as a moral force, encouraging order and obedience to law. Moreover, "[c]hurches exist in the Republic to remind this sovereign ruler [in America, the people], 'You, too, are mortal; you are not God.' "[68] Of course, each church would do this job in its own way, as it set forth its own doctrine. To this extent, Mead's vision depended in part on a pluralistic set of allies. He could not want to see the various churches collapse, even with all their particularity, because of the function they carried out. As with Marty, but in a different way, pluralism ended up doing better in Mead's prospect than transcendence did.

CONCLUSION

In 1972 Sidney Mead delivered an address at Concordia Theological Seminary, Springfield, Illinois. His remarks bore great similarity to one of his essays cited above. But on that occasion he also said that he had been trying for at least 25 years to get theologians to see the theological conflict between the religion of the Enlightenment and any contemporary religion. He added, "I long ago concluded that the most likely place in Protestantism to expect an adequate theological clarification of the issue posed by the two conflicting traditions at war was in Lutheranism."[69] Mead did not say so, but presumably this conclusion occurred to him because of the classic Lutheran teaching of God's governance in two realms.

This teaching relieves some of the problems that Mead thought were so endemic for American Christians. That is, Christians can acknowledge God's lordship in both realms. Broadly speaking, He rules His church on one hand through the Gospel and on the other hand He rules the world and all its nations via the Law, also natural law. We Christians recognize the only true God, the God and Father of our Lord Jesus Christ, as the "Creator" and "nature's God" mentioned in the Declaration of Independence. Yet we do not have to insist on the same recognition by our fellow citizens before civil order or national unity can ensue. Still, Mead's work can remind us that some of those fellow citizens tend to take it for granted that when any real or perceived ideological conflict arises between being a "good American" and adhering to our confession of Christ, it will tend in practice to be resolved on the "American" side.

Against Mead, Martin Marty was right to hold the door open to plural commitments. His problem was keeping those commitments rightly ordered. He made a clearer distinction than Mead did between "saving faith" and "ordering faith."[70] But the line between the two cannot be drawn adequately using natural tools alone, Marty should have realized, for the teaching of God's twofold rule is an article of faith that must be based upon Scripture. Religious function can take people involved in public religion only so far, be they participants in it or commentators upon it.

Notes

1. The Rev. Dr. Ken Schurb is pastor of Zion Lutheran Church, Moberly,

Missouri. He holds M. Div. and S.T.M. degrees from Concordia Theological Seminary in Ft. Wayne, Indiana, and M.A. and Ph.D. degrees in history from Ohio State University.

2. Robert N. Bellah, "Civil Religion in America," in *American Civil Religion,* ed. Russell E. Richey and Donald G. Jones (New York: Harper & Row, 1974), 21–44. See the introduction to this book.

3. Martin E. Marty, *The New Shape of American Religion* (New York: Harper & Row, 1959), 37–39.

4. Marty, *New Shape of American Religion,* 166.

5. Marty, *New Shape of American Religion,* 55. See also Marty, *New Shape of American Religion,* 23 and 42.

6. Marty, *New Shape of American Religion,* 78–84.

7. Marty, *New Shape of American Religion,* 73.

8. Marty, *New Shape of American Religion,* 85.

9. Jacques Maritain, *Reflections on America* (New York: Scribner's, 1958), 188; quoted in Marty, *New Shape of American Religion,* 86.

10. Marty, *New Shape of American Religion,* 89. Marty was echoing Will Herberg's criticism of "the religiousness characteristic of America today," that is, "a religiousness without serious commitment, without real inner conviction, without genuine existential decision" (*Protestant—Catholic—Jew: An Essay in American Religious Sociology* [New York: Doubleday, 1955], 276).

11. Marty, *New Shape of American Religion,* 159, 166.

12. Marty, *New Shape of American Religion,* 167, *emphasis original.*

13. Marty, *New Shape of American Religion,* 86.

14. In fairness, it should be observed that also toward the end of his book, Marty quoted Acts 4:12 about the only name given under heaven for human salvation. "Religion-in-general fuses this name with all others," he pointed out, "and this fusion dulls the impetus of Christian missionary endeavor." Here, as elsewhere in the book, Marty was clearly critical of "different boats heading for the same shore" sort of thinking. He added, however: "I am not saying that an implied universalism with its belief that ultimately the love of God will overcome the wrath and justice of God is a base motive. It may proceed from the deepest resources of love and may prove somehow to be 'true.' But when Protestant Christianity becomes the propagandizer of such a vision it is arrogating to itself something which is God's own province to declare, and which is not declared in the revelation that gives birth to the Christian faith and its mission" (*New Shape of American Religion,* 166). Marty did not do justice to the

exclusive claim made in the very passage he went on to quote, Acts 4:12.

15. Sidney E. Mead, "Christendom, Enlightenment, and the Revolution," in *Religion and the American Revolution*, ed. Jerald C. Brauer (Philadelphia: Fortress, 1976), 42.

16. Marty later acknowledged the debt he owed at the time to neo-orthodox theologians such as Karl Barth: "In a nation that was tempted to identify divine purpose with our righteous 'crusade against atheistic communism' and for 'the American Way of Life,' Barth was at least a corrective" (Martin E. Marty, "Barth," *How Karl Barth Changed My Mind* [Grand Rapids: Eerdmans, 1986], 104).

17. Marty, *American Religion*, 167.

18. Marty, *American Religion*, 88. John Warwick Montgomery pointed out that by taking this position, the Puritans "unwittingly laid the groundwork for a depreciation of the very Scriptures they held so high, for any encouragement to regard one's people as a revelatory community opens the gates to sectarian claims that appear, in the eyes of unbelievers, to reduce the Bible to relativism" (*The Shaping of America* [Minneapolis: Bethany Fellowship, 1976], 117).

19. Karl Barth, *The Word of God and the Word of Man* (New York: Harper & Row, 1957), 229–230.

20. Martin E. Marty, "The Status of Societal Religion in the United States," *Concordia Theological Monthly* 36 (November, 1965): 687–705. See "Societal Religion," 697.

21. Marty, "Societal Religion," 704; see 700 and 703.

22. Martin E. Marty, "Two Kinds of Two Kinds of Civil Religion," in *American Civil Religion*, eds. Russell E. Richey and Donald G. Jones (New York: Harper & Row, 1974), cited in the present essay in a slightly revised form: "Civil Religion: Two Kinds of Two Kinds," chapter four in Martin E. Marty, *Religion and Republic: The American Circumstance* (Boston: Beacon Press, 1987), 77–94.

23. Marty, "Two Kinds," 82. Interestingly, Marty's sentence continues: " . . . nor need Sidney E. Mead have had to declare it superior to church religion." See below on Mead.

24. Marty, "Two Kinds," 93.

25. Martin E. Marty, *A Nation of Behavers* (Chicago: University of Chicago Press, 1976), 196–97. See also *Nation of Behavers*, 182, 187–90, 194–95.

26. Martin E. Marty, "A Sort of Republican Banquet," *Journal of Religion* 59 (October 1979), cited in the present essay in a slightly revised

form: "Public Religion: The Republican Banquet," chapter 3 in Marty, *Religion and Republic*, 53–76. This essay in large measure responded to the work of Marty's former teacher Sidney Mead.

27. Marty, "Republican Banquet," 64–66. Marty distinguished the approach of Franklin from that of Jefferson, who had less use for the churches. Marty preferred Franklin's concept of a "Publick Religion" that would profess "the essentials of every religion," namely, "the existence of the Deity, that he made the world, and govern'd it by his Providence; that the most acceptable service of God was the doing good to men; that our souls are immortal; and that all crime will be punished, and virtue rewarded, either here or hereafter." Franklin was prepared to respect the respective churches depending on the degree to which they instilled these "essentials" in their adherents (as quoted in Marty, "Republican Banquet," 60–61).

28. Marty, "Republican Banquet," 73.

29. Marty, "Republican Banquet," 64. The phrase is from William James. See "Republican Banquet," 57.

30. Martin E. Marty, *The Public Church: Mainline—Evangelical—Catholic* (New York: Crossroad, 1981), 16; see 3ff.

31. Marty, *Public Church*, 129.

32. Marty continued: "In American history the outlook finds prefigurement and embodiment in the Declaration of Independence, the tradition of republican and democratic thought, the legal heritage, and the Constitution" (Marty, *Public Church*, 109).

33. Marty, *Public Church*, 168.

34. Marty, *New Shape*, 69. In 1997 Marty reflected: "For some years I have been taking issue with those who see all plural commitments as 'all or nothing' rivalries within the original group and, one might add, the individual person" (Martin E. Marty, *The One and the Many: America's Struggle for the Common Good* [Cambridge: Harvard University Press, 1997], 150).

35. Marty made perhaps his best brief formulation of the continuity (with no mention of the discontinuity) within his thought in a popular book published the year before the bicentennial observance. He wrote of "dangerous attempts to identify God's purposes with a nation's way of life. Sometimes these attempts focus on what is called 'civil religion,' a possibly creative way of seeing the nation itself as a matrix or repository of religious symbols and purpose. But the 'way of life' religion may encompass more. It can include behavior patterns, customs, mores, and sanctions for success seeking" (Martin E. Marty, "Con," in *The Pro and Con Book of Religious America: A Bicen-*

tennial Argument [Waco, Texas: Word, 1975], 134). Presumably, the "way of life" religion is what Marty was willing to own up to having attacked during the 1950s. Civil religion itself, however, was "possibly creative."

36. Marty did point out, wisely, that "the civic realm makes room for what has been called 'religiocification' more readily than do most other modes or locales of human activity" (Marty, "Two Kinds," 77).

37. Luther wrote, for example: "Wherever God hides Himself, and wills to be unknown to us, there we have no concern. . . . Now, God in His own nature and majesty is to be left alone; in this regard, we have nothing to do with Him, nor does He wish us to deal with Him. We have to do with Him as clothed and displayed in his Word, by which He presents Himself to us" (*Martin Luther on The Bondage of the Will,* trans. J. I. Packer and O. R. Johnston [Old Tappan, N. J.: Fleming H. Revell, 1957], 170; Latin text in WA 18:685).

38. Sidney E. Mead, "The Nation with the Soul of a Church," in Richey and Jones, 45–75. The present essay cites this article not from Mead's own collection of his essays (which took its title from this article; see next note) but rather from the Richey and Jones anthology that gave it to readers as it had originally been published in the 1967 volume of *Church History.*

39. Sidney E. Mead, preface to *The Nation with the Soul of a Church* (New York: Harper & Row, 1975), viii and 129–30 n. 3. This volume collected Mead's essays published over the previous decade or so, his "Iowa years."

40. Sidney E. Mead, "Religion of (or and) the Republic," in *The Nation with the Soul of a Church,* 119 (*emphasis original*). See also Mead, *Nation with the Soul of a Church,* 52–53.

41. Sidney E. Mead, "Reinterpretation in American Church History," in *The Lively Experiment Continued,* ed. by Jerald C. Brauer (Macon, Ga.: Mercer University Press, 1987), 237. See Daniel F. Rice, "Sidney E. Mead and the Problem of 'Civil Religion,'" *Journal of Church and State* 22 (Winter 1980): 61.

42. Mead, "The Post-Protestant Concept and America's Two Religions," in *The Nation with the Soul of a Church,* 18–19. This essay, originally published in 1964, constituted Mead's most direct answer to the claims launched during the 1950s by Marty and Herberg (and also Winthrop Hudson).

43. Mead, "Nation," 56.

44. Mead, "Post-Protestant Concept," 22, *emphasis original.* Similarly, over a decade later Mead argued that "every ardent defense of sectar-

ian Christianity, however unintentional, was by implication an attack on the mainspring of the Republic" (Sidney E. Mead, "Christendom, Enlightenment, and the Revolution," in *Religion and the American Revolution*, ed. Jerald C. Brauer [Philadelphia: Fortress, 1976], 52).

45. Martin Marty summarized: "Some days Mead sounded militant against the pluralism of the distracting sects, but more often he was merely explicit and asked that the sects be exposed as irrelevant to the public weal. Leave them alone and they'll go home, to tend private hungers for salvation that have nothing to do with public order" (Marty, *Public Church*, 158).

46. Sidney E. Mead, "The Fact of Pluralism and the Persistence of Sectarianism," in *The Nation with the Soul of a Church*, 47.

47. Mead, "Post–Protestant Concept," 20. Mead had borrowed the phrase "the nation with the soul of a church" from Chesterton.

48. See Mead, "Post–Protestant Concept," 17–18. Herberg specifically disclaimed this position (Will Herberg, "America's Civil Religion: What It Is and Whence It Comes," in *American Civil Religion*, 86). Yet as already noted above (see n. 10), Herberg had criticized mid-century American religiousness for not standing out as existentially compelling. A bit later, he added: "Civic religion is a religion which validates culture and society, without in any sense bringing them under judgment" (Herberg, *Protestant—Catholic—Jew*, 279). From these assertions the inference could fairly be made that so far as Herberg was concerned, civil religion was hardly worthy of the name "religion."

Mead vouched for the integrity of the religion of the republic at every stage of the historical game. Accordingly, he crossed interpretative swords once again with Marty, who claimed that in the flurry of the early nineteenth century, America became Protestant also in its basic political assumptions. Mead exclaimed incredulously: "Surely Marty does not mean that the Declaration of Independence was converted and baptised by Protestants so that its assumptions were Christianized" (Mead, "Post–Protestant," 134 n. 34.)

49. Mead, "Nation," 55. Rice correctly noted that no airtight distinction can be made here because Herberg (and, it might be added, the early Marty) also drew upon Tillich. See Rice, "Mead and the Problem of 'Civil Religion,'" 59 n. 27. Also see J. Ronald Engel, "The Religion of the Republic," in *The Lively Experiment Continued*, ed. Jerald C. Brauer (Macon, Ga.: Mercer University Press, 1987), 49–67; and LeRoy Moore, "Sidney E. Mead's Understanding of America," *Journal of the American Academy of Religion* 44 (1976): 133–53, repr. in *Modern American Protestantism and Its World: Historical Articles on Protes-*

tantism in American Religious Life, Vol. 1: *The Writing of American Religious History*, ed. Martin E. Marty (Munich: K. G. Saur, 1992), 106–26.

50. Mead, "Religion of (or and) the Republic," 121.

51. Paul Tillich, *Christianity and the Encounter of the World Religions* (New York: Columbia University Press, 1963), 97, quoted in Mead, "In Quest of America's Religion," in *The Nation with the Soul of a Church*, 8. Mead had a hunch that such statements helped account for Tillich's appeal to American students. Tillich offered young people conditioned by pluralism a way to satisfy their curiosity about religion while rejecting "sectarian institutional forms of religion" (Mead, "Quest," 9).

52. See Mead, "Nation," 58, where Mead also quoted Tillich.

53. See Engel, "Religion of the Republic," 53–56.

54. See Sidney E. Mead, "History and Identity," *Journal of Religion* 51 (January 1971): 1–14. Mead formulated "the primary question confronting the denominations today" as: "What is that '*common type* of faith and life' that God has permitted to emerge out of the American experience of Christianity?" (Mead, "Fact of Pluralism," 47, *my emphasis*).

Over time, as Marty put it, "[t]he community that provided identity had been progressively enlarged in Mead's vision." While Mead had been "most concerned with the Christian past" in 1953, by 1970 "he needed cosmic space and geological time" when he wrote: "We find a stable identity only through an imaginative grasp that we are one with all of life in time and space . . . human life is the planet become conscious of itself" (Mead, "History and Identity," 14; Martin E. Marty, "The Historian as Teacher," in *The Lively Experiment Continued*, ed. Jerald C. Brauer [Macon, Ga.: Mercer University Press, 1987], 34). Rice characterized Mead's thought as eventually having evolved to a "cosmic mysticism whose universality transcends all residual elements of an Enlightenment universalism tied to the reality of historic communities" ("Mead and the Problem of 'Civil Religion,' " 73).

55. Mead, "Nation," 56; Mead, "Post-Protestant Concept," 23.

56. Mead, "Religion of (or and) the Republic," 125.

57. Mead, "Post-Protestant Concept," 25. See also "Post-Protestant Concept," 17–18. Marty had indicated much the same thing when he wrote, toward the beginning of his 1959 book, that "a sort of casually Deist natural religion . . . informed by the Enlightenment" had been present since the beginnings of the United States as a nation. Marty's concern was that "this attitude is coming to new maturity in the mid-

dle of the twentieth century" with "corrosive influences" (Marty, *New Shape*, 4).

58. Mead, "Nation," 57.

59. Mead, "Quest," 9–10. Mead modestly refrained from claiming to know precisely what Tillich meant when he wrote of the "that" indicated by every living religion. See the quote from Tillich in the text corresponding to n. 51 above.

60. Mead, "Quest," 4–5, *emphasis original*.

61. Alexis de Tocqueville, *Democracy in America*, ed. and abridged by Richard D. Heffner (New York: New American Library, 1956), 148.

62. Mead, "Nation," 71. See Moore, "Mead's Understanding of America," 118.

63. See above, the text corresponding to n. 47.

64. Paul Tillich, *The Courage to Be* (New Haven: Yale University Press, 1952), 177–85; the quotation is from 185.

65. "My primary interest in this discussion is not what religion *is*, but what it *does* . . . I think the method of the outsider must be functional; that his ideal purpose is to delineate the effect religious beliefs and convictions have had upon what people did and the way they did it" (Mead, "Religion of (or and) the Republic," 117, *emphasis original*).

66. See the quote in the text at n. 59 above.

67. Mead, "Quest," 9–10.

68. Mead, "Quest," 10. In 1979 Marty sensed delicious irony in the picture Mead had painted. Marty wrote that "at the republican banquet today the burden of supporting public religion has fallen largely to the very inept and distracted sectarians whom the enlightened expected to see excluding themselves, suffering indigestion, or dying at the banquet door." That is, near the end of the twentieth century Marty found very few people talking about God in any way conducive to public religion except within "denominational religion" (Marty, "Republican Banquet," 70).

69. Sidney E. Mead, "An Address to Lutherans," *The Springfielder* 37 (June 1973): 15.

70. The latter term, however, can be misleading. See the essay in this book by Alvin J. Schmidt.

5

"In _____ We Trust": Filling in the Blank

American Religion and Biblical Christianity

JOEL P. OKAMOTO[1]

INTRODUCTION

There is no simple yet coherent way to handle this theme. "American religion" and "biblical Christianity" are very large and complex topics. Drawing comparisons and identifying contrasts between them is complicated because almost every notion of "American religion" involves American Christians. And the theme itself reflects important concerns and implies important issues for American Christians today, especially those in The Lutheran Church—Missouri Synod.

A choice needs to be made: simplicity or coherence. In this presentation I have pursued simplicity rather than coherence. I have simply tried to consider religion in America from both a sociological and a theological viewpoint. First, I consider the prevailing religious sensibility in American society today. Next, I consider the prevailing "theology" or "doctrine of God" in America, in particular the way the God of Israel and of Jesus Christ is characterized in the United States today. Finally, I try to draw together some of the themes and issues that emerge and propose some lessons for the church today.

SOME PERSPECTIVES ON RELIGION IN AMERICA

Not so long ago—that is to say, in the 1960s—the future for American religion looked grim. It was respectably argued and seriously feared that secularization was eroding the foundations of religious belief and threatening the viability of religious communities. One could find no more important indication of this threat than what Peter Berger called "the alleged demise of the supernatural." As he observed, "If commentators on the contemporary situation of religion agree about anything, it is that the supernatural has departed from the modern world." Although people responded to this situation in different ways, they all agreed, "the divine, at least in classical forms, [had] receded into the background of human concern and consciousness."[2] As far as modern societies were concerned, secularization had reduced talk about God, angels, and all things transcendent to the status of "rumors—and not very reputable ones at that."[3]

But as time passed, prospects for religion brightened. It turned out that unbelief, not religion, was the rumor. The "alleged demise of the supernatural" was just that: *alleged*. Religion in America endured.

But it has not endured intact. Religion in America has always been fluid, but the past fifty years have witnessed changes in and about religion remarkable even for American history. Not only have attitudes about religion changed, but the very conception of religion itself has changed. Not only do Americans, now more than ever, hold a wide range of religious beliefs, but their very perspective on believing has changed. Not only have the composition and number of religious communities changed, but the very significance of religious communities.

As one might expect, observers differ about what is most significant in these changes.

"A New Religious America"

One apparent change in American religion is that it has become visibly more diverse. When I was a child, the answer to the question "What is your religion?" was "Lutheran," "Catholic," or "Methodist." Religious identity was denominational identity. To learn about others and their religion, you visited other churches. This, at any rate, was my experience.

This experience fit well with the map of the religious landscape that Will Herberg drew in his 1955 study *Protestant— Catholic—Jew*.[4] Of course, even then, these categories did not fully do justice to the variety of American religious belief and practice. This map ignored Eastern Orthodoxy, and it took too little notice of such American phenomena as Mormonism and Pentecostalism. Nevertheless, it seemed plausible because it corresponded to widespread experience and common judgments.

But the composition of American religion has changed dramatically even since the 1950s and 1960s. It is now shifting from a diversity largely within the context of Christianity and Judaism to a plurality of the world's religions. As Diana Eck points out in her book *A New Religious America*, the signs of this plurality may be seen across the country. The United States, in the space of a generation, has become a nation with mosques in places such as cornfields near Toledo, with Hindu temples in the suburbs, with Minneapolis as the home of a Cambodian Buddhist temple and monastery, and with Sikhs gathering near San Jose.[5]

RELIGION AND THE CULTURE WARS

More has changed, however, in American religious life than simply more and/or more visible religious communities. This way of looking at American religion, for instance, does little to help us understand the unprecedented religious alignments in the American "culture wars." Lutheran theologian Robert Jenson gives a typical picture of the odd alliances that Americans form in their fights about such issues as abortion, fundamentalism, and ideological pluralism.

> Old-fashioned rationalists and new-age mystagogues have no public worries about each other, though both worry much about the lamentably sectarian views of practicing Jews or Christians. Gender feminists and predatory males join hands to fortify abortion clinics against an almost equally surprising league of Catholic bishops and Baptist populists. The Republican Party depends about evenly on evangelical Christians and amoralist libertarians. And so on and on.[6]

One does not have to believe that religion has only or primarily moral functions to recognize that religion plays a decisive role in civil life in general, and in the American cultural conflicts in particular. James Davison Hunter traced out this development in his book *Culture Wars*.

> [T]he cultural hostilities dominant over the better part of American history have taken place *within* the boundaries of a larger Biblical culture—among numerous Protestant groups, and Catholics and Jews—over such issues as doctrine, ritual observance, and religious organization. Underlying their disagreements, therefore, were basic agreements about the order of life in community and nation—agreements forged by Biblical symbols and imagery. But the old

arrangements have been transformed . . . The older agree-
ments have unraveled. The divisions of political conse-
quence today are not theological and ecclesiastical in character but the result of differing worldviews. That is to say,
they no longer revolve around specific doctrinal issues or
styles of religious practice and organization but around our
most fundamental and cherished assumptions about how
to order our lives—our own lives and our lives together in
this society.[7]

Jenson explicitly argues what Hunter suggests: that the "culture
wars" are "God-wars," conflicts over religion. He argues that these
fights and the alliances they generate only manifest an underlying
religious conflict. For centuries, Christianity had been both the
basic source and the perennial critic of Western civilization. Now,
however, this long "love-hate relationship" is coming to an end.
Christians, especially in America, find themselves having to be
either for the Lord or against Him. Therefore, Jenson concludes,

many who supposed they were for him line up practically
on the other side; many who thought themselves serenely
beyond religious concerns are revealed as lifelong zealous
opposers. It even happens that some who thought themselves apostate rally to what is in fact his cause.[8]

Beyond the question, however, of whether America was ever
really Christian, we might ask whether it is really as simple as being
"for or against the Lord." After all, on abortion, Americans who
genuinely regard themselves as Christian are lining up against
other Americans who also genuinely regard themselves as Christian. Furthermore, not all issues produce the same alliances. For
instance, Catholics who stand together in opposition to abortion
rights may stand apart on the use or application of the death
penalty.[9] Ultimately, of course, one must be either for or against
the Lord, and so the question is ultimately significant. But this distinction is not particularly helpful in sorting out American religious life. You might say that this question helps us to show *that*

something has happened but not necessarily *what*. It is far from obvious that moral disagreements alone have precipitated a fundamental change in the religious landscape. For that matter, it is far from obvious that these alignments are much more than *ad hoc* coalitions. And it does not help to explain the kind of "spiritual journeys" and changing character of spirituality that became obvious to so many in the last forty years.

"FROM DWELLING TO SEEKING"

A 1993 *Time Magazine* cover story on the Baby Boom generation and religion began with the story of Emil and Kathleen Walcek and their nine children. Growing up in the 1950s and 1960s, this Catholic family prayed before every meal, went to Mass every morning, and sent every one of their kids to parochial schools. Then, one by one, the children went out into the world and set off on what are turning out to be quite varied spiritual paths.

Emil Jr., 45, and Edward, 32, dropped out of church and stayed out. John, 43, was married on a cliff overlooking Laguna Beach, then divorced—and returned to the Catholic Church, saying, "[m]aybe the traditional way of doing things isn't so bad." Joe, 41, also returned to the fold after marrying a Ukrainian Catholic. Mary, 40, married a lapsed Methodist and worships "God's creation" in her own unstructured fashion. Rosie, 38, drifted into the Hindu-influenced Self-Realization Fellowship. Chris, 34, picked Unitarianism, which offered some of Christianity's morality without its dogma. Theresa, 36, spent five years exploring the "Higher Power" in 12-step programs. Ann, 30, called off her wedding when her nonpracticing Jewish fiancé embraced Orthodoxy, a crisis that "sparked a whole new journey for me."[10]

The Walceks may not have been your typical postwar family, but they were a microcosm of today's "lead generation," the Boomers.

The shift in religious outlook and understanding that is captured in the Boomer generation, however, extends through much of American society. The local chain bookstore provides a ready illustration of this shift: The "old 'religion' section is gone and in its place is a growing set of more specific rubrics catering to popular topics such as angels, Sufism, journey, recovery, meditation, magic, inspiration, Judaica, astrology, gurus, the Bible, prophecy, Evangelicalism, Mary, Buddhism, Catholicism, esoterica, and the like."[11] Other indications are also easy to discern. People today regularly talk about religious matters in terms of "journey," "search," and "discovery," and a significant number of people will speak of themselves as "spiritual" but not necessarily as "religious." People now look for direction and guidance in many ways and from many sources: self-help seminars, support groups, retreat centers, parachurch organizations, coffeehouses, talk shows, and the Internet. People, like the Walcek children, may try any number of ways, sometimes simultaneously.

Of course, there has long been a stream of American religion that has emphasized the personal over the institutional and set the individual's experience over against established religious communities, doctrines, practices, and leaders. The transcendentalism of nineteenth-century New England is one well-known example. But such movements have been largely on the margins of religious life. Today this emphasis on the internal and the personal over against the external and institutional is increasingly a decisive characteristic of American religion.

Sociologist Robert Wuthnow calls this shift in the "spirituality" of Americans (by "spirituality" he means the beliefs and activities by which individuals relate themselves and their lives to a divine being or transcendent reality) a shift from a traditional "spirituality of dwelling" to a new "spirituality of seeking." As the term suggests, a spirituality of dwelling stresses "habitation":

God occupies a definite place in the universe and creates a sacred space in which humans too can dwell; to inhabit sacred space is to know its territory and to feel secure.[12]

A spirituality of seeking emphasizes "negotiation":

[I]ndividuals search for sacred moments that reinforce their conviction that the divine exists, but these moments are fleeting; rather than knowing the territory, people explore new spiritual vistas, and they may have to negotiate among complex and confusing meanings of spirituality.[13]

Wuthnow compares the shift in spirituality to the shift in the way the American people relate to their homes. At one time, most people lived where they worked, shopped, and went to church. They lived in readily defined communities. Now, many people commute to work, travel to shopping centers and malls, and shop for a church. They often complain about the lack of community. In the same way, he explains: "At one time, people identified their faith by membership; now they do so increasingly by the search for connections with various organizations, groups and disciplines, all the while feeling marginal to any particular group or place."[14]

He also represents the shift in economic terms, as a move from spiritual *production* to spiritual *consumption*:

They used to produce offspring, for their churches and synagogues, send out missionaries and evangelists to convert others, and spend their time working for religious committees and guilds; they now let professional experts—writers, artists, therapists, spiritual guides—be the producers while they consume what they need in order to enrich themselves spiritually.[15]

As these images suggest, this shift in spirituality is quite apparent among Christians and their churches. But just as the culture wars make for unexpected alignments, so does the current spiritual climate. Wade Clark Roof has studied Boomers and their religious sensibilities for nearly a decade, and his views parallel those of

Wuthnow. He refers to the Boomers as "a generation of seekers" and has characterized them as "believers, not belongers." Like others, he uses the language of marketing and business to describe the contemporary religious landscape, which he argues is a "spiritual marketplace" set in a "quest culture" and serviced by "spiritual suppliers." Key to his studies is a distinction between "religious identity" and "spiritual identity."[16]

Roof finds that many self-described Evangelicals, Pentecostals, and Charismatics not only describe themselves like many mainstream liberal Protestants (e.g., they both identify themselves as "religious" and as "spiritual"), but they also share similar characteristics in terms of religious themes. Both, moreover, have some important affinities with those New Agers and Neopagans. As Roof explains:

> Because of so widespread a cultural mood at present, Christian evangelicals and New Age movements within the United States, despite obvious differences, share many themes: an emphasis on direct experience, physical and emotional healing, personal and social transformation, the democracy of believers and of followers, expectations of future change, a deeply based quest for wholeness.[17]

The image of a "seeker-oriented spirituality" and the complex of identity, perception, reflection, practices, and relationships that it represents obviously have many implications. One fundamental implication is that the "God" of the emerging American religious life is increasingly to be characterized as a god of personal experience rather than the God of the Bible. Of course, even the use of the term "God" cannot be taken for granted, but contemporary America continues to say that it overwhelmingly believes in "God."[18] The spirituality of seeking *in a context of religious plurality*, however, will characteristically regard the God of the Bible as only one way to conceive of the divine. To be sure, many Americans were raised as Christians, and Christian churches continue to be socially significant, at least compared to many other religious institutions and spiritual traditions. Therefore, the Bible, its teachings, and its conception of God will remain important and recognizable. But the future of that influence is clearly in question.

Perhaps the most telling sign that this future influence is in doubt comes from Christian churches themselves. An April 2000 article in the *Wall Street Journal* strikingly illustrated and neatly summarized this trend:

> With its Tiffany windows, tall organ pipes and stone exterior, century-old West-Park Presbyterian Church in New York seems like a bastion of traditional Protestantism— that is, until the minister starts talking about God.
>
> "O burning mountain, O chosen sun, O perfect moon," intones the Rev. Robert Brashear during his Wednesday night services, invoking earthly images of the deity that sound more like Greek myths than Christian liturgy. "O fathomless well, O unattainable height, O clearness beyond measure . . . "
>
> Across the country, the faithful are redefining God. Dissatisfied with conventional images of an authoritarian or paternalistic deity, people are embracing quirky, individualistic conceptions of God to suit their own spiritual needs. . . . While these adaptations have been in vogue in feminist and fringe circles for years, they haven't moved into the mainstream until now.[19]

This suggests a second implication, namely, that religious institutions, including congregations and denominations, are involved in this shift. But, as our example suggests, it is harder to see which is the chicken and which is the egg. Certainly widespread social changes (e.g., modernization) and particular historical events (e.g., the Vietnam War) helped to shape the religious outlook of individual Americans. But churches and traditions themselves have responded to these changes and, because of their response, have contributed to the shaping of individual Americans. In any case, it is clear that the shape of institutional religion in

America has also changed. Many traditional institutions (e.g., congregations) have recast themselves to respond either affirmatively to the seeker-oriented spirituality or defensively by stressing traditional practices and values. Further, new institutions such as parachurch organizations and media outlets have emerged and are flourishing.

A third implication concerns American civil religion. It is sometimes thought that the separation of church and state means that civil government in the United States has been denied a religious dimension. This, however, has never been the case. As Robert Bellah puts it, there has long been "an elaborate and well-institutionalized civil religion in America."[20] The core of what Lincoln called "our ancient faith" is summed up in the Declaration of Independence and affirmed for Americans particularly through Lincoln's Gettysburg Address.[21] This national faith believes in "Nature's God," by whom and under whom the United States is dedicated to securing "certain unalienable rights," in particular, "life, liberty, and the pursuit of happiness." The conviction that this is a nation "under God" has been repeated in one way or another from George Washington to the present day.

For a long time, American religious life had a core largely if vaguely related to the Christian faith, and so did civil religious events. But as religious pluralism has emerged and American spirituality has shifted, one should expect the contours of civil religion to change as well. The emergence of Wiccans in the military is one sign of changes in civil religion. In the past few years they have become the focus of considerable attention as the armed forces have tried to secure religious services for them. But perhaps no more clear indication of the importance of this shift for civil religion was seen than in the choice for master of ceremonies at the "Prayer for America" service following Septemter 11: Oprah Winfrey.

GOD AND AMERICA

Talk about civil religion also helps to introduce our second line of reflection about "American religion" and biblical Christianity, which is *theological.*

The God of American Civil Religion

Let us begin by considering the god of civil religion. It is easy to see that the "god" of the institutionalized civil religion is a generic god. The god who is invoked in the pledge of allegiance and who is asked to bless America is no god in particular. Historically, it is clear that he has been related to the God whom Christians call "Our Father," but this identification has always been implied.[22] The god of civil religion is a unitarian god who resembles the divine reality of deism. But he is, as Robert Bellah puts it, "by no means simply a watchmaker God. He is actively interested and involved in history, with a special concern for America."[23]

As one might expect, this god's concern for America comes out especially in times of national tragedy. This conviction came through when President Lyndon Johnson addressed the Congress and the American people shortly after Kennedy had been assassinated, closing his speech with lines from "America the Beautiful":

America, America,
God shed His grace on thee,
And crown thy good with brotherhood
From sea to shining sea.

This sense was also pronounced after the attacks of September 11. When President George W. Bush spoke at the National Cathedral on the National Day of Prayer and Remembrance, he sought repeatedly to comfort and reassure Americans that God cared for them. He told Americans that their prayers "are known and heard and understood." He explained: "Grief and tragedy and hatred are only for a time. Goodness, remembrance, and love have no end. And the Lord of life holds all who die, and all who mourn." He called on Americans to "thank Him for each life we now must mourn, and the promise of a life to come." And he concluded by selectively quoting St. Paul: "As we have been assured, neither death nor life, nor angels nor principalities nor powers, nor things present nor things to come, nor height nor depth, can separate us from God's love. May He bless the souls of the departed. May He comfort our own. And may He always guide our country."

God and the Americanization of the Church

Observers often pay attention to the vague idea of the god of civil religion. But it is vital also to realize that the *characteristics* of the god of civil religion are not much different from those of the God of many American Christians. In other words, Christians in America differ little from other Americans when they talk about "God." Stanley Hauerwas was right when he said: "There is no better indication of the Americanization of the church than the god worshiped by Christians in America. For most American Christians, the crucially important things about God are that God exists and that God's most important attribute be love."[24]

This identification was brought home after 9/11. In the minutes, hours, days, and weeks after the terrorist attacks of September 11, 2001, we saw some of the best from Americans. Across the country there was a heightened sense of unity, deep sensitivity and sympathy for the victims and their families and friends, unstinting generosity of time and resources, and universal appreciation for those who helped, particularly for those who also fell as victims. Unfortunately, at the same time, we saw some of the worst from Christians in America. The problem was neither insensitivity nor indifference on the part of Christians, nor was it a lack of generosity or participation. No, the problem had to do with Christian witness about God.

Time and again, people wondered "Where was God?" and "How could God let this happen?" Time and again, Christians seemed compelled to answer in ways that would allow them to say unambiguously, "God is love." Where was God? Along with President Bush, Christians said, "Holding all who die and all who mourn"; with the passengers and flight crews; with desperate office workers and trapped firemen; with their families, friends, and colleagues; with all America in its shock and grief.

And what was God doing? Pastors and preachers were quick to point out that God had nothing to do with those attacks. What, then, was He doing? Some, like this New York pastor and hospital chaplain, said:

> For the people I've counseled, the idea that God was working through the rescue workers, the firemen and policemen, is a very powerful image . . . we can see God's presence at work in the ways that people dealt with this terrible event, the ways that people were delivered from it.[25]

Others assured us of God's own suffering with the proclamation that God not only suffers with us but knows suffering personally through the cruel death of His own Son.

America and Theologians of Glory

Such speaking reflects what Luther called the "theology of glory."[26] Theologians of glory, in Luther's estimation, do not deserve to be called "theologians" because they believe that they can and must look through creation, through the events of our lives, and even through the cross of Christ to see virtue, wisdom, justice, and goodness in God. This, however, leads the theologian of glory to call evil good and good evil because he cannot bear the sight of God at work. The theologian of the cross, on the other hand, "deserves to be called a theologian" because he "comprehends the visible and manifest things of God through suffering and the cross." For this reason, they are willing to say what a thing actually is.[27]

Where was God on 9/11? If you were to ask Job, he would have said, "The LORD gave, and the LORD hath taken away; blessed be the name of the LORD" (Job 1:21).[28] If you were to ask Moses, he would have said, "The LORD turns men back to dust, saying, 'Return to dust, O sons of men,' " and "He sweeps men away in the sleep of death; they are like the new grass of the morning—though in the morning it springs up new, by evening it is dry and withered" (see Psalm 90:3, 5–6 NIV). In death and destruction, they saw God at work. They feared; they grieved; they glorified the Lord.

After 9/11, however, many Christians could not, would not, see God at work in death and destruction. Where was God? Not there, for sure. They had to look through the rubble and smoke, past the fallen buildings and falling bodies to see God's virtue, justice, and goodness. And they found it: God holding "all who die and all who mourn"; God in the rescue workers and office "Good Samaritans"; God suffering with all who suffer unjustly.

In an American context that believes in a God who cares, the thought that God suffers is particularly attractive. In a tradition that says that the true theologian, the theologian of the cross, is one who "comprehends the visible and manifest things of God through suffering and the cross," the thought that God suffers also seems particularly apt. But it is in fact particularly misleading.

To be sure, what Christians said and did after 9/11 only reflected a perennial problem. Gerhard Forde characterized this problem in his book *On Being a Theologian of the Cross*:

> Jesus is spoken of as the one who "identifies with us in our suffering," or the one who "enters into solidarity with us" in our misery. "The suffering of God," or the "vulnerability of God," and such platitudes become the stock-in-trade of preachers and theologians who want to stroke the psyche of today's religionists. But this results in rather blatant and suffocating sentimentality. God is supposed to be more attractive to us because he identifies with us in our pain

and suffering. "Misery loves company" becomes the unspoken motif of such theology.[29]

In a 1986 *Christian Century* article, Ronald Goetz went so far as to say that the idea of "the suffering God" was the "new orthodoxy."[30] He cited several reasons for this development, including the demise of Christendom (this made the idea that God controls history difficult to maintain), the conviction of the rightness of liberal democracy (the idea of a sovereign God does not fit well with a belief in freedom), and the widespread acceptance of critical-historical interpretation of the Bible. But the most obvious reason for this development is the problem of suffering and evil. How can a loving God who is all-powerful allow suffering and evil? Events such as the terrorist attacks of September 11 only make such questions more urgent to address. And so it is understandable that pastors and preachers so often responded by saying that "God had nothing to do with those attacks" and by reassuring their hearers that "God not only suffers with them, but He knows all about suffering personally through the cruel death of His own Son."

Such thoughts can be made to fit with Luther's claim that the theologian of the cross "comprehends the visible and manifest things of God through suffering and the cross." At this point many will say something like this: "God's love can only be seen in the suffering Christ." But this move turns out to reflect the theology of glory. "You might say," Forde explains, "that this kind of theologian treats the cross as though God were merely giving some kind of illustrated lecture about himself. The cross dramatically portrays a truth about God which we already knew anyway—that 'God is love' or something of that sort."[31] But this is exactly the point of saying that God "knows all about suffering personally through the cruel death of His Son."

The idea that God suffers with us seems attractive in the sense that "there is a certain immediate psychological comfort in the notion that God does not require of us a suffering that he himself will not endure."[32] But this idea requires more than God's suffering. As Goetz explains:

> To anyone who feels compelled to affirm divine suffering, the fact that God is deeply involved in the anguish and the blood of humanity forces a drastic theological crisis of thought vis-à-vis the question of evil. The mere fact of God's suffering doesn't solve the question; it exacerbates it. For there can no longer be a retreat into the hidden decrees of the eternal, all-wise, changeless and unaffected God. The suffering God is with us in the here and now. God must answer in the here and now before one can make any sense of the by and by. God, the fellow sufferer, is inexcusable if all that he can do is suffer.[33]

For the thought of the suffering God to give lasting comfort, it must be shown how His suffering deals with evil. Otherwise God who is preached is useless.

"AMERICAN RELIGION" AND "SAYING WHAT A THING ACTUALLY IS"

In this presentation I have tried to discuss "American religion" from both sociological and theological viewpoints. Now I shall try to tie together some themes and address a few of the issues that this discussion suggests.

Both viewpoints suggest that Christians in America cannot be readily distinguished from American religion. Christians are very much part of the fabric of American religious life. On the one hand, the prevailing American seeker-oriented spirituality has influenced many Christians and their churches. On the other hand, many Christians have given and continue to give shape and vitality to this spirituality. Seeker services might be an instance of the first; small groups might be an instance of the second. The same likely holds for civil religion. American civil religion often finds expression in Christian churches, but Christian churches are probably shaping the theology and practice of civil religion as well.

But if Christians are as deeply involved in American religious viewpoints and sensibilities as I have suggested, then something more extensive than a short list of things to do and things to avoid needs to be recommended.

A first step might be to recall Karl Barth's remark about continuing to do theology "as if nothing had happened." What had happened when he made that remark was the advent of Adolf Hitler. This comment, however, had nothing to do with quietism or indifference. Rather, it was Barth's way of recognizing that the world had not really changed with Hitler, just as it had not really changed two decades earlier with the outbreak of what was still called the "Great War." It had changed a long time before, with the death and resurrection of Jesus Christ.

Stanley Hauerwas echoed Barth's position when he recently commented:

> September 11, 2001, is not the day that changed our world. The world, the cosmos, what we call history, was changed in A.D. 33. Preaching after September 11, 2001, requires that what happened on September 11, 2001, be narrated in the light of cross and resurrection. To be sure, this is a task easier said than done.[34]

It is a point that is simple, but perhaps deceptively so. In any case, it needs to be made. In the questions "Where was God?" and "How could God let this happen?" and "How could this happen to us?" it is clear that this point, that this story and its place in our lives, has been obscured amid the death and destruction, loss and pain, fear and uncertainty that Americans refer to as "9/11." But the terrorists did not suddenly cause that point, that perspective, to be lost. That must have happened quite some time ago.

Therefore, I agree with Hauerwas when he made these observations about a collection of sermons preached after September 11:

[S]ome of these sermons seem to try to "get God off the hook" or, failing that, to show that even though we cannot understand how God could allow this to happen to people like us, believing in God remains important if we are not to be crushed by the terror of September 11, 2001. As understandable, as human as these responses are, I think they fail to be appropriately disciplined by the gospel. Christians— at least Christians who Sunday after Sunday read the psalms—should know the question "Why do bad things happen to good people?" is not a question Christians should ask.

Which is but a reminder that more important than sermons preached after September 11, 2001, is the kind of preaching that shaped the life of congregations prior to September 11, 2001. For if Christians had no way of discerning how their being Christian might involve tension with being American prior to September 11, you can be sure that they, or those who preached to them after that date, would be unable to say how the Christian response can and must be distinguished from the American response. The sentimentality and pietism that is so prominent in American sermonizing could not help but grip our imaginations and speech when confronted by the horrible events of this day.[35]

As the career of Stanley Hauerwas shows, it is a life's work to begin to answer comprehensively what kind of preaching, and what kind of congregational life, Christians might need to distinguish themselves rightly from America or from the prevailing spiritual winds. But, as he said, it begins with recognizing that the world changed with the death and resurrection of Jesus. And it is therefore true that "Christians can do nothing more significant in America than to be a people capable of worshiping a God who is to be found in the cross and resurrection of Jesus of Nazareth."[36]

Second, we should acknowledge that being faithful Christians, being theologians of the cross, is not only essential but also hard.

Stanley Fish has remarked: "Whenever I teach *Paradise Lost*, the hardest thing to get across is that God is God."[37] According to Fish, students invariably hold the position that William Empson laid out in his book *Milton's God*. In Empson's view, *all* characters are on trial in any civilized narrative, that is, readers should hold every character accountable to some universal standard, such as goodness or justice. Fish, however, points out that in *Paradise Lost*, Milton's God is truly "God." He is and will be accountable to no one.

What is hard in understanding a piece of literature is much harder when it comes to acknowledging personally that the Lord is God. Of course, it is utterly inconceivable without the Spirit of God, but the regenerate will inevitably find it difficult because it is precisely in such situations that the old Adam is under direct attack and therefore fights hardest for survival.

But it is precisely because the truth that "God is God" attacks our sinfulness so directly that we can also see a practical reason why it must not be given up. As Luther said, "Although the works of God always seem unattractive and appear evil, they are nevertheless really eternal merits."[38] The point is soteriological. What Luther speaks of here is also confessed in the Apology of the Augsburg Confession, which says that the two chief works of God in human beings are "to terrify and to justify the terrified or make them alive."[39]

Third, the notion of the theologian of the cross bears directly on the issue of Christian witness. The current civil religious climate goes hand in hand with the prevailing religious and spiritual trends of society. One temptation when faced with the unfamiliar and the challenging is simply to say no. And sometimes that is exactly what needs to be done. But we need to be careful not to let the world, as it were, set the theological and ecclesial agenda. If accommodation is one form of capitulation, then separation is often another form, for it can easily permit "civil religion" or the "spiritual marketplace" to shape one's identity.

But if we consider that both American civil religion and the spiritual seeker are theologians of glory, then I think we can see more clearly how a faithful Christian witness relates to "American religion." A faithful Christian witness says what a thing is, ugly, even harsh, as that truth often will be. Take the matter of being asked by the public for words of comfort at time of tragedy. One cannot act as if Americans are, plain and simple, God's people; they have no claim as such on God's promises. That means there is little obvious or transparent comfort to give those who are not in Christ Jesus. God only knows the state of the heart of each of the individual passengers, office workers, firefighters, and military personnel who died on 9/11. Christians don't, and they ought not act like they do.

But a faithful Christian witness does just what God wants; and where and when it pleases God, there will be death, but there will be life; there will be repentance, and then there will be faith. And the mission of God in the world will advance.

Notes

1. The Rev. Dr. Joel P. Okamoto is assistant professor of systematic theology at Concordia Seminary, St. Louis, Missouri. He holds M. Div., S.T.M., and Th.D. degrees from Concordia Seminary. This paper was prepared and read as a part of the annual theological symposium of Concordia Seminary in September 2002.

2. Peter L. Berger, *A Rumor of Angels: Modern Society and the Rediscovery of the Supernatural* (Garden City, N. Y.: Doubleday, 1970), 1–2.

3. Berger, *Rumor of Angels*, 120. Berger helpfully discusses the conceptions of "secularization" and "modernization," and also their implications for modern life, in *The Sacred Canopy: Elements of a Sociological Theory of Religion* (Garden City, N. Y.: Doubleday, 1967) and *The Homeless Mind: Modernization and Consciousness,* with Brigitte Berger and Hansfried Kellner (Garden City, N. Y.: Doubleday, 1973). He discusses the pluralizing implications of modernization for religious belief and practice in the first chapter of *The Heretical Imperative: Contemporary Possibilities of Religious Affirmation* (Garden City, N. Y.: Doubleday, 1979).

4. Will Herberg, *Protestant—Catholic—Jew* (Garden City, N. Y.: Anchor Books, 1955).

5. Diana L. Eck, *A New Religious America: How a "Christian Country" Has Now Become the World's Most Religiously Diverse Nation* (New York: HarperCollins, 2001), 1.

6. Robert W. Jenson, "The God-Wars," in *Either/Or: The Gospel or Neo-paganism*, ed. Carl E. Braaten and Robert W. Jenson (Grand Rapids: Eerdmans), 23.

7. James Davison Hunter, *Culture Wars: The Struggle to Define America* (New York: Basic Books, 1991), 42. Earlier in the book Hunter sketches out some of these conflicts, including anti-Catholic sentiments, anti-Semitism, and hostility toward the Mormons (35–41).

8. Jenson, "God-Wars," 24.

9. For example, see the October 2002 issue of *First Things*, in which Avery Cardinal Dulles takes issue with Justice Antonin Scalia, a fellow Catholic, about the *use* or *application* of the death penalty. It is also worth noting that Scalia had dissented from the pope on this issue.

10. Richard N. Ostling, "The Church Search," *Time* (April 5, 1993): 45.

11. Wade Clark Roof, *Spiritual Marketplace: Baby Boomers and the Remaking of American Religion* (Princeton, N. J.: Princeton University Press, 1999), 7.

12. Robert Wuthnow, *After Heaven: Spirituality in America since the 1950s* (Berkeley: University of California Press, 1998), 3–4.

13. Wuthnow, *After Heaven*, 4.

14. Wuthnow, *After Heaven*, 7.

15. Wuthnow, *After Heaven*, 7–8.

16. See Wade Clark Roof, *A Generation of Seekers: The Spiritual Journeys of the Baby Boom Generation* (New York: HarperCollins, 1993) and *Spiritual Marketplace* for research and analysis of the postwar Boomer generation on religious outlook and attitudes. In the later book, he studies American religion in terms of the ways people identify themselves as "religious" and as "spiritual."

17. Roof, *Spiritual Marketplace*, 154.

18. As is widely known, polls have shown with remarkable consistency that about 19 out of 20 Americans say that they believe in "God," and the great majority of these (about 85 percent of Americans, according to the latest edition of the *World Christian Encyclopedia*) identify their God with the Christian God.

19. Lisa Miller, "Redefining God," *The Wall Street Journal* (April 21, 2000): W1. Reprinted by permission of *The Wall Street Journal*, Copy-

right © 2000 Dow Jones & Company, Inc. All Rights Reserved Worldwide. License number 1083150390922.

20. Robert Bellah, "Civil Religion in America," *Daedalus* 96, no. 1 (1967): 1.

21. In his essay "The Revolution and the Civil Religion" (in *Religion and the American Revolution*, ed. Jerald C. Brauer [Philadelphia: Fortress Press, 1970]) Robert Bellah cites the Declaration of Independence as the "primary text" of the American civil religion, particularly its opening, which claims that "the Laws of Nature and Nature's God entitle them" to a "separate and equal station" among nations, and which holds "these truths to be self-evident, that all men are created equal, that they are endowed by their creator with certain unalienable rights, that among these are life, liberty, and the pursuit of happiness." He also regards the Gettysburg Address as "a rededication to and renewal of that primary text," particularly in its opening and closing statements: "Four score and seven years ago our fathers brought forth on this continent, a new nation, conceived in Liberty, and dedicated to the proposition that all men are created equal . . . It is rather for us to be here dedicated to the great task remaining before us . . . that this nation, under God, shall have a new birth of freedom—and that government of the people, by the people, for the people, shall not perish from the earth" (55–56). See also Garry Wills on the Gettysburg Address as a central reinterpretation of the Declaration of Independence in *Lincoln at Gettysburg: The Words that Remade America* (New York: Simon & Schuster, 1992), 90–120.

22. Bellah illustrates the dimensions and function of civil religion particularly by reference to President John F. Kennedy's inaugural address. The choice was telling, for Kennedy was the first Catholic president of the United States, and his Catholicism had been a campaign issue. But while his address mentioned God three times, he did not refer specifically to the God in whom Catholics believe. "In fact," says Bellah, "his only reference was to the concept of God, a word which almost all Americans can accept but which means so many things to so many people that it is almost an empty sign" ("Civil Religion in America," 3).

23. Bellah, "Civil Religion in America," 7.

24. Stanley Hauerwas, *A Better Hope: Resources for a Church Confronting Capitalism, Democracy, and Postmodernity* (Grand Rapids: Brazos Press, 2000), 33.

25. John Horgan and Francis H. Geer, *Where Was God on September 11? A Scientist Asks a Ground Zero Pastor* (San Francisco: Browntrout Publishers, 2002), 66.

26. Martin Luther, "Heidelberg Disputation, 1518," LW 31:35–70.

27. LW 31:52–53.

28. Unless otherwise indicated, Scripture quotations in this essay are taken from the KJV.

29. Gerhard O. Forde, *On Being a Theologian of the Cross: Reflections on Luther's Heidelberg Disputation, 1518* (Grand Rapids: Eerdmans, 1997), viii.

30. Ronald Goetz, "The Suffering God: The Rise of a New Orthodoxy," *The Christian Century* (April 16, 1986): 385.

31. Gerhard O. Forde, *Where God Meets Man: Luther's Down-to-Earth Approach to the Gospel* (Minneapolis: Augsburg, 1972), 33.

32. Goetz, "Suffering God," 33.

33. Goetz, "Suffering God," 33.

34. Stanley Hauerwas, "The Sunday after Tuesday: An Afterword," in *The Sunday after Tuesday: College Pulpits Respond to 9/11* (Nashville: Abingdon, 2002), 193.

35. Hauerwas, "Sunday after Tuesday," 195–96.

36. Hauerwas, *Better Hope*, 34.

37. Stanley Fish, "Why We Can't All Just Get Along," *First Things* 60 (February 1996): 18.

38. LW 31:44.

39. Ap. XII, 53 (K-W, 195).

6

Patriotism Gone Awry?

The Church Used for Civic Ends

RONALD R. FEUERHAHN[1]

T he main concern that I would address is that of American civic religion (or "civil religion" as Sydney Ahlstrom called it). It appears to be as old as America. It is therefore well entrenched. I want to examine the history of the civic use of the church for its purposes but also the opposite.

CAESAR'S PANTHEON

The Roman emperor Hadrian erected the Pantheon in Rome in A.D. 120–124. It was a temple dedicated to all (*pan*) the gods (*theon*).[2] Caesar always wants his/its Pantheon, to co-opt the church. Caesar, in our day, includes the social pressures to make the church conform to the expectations of a community for comfort and happiness, of niceness and support.[3]

When we learn that two centuries later the Emperor Constantine had not only "converted" to Christianity but also had taken over control of the church's affairs in many regards, do we thereby understand this to be the first attempt by the ruler, or the people, to mix the kingdom of Christ with that of the State? Surely not, for this had been part of the false expectation of the early Jews who wanted to make Christ King.

> Jesus saw Nathanael coming to Him, and said of him, "Behold, an Israelite indeed, in whom is no guile!" Nathanael said to Him, "How do You know me?" Jesus answered him, "Before Philip called you, when you were under the fig tree, I saw you." Nathanael answered Him, "Rabbi, You are the Son of God! You are the King of Israel!"[4] Jesus answered him, "Because I said to you, I saw you under the fig tree, do you believe? You shall see greater things than these." (John 1:47–50)[5]

It was seeing such great things that caused them all the more to have Him as King.

> When the people saw the sign which He had done, they said, "This is indeed the prophet who is to come into the world!" Perceiving then that they were about to come and take Him by force to make Him king, Jesus withdrew again to the hills by Himself. (John 6:14–15)

Finally, right before His death on the cross, it appears as if they were to get their way with Him:

> The next day a great crowd who had come to the feast heard that Jesus was coming to Jerusalem. So they took branches of palm trees and went out to meet Him, crying, "Hosanna! Blessed is He who comes in the name of the Lord, even the King of Israel!"[6] And Jesus found a young ass and sat upon it; as it is written, "Fear not, daughter of Zion; behold, your king is coming, sitting on an ass's colt!" (John 12:12–15)

But, alas, God had other plans; nevertheless, His projected kingship was not to be given up even then:

> Pilate entered the praetorium again and called Jesus, and said to Him, "Are You the King of the Jews?" Jesus answered, "Do you say this of your own accord, or did others say it to you about Me?" Pilate answered, "Am I a Jew? Your own nation and the chief priests have handed You over to me; what have You done?" Jesus answered, "My kingship is not of this world; if My kingship were of this world, My servants would fight, that I might not be handed over to the Jews; but My kingship is not from the world." Pilate said to Him, "So You are a king?" Jesus answered, "You say that I am a king. For this I was born, and for this I have come into the world, to bear witness to the truth. Every one who is of the truth hears My voice." Pilate . . . went out to the Jews again, and told them, "I find no crime in Him. But you have a custom that I should release one man for you at the Passover; will you have me release for you the King of the Jews?" (John 18:33–39)

Finally, they got the picture, without, of course, understanding anything about His kingship:

> They came up to Him, saying, "Hail, King of the Jews!" and struck Him with their hands. . . . [Pilate] said to the Jews, "Here is your King!" They cried out, "Away with Him, away with Him, crucify Him!" Pilate said to them, "Shall I crucify your King?" The chief priests answered, "We have no king but Caesar." . . . Pilate also wrote a title and put it on the cross; it read, "Jesus of Nazareth, the King of the Jews." . . . The chief priests of the Jews then said to Pilate, "Do not write, 'The King of the Jews,' but, 'This man said, "I am King of the Jews."'" (John 19:3, 14–21)

Even Herod wanted to have Jesus play king, or at least magician:

> When Pilate heard this, he asked whether the man was a Galilean. And when he learned that He belonged to Herod's

171

jurisdiction, he sent Him over to Herod, who was himself in Jerusalem at that time. When Herod saw Jesus, he was very glad, for he had long desired to see Him, because he had heard about Him, and he was hoping to see some sign done by Him. So he questioned Him at some length; but He made no answer. (Luke 23:6–9)

John tells us what was wrong: "He was in the world, and the world was made through Him, yet the world knew Him not. He came to His own home, and His own people received Him not" (John 1:10–11).

By the fourth century it appeared that the world was finally ready to embrace this Messiah, the King of the Jews. At least Constantine the Great was. *The Oxford Dictionary of the Christian Church* summarizes his attitude succinctly in these terms:

- His policy was to unite the Christian Church to the secular State by the closest possible ties.

- He became concerned with the internal affairs of the church.

- He held the Byzantine theory of the emperors as supreme ruler of Church and State alike.

- He exempted Christian clergy from the decurionate. ["Decurions" were members of the senate of an ancient Roman colony or municipality, a decury.[7]]

- His centralization of the empire at Constantinople led to an increasing Imperial control of the church, esp. in the East.[8]

In addition, the *Oxford Dictionary of the Christian Church* says of Constantine that "[i]n the Eastern Church he has been named the 'Thirteenth Apostle' and is venerated as a saint."[9] The *Lutheran Cyclopedia* adds of him that "[h]e saw himself as 'bishop of bishops.'"[10]

Thus began the so-called "Constantinian Era." At least one historian has suggested the church has lived in its "Constantinian Era" until the twentieth century, "[a]nd that we are now going through a crisis connected with the end of that long era."[11] With this era came the "Imperial Church."[12] The title tells a story.

From A.D. 313, Constantine had chosen as his ecclesiastical adviser,[13] Hosius (or Ossius, ca. A.D. 256–357/8), the bishop of Cordoba. This, the first "minister of religion"[14] in the history of the church, would later be one of the first to warn against the idea of an "Imperial Church." In A.D. 355 he was banished to Sirmium for his support of St. Athanasius, and from his exile he addressed to Constantius II a letter in which, on the basis of Matthew 22:21, he affirmed the independence of ecclesiastical authority from political power.[15]

> Do not intrude[16] into ecclesiastical matters, and do not give commands to us concerning them; but learn them from us. God has put into your hands the kingdom; to us he has entrusted the affairs of the Church; and, as he who should steal the Empire from you would resist the ordinance of God, so likewise fear on your part lest, by taking upon yourself the government of the Church, you become guilty of a great offence. It is written, Render unto Caesar the things that are Caesar's, and unto God the things that are God's. [Matthew 22.21] Neither, therefore is it permitted us to exercise an earthly rule, nor have you, Sir, any authority to turn incense. These things I write to you out of a concern for your salvation.[17]

Another bishop, Ambrose of Milan (ca. A.D. 339–397), was also in close touch with successive Western emperors. He also maintained the independence of the church against the civil power.[18] It was at this time that Theodosius (r. A.D. 379–395) declared the Christian religion the religion of the empire (A.D. 380).[19] As the *Oxford Dictionary of the Christian Church* notes: "He founded the orthodox Christian state: Arianism and other heresies became legal offences, sacrifice was forbidden, and paganism almost outlawed."[20]

Of course, Constantine and the other Roman Emperors were not the last to seek the support and authority of the church as the "cement of the Empire." In 1530 Emperor Charles V called for the Diet of Augsburg as an appeal to all parties to stay together in the face of the threat from the Turks who were at the doors of Vienna. Elizabeth I in England less than 30 years later was calling for a unified church in the face of threats imagined and real.

THE REFORMERS

I will assume here a basic knowledge of the attitude of the reformers with regard to the relation of church to state. It should be noted that while Luther called upon the princes to act in the role of *Notbischof*, "emergency bishop," they actually took the role permanently as *summus episcopus*[21] or "chief bishop," at least until the Revolution of 1918 in Germany.

Luther

Luther's teaching on the two kingdoms (or regimens) is well summarized in the Augsburg Confession:

> [O]ne should not mix or confuse the two authorities, the spiritual and the secular. For spiritual power has its command to preach the gospel and to administer the sacraments. It should not invade an alien office. It should not set up and depose kings. It should not annul or disrupt secular law and obedience to political authority. It should not make or prescribe laws for the secular power concerning secular affairs. For Christ himself said [John 18:36]: "My kingdom is not from this world." And again [Luke 12:14]: "Who set me to be a judge or arbitrator over you?" And St. Paul in Philippians 3[:20]: "Our citizenship is in heaven."[22] And in 2 Corinthians 10[:4–5]: "For the weapons of our warfare are not merely human, but they have divine power to destroy strongholds . . . arguments and every proud obstacle raised up against the knowledge of God."

In this way our people distinguish the offices of the two authorities and powers and direct that both be honored as the highest gifts of God on earth.[23]

Calvin

Calvin saw that the task of "constituting religion aright" is assigned to the civil government.

Its object is not merely, like those things, to enable men to breathe, eat, drink, and be warmed, (though it certainly includes all these, while it enables them to live together); this, I say, is not its only object, but it is that no idolatry, no blasphemy against the name of God, no calumnies against his truth, nor other offences to religion, break out and be disseminated among the people; that the public quiet be not disturbed, that every man's property be kept secure, that men may carry on innocent commerce with each other, that honesty and modesty be cultivated; in short, that a public form of religion may exist among Christians, and humanity among men. Let no one be surprised that I now attribute the task of constituting religion aright to human polity . . . .[24]

And, moreover, he specifically declares that it is the responsibility of civil magistrates to enforce the First Table of the Law:

The duty of magistrates, its nature, as described by the word of God, and the things in which it consists, I will here indicate in passing. That it extends to both tables of the law, did Scripture not teach, we might learn from profane writers, for no man has discoursed of the duty of magistrates, the enacting of laws, and the common weal, without beginning with religion and divine worship. Thus all have confessed that no polity can be successfully established unless piety be its first care, and that those laws are absurd which disregard the rights of God, and consult only for men.[25]

Thus for Calvin, and for those who have followed or been influenced by him, the civil authority has a far different relationship with the church than it had for Luther and the heirs of the Lutheran Confessions.

England

We turn our attention particularly to England. For here is the chief source of the religious and political thought for America. It is for this reason that Sydney Ahlstrom gave "special emphasis to the character of the Reformed tradition":

> Because this phase of the Continental Reformation struck Great Britain with far greater transforming power then either the Lutheran or Radical movements, special attention must be given to its driving concerns and central ideas. ... It ultimately generated its own Anglo-American type of radical "Puritanism," which would in turn become one of the most vital elements in the foundations of American thought and culture.[26]

The American Colonies

In the Puritan colonies of New England, church and state cooperated closely, and Reformed ideas, as modified by covenant theology, held sway. Biblical covenants provided models for political order as well as ecclesiastical. There was a cooperation of church and state in the Bay Colonies that was to be a strong example for early America.

Town meetings were at first both civil and ecclesiastical in their scope. The General Court in turn made such support obligatory and in many ways sought to uphold the churches and protect them from their enemies. The civil government also enforced the 'First Table' of the Decalogue, punishing blasphemy, heresy, and vain swearing, and requiring that the Sabbath be kept. The theory behind this close cooperation is stated by Urian Oakes, minister in Cambridge and sometime president of Harvard:

> According to the design of our founders and the frame of things laid by them the interest of [a] righteousness in the commonwealth and [b] holiness in the Churches are inseparable. . . . To divide what God hath conjoined . . . is folly in its exaltation. I look upon this as a little model of the glorious kingdom of Christ on earth. Christ reigns among us [a] in the commonwealth as well as [b] in the Church and hath his glorious interest involved and wrapt up in the good of both societies respectively.[27]

The consequences of this attitude are summarized by Ahlstrom:

> There was a consequent religious tension which arose in the Puritan community of New England. It was about Nature and Grace: "the place of law and 'legal obedience' under the gospel order, a matter with which the American churches were still wrestling in the later twentieth century and which in one form or another has aroused heated controversies during most of the intervening decades."[28]

There were, nonetheless, attempts at a separation of church and state. This was the result in large part of religious pluralism and to a certain degree the Anabaptist influences.[29]

America as New Jerusalem

In 1630, John Winthrop, governor of the Massachusetts Bay Colony, preached to his fellow immigrants aboard the ship *Arbella*. His sermon, "Christian Charity: A Model Hereof," would have remained known only to the elite class of Puritan scholars were it not for his use of the biblical image of the "city set on a hill" to describe the moral purpose of the Pilgrim adventure into the unknown. That image, from Jesus' Sermon on the Mount in Matthew's Gospel,[30] is what gave Winthrop's sermon life and Matthew's text a new context, providing perhaps the most enduring metaphor of the American experience, that of the exemplary nation called to virtue and mutual support.[31]

Perry Miller has argued that this sermon, given on board the ship in Salem Harbor before the colonists had landed, stands at the beginning of American consciousness.[32] In it the settlers were addressed as both members of a church and a society.

Ahlstrom is particularly helpful when he suggests that the employment of this biblical metaphor gives a "mythic quality" to American historiography: "This mythic theme of America as a beacon on a hill and as exemplar for the world became a constituent element in historical interpretations of the nation's religious life."[33]

He connects this with the additional biblical motif of "the elect nation."[34] Later he identifies it with a *theologia gloria* (theology of glory), "in which patriotism and religion are inextricably entwined."[35] In another place he describes this as a "pious providentialism."[36]

Equally powerful as an integrating idea was the metaphor of the melting pot as a crucible in which the diverse base metals of the world would be marvelously transformed into pure Anglo-Saxon Protestant gold.[37]

The effect that this sense of national calling has had on the American understanding of its place in the world is described by Hermann Sasse in his book about American Christianity (literally Churchdom) in 1927:

> Led to the head of humanity, today the Americans are the leading people on earth. The prospects are bright for a glorious future, and they deeply believe that God has called upon them to ensure the security of all humanity. America has been summonsed to nurse to health the suffering, shattered, and helpless world.[38]

Sasse also observes the American sense of the divine blessing upon America, which holds that

[i]f Jesus were living today he would, in principle, affirm American civilization. The basic idea behind this piety is that Christianity is something which belongs in this world, and in this American culture. There is a pre-established harmony between Christianity and civilization. If they do not coincide then we are still incomplete Christians in an unfulfilled civilization. But both have the same goal: The perfection of the church coincides with the perfection of civilization. The kingdom of God, the goal of the church, cannot be considered, unless it is simultaneously thought of as the final goal of all of human culture.[39]

Sasse also observed ideas in early America that are still in force today: "Benjamin Franklin tried [?] to speak of 'the religion in which we all agree': It is an idea and expression common to the early Free Masons of the 18th century."[40] And Sasse described the impact of Calvinism on the development of this American religious consciousness:

If we are to understand this close connection between church and civilization, we must consider that this modern American Protestantism is of Calvinistic origin. And Calvinism, early on, forged a positive relationship to the economic questions and tasks of modern culture, in a way quite different from Lutheranism.[41]

Strictly speaking, what came to be in America was not such a clear separation of church and state; nor was it so much of Calvin, for he

upheld a theocratic polity, subjecting state to church. In the words of the Second Helvetic Confession 1566, it is the duty of the magistrate to "advance the preaching of that truth and the [pure and] sincere faith."[42]

This, too, was noted by Hermann Sasse:

America has never known this opposition between church and culture, because it has never had a Middle Ages which had to be overcome. In America the church never has been an obstacle for civilization, an enemy of advancement, or whatever other form the accusations may take.[43]

He noted that which sets America apart from Europe religiously:

Since colonial times there has been a strong churchly tradition in America, an unbroken, naive churchliness. Religion is part of life, part of the existence of the nation, of the civilization. A peace between church and secular culture rules undisturbed.[44]

Kingdom of God Motif

Earlier we mentioned the Rev. Urian Oakes, president of Harvard, who declared:

I look upon this as a little model of the glorious kingdom of Christ on earth. Christ reigns among us [a] in the commonwealth as well as [b] in the Church and hath his glorious interest involved and wrapt up in the good of both societies respectively.[45]

It is this notion of the kingdom of Christ or of God that would grow. H. Richard Niebuhr has argued that the kingdom of God is the master symbol of American Christianity.[46]

Reformed "One Kingdom" / "One Word"

Often there is a particularly Reformed twist to this idea. It follows a Reformed view of a "one kingdom" theology, denying the two kingdoms or two regimens of Luther. This "one kingdom" theology is reflected in Karl Barth's "one word" theology, which denies the distinction between Law and Gospel. This "Reformed twist" becomes apparent when Americans think of prayer as a civic rite as well as a religious rite. We often make no distinction.[47] This explains in large part why in America we so readily confuse the civic and religious realms. The Puritans had seen the two as one. And as much as we talk about the separation of church and state, in actual practice the opposite is often the case. The First Amendment, after all, does not prohibit religion but rather a single religion. We are a nation comfortable with syncretism: "One nation under God" is almost synonymous with "One nation, many gods." So one speaker at the event in Yankee Stadium in September 2001 could describe America as: "People of many faiths but one nation . . . under God."

SYNCRETISM

The term *syncretism* came into prominence in the seventeenth century when it was applied to the teaching of Georg Calixtus, who undertook to unite the Reformation churches with one another, and with the Catholic Church, on the basis of the Apostles' Creed and the doctrine of the first five centuries (the so-called *consensus quinquesaecularis*).[48] It also includes efforts to inculturate the Gospel, to make the Gospel conform to our cultural expectations.[49] Syncretism is a problem today: There is more of it about than ever before. How strange these words of the Bible must sound to American ears today:

> I am the LORD, and there is no other, besides Me there is no God; I gird you, though you do not know Me, that men may know, from the rising of the sun and from the west, that there is none besides Me; I am the LORD, and there is no other. (Isaiah 45:5–6)

> I, I am the LORD, and besides Me there is no Savior. (Isaiah 43:11)

> Then Jesus said to him, "Begone, Satan! for it is written, 'You shall worship the Lord your God and Him only shall you serve.'" (Matthew 4:10)

It is hardly surprising that a Christianity that affirms these truths will be an offense to those who hold that America must be "[p]eople of many faiths but one nation . . . under God."

UNIONISM

In association with syncretism we think of *unionism*. The noted historian of American Lutheranism, Abdel Ross Wentz, has noted:

> The second problem that vexed the church in the youth of the Republic was unionism. Partly the offspring
>
> [1] of religious indifference. . . .
>
> [2] of lessening confessional convictions. . . . Motives
>
> [3] of expediency also played their part—union with other church bodies seemed the line of least resistance. . . .
>
> for the Lutheran church it meant the decline of her denominational consciousness, for a time the new American impulse to union threatened the very existence of the church in this country.[50]

FIDEI DEFENSOR

Shifts in our religious thinking are illustrated in sometimes rather dramatic ways. An example will illustrate how a small shift in words can reflect a tidal shift in underlying religious understanding. Some time ago, Prince Charles, as the current Prince of Wales and heir apparent to the British crown, announced that he would not take the royal title *Fidei Defensor* (Defender of the Faith). Rather, he would accept a modified title of "Defender of Faiths." To understand the significance of this subtle change, a bit of history is in order.

The honored title *Fidei Defensor* was originally bestowed, at his own request, on Henry VIII in 1521 by Pope Leo X in recognition of his treatise against Luther.[51] By 1534, after his break with Rome, Henry kept the pope's title and added another: "the only supreme head in earth of the Church of England, called *Anglicana Ecclesia*." This title was repealed under Mary by the See of Rome Act (1554), and the repeal was initially confirmed by Elizabeth I. But Elizabeth's Act of Supremacy (1558) restored the Henrician appellation in a revised form. The monarch's title was now more modest in view of her gender; the Queen now declared herself to be "the only supreme governor of this realm, and of all her highness's dominions and countries, as well in all spiritual and ecclesiastical things or causes as temporal."[52] The *Oxford Dictionary of the Christian Church* characterizes this act as "an assertion of the monarch's responsibility before God for the welfare of the Church, and annexed 'for ever' the power of reforming abuses to the Crown."[53] To this day the appointment of bishops includes a process of royal assent known officially as *congé d'élire* ("permission to elect").[54]

The title *Fidei Defensor* is not merely symbolic but represents both the monarch's legal role as head of the Church of England and the Anglican Church's special position in English law and national identity. When Prince Charles announced some time ago that he would accept the modified title of "Defender of Faiths," he stated his intention that the monarch would protect the rights of all religions, thus reflecting the tidal shift that has occurred in how the English nation thinks about religion and the place of its national church.

THE ATTITUDE TODAY:
CONFUSION OF CHURCH AND CHRISTIAN

Today there seems to be a confusion of expectations with regard to the church and the Christian in addressing the public arena on matters political or moral. Religious leaders are summoned by a general attitude of the public to pronounce on, or at least advise on, matters of moral and/or political concern. Even the president of the United States solicits the advice and support of church leaders rather frequently.

But, we must ask, by what authority do these churchmen, as churchmen, offer such advice to the state? This is not their realm. For the individual, even the individual Christian, to address issues in his/her community is part of our stand (or "station") as citizens. As such we remind the state, or other citizens, of God's will under the Law, the first use of the Law,[55] but not the Gospel.

The Gospel is not spoken to the state because the state is not a community of faith. It cannot hear the Gospel. The Law alone, particularly the Law in what has been called the first *usus* (use), is to be addressed to the public community.

THEOLOGIA GLORIAE

The expectation that the church and the Christian should address the public arena on matters political or moral reflects the theology of a God of glory, not the theology of the hidden God. It often calls on God to do what He has never promised to do or to act in a way that He has not promised to act. The American religious consciousness that mixes church and state is a theology of glory.[56] It is often outside the church. In any case, it is not particularly dependent on the church, which means it is separated from the means of the Spirit. Fundamentally, it is a false ecclesiology, an individualistic, Nestorian ecclesiology.[57]

BOUNDARIES

In our relations with other faiths or even other confessions, there are boundaries. It has always been the task of the people of God to acknowledge these boundaries. St. Paul asserts a very definite separation from those who teach another gospel (Galatians 1, etc.). Always the pastor, Paul teaches us in the Pastoral Epistles that we must not only proclaim the Gospel positively but also must speak against those who proclaim another gospel. His language is firm: We must "refute" them (e.g., Titus 1:9). The church has always, at least up to modern times, asserted these differences for the sake of making a clear confession.[58] Robert Bellah describes this need:

> It may seem obvious that in order for me to know who I
> am I need to know who I am not. I am not you; that is the

beginning of the definition of me. It is the same with groups. In order to know what my group is, I need to know what it is not—I need to know its boundaries. Thus inclusion and exclusion are basic to the very idea of identity.[59]

In its whole history the church has always confessed both the positive, "We believe, teach and confess," and also the negative, "We condemn" (*Anathama/Damnamus*). For the first time in the history of the church, a council did not offer such rebukes when "cuddly"[60] Pope John XXIII instructed Vatican II not to offer the decrees with such negative references but rather to affirm as much as possible the fellowship of those of other faiths.

To fail to say no to that which we cannot accept is the first step toward giving up our distinctive identity. Even more troubling, it makes ambiguous everything else that we do say. As Avery Cardinal Dulles once remarked regarding another denomination, "It's so hard to tell what the ELCA means by 'Yes' because they never say 'No'!"[61]

CONCLUSION

Therefore, the question for the pastor invited to participate in a civic event in which religious elements are mixed may not be, "Does one participate with clerics of other denominations or other faiths?" but rather, "Does one even participate alone, given the 'religion' present?"

That religion is the collection of all religions; it makes no difference.

That religion sees all faiths as equal.

That religion does not distinguish one confession from another; they are all of the same truth. (Perhaps a collection of many partial truths, brought together to form a greater truth.)

It is easy in such contexts to confuse love of neighbor with tolerance of error simply because in our culture renouncing error, or even calling attention to it, will often be labeled as "unloving." The greatest love (charity) for our neighbor, however, is best expressed in a clear proclamation of the Gospel of Christ. Luther is very clear in this matter:

> Hence this passage must also be considered carefully in opposition to the argument by which they accuse us of offending against love and thus doing great harm to the churches. We are surely prepared to observe peace and love with all men, provided that they leave the doctrine of faith perfect and sound for us. If we cannot obtain this, it is useless for them to demand love from us. A curse on a love that is observed at the expense of the doctrine of faith, to which everything must yield—love, an apostle, an angel from heaven, etc.! . . . they would know that one Word of God is all and that all are one, that one doctrine is all doctrines and all are one, so that when one is lost all are eventually lost, because they belong together and are held together by a common bond.

> Therefore let us leave the praise of harmony and of Christian love to them. We, on the other hand, praise faith and the majesty of the Word. Love can sometimes be neglected without danger, but the Word and faith cannot. It belongs to love to bear everything and to yield to everyone. On the other hand, it belongs to faith to bear nothing whatever and to yield to no one. Love yields freely, believes, condones, and tolerates everything. Therefore it is often deceived.[62]

It has become commonplace in our church in recent discussions and publications to pit the "mission of the church" over against the concerns for "doctrinal purity" or confessional faithfulness. The expression of concerns about the actions of church officials in what have been characterized as "civic events" have sometimes been charged as an irresponsible detraction from the mission of the church. This way of speaking would seem to indicate that the concern for a faithful confession of the doctrine of God's Word is somehow different from the so-called "Great Commission." Such a distinction must be challenged and discussed by our churchmen.

It is precisely through our faithful confession of the "sound doctrine" of God's Word (Titus 1:9) that we best serve the world. This is our great commission indeed. Again, Luther speaks clearly and firmly about this:

> With the utmost vigor we demand that all the articles of Christian doctrine, both large and small—although we do not regard any of them as small—be kept pure and certain. This is supremely necessary. For this doctrine is our only light, which illumines and directs us and shows the way to heaven; if it is overthrown in one point, it must be over-thrown completely. And when that happens, our love will not be of any use to us. We can be saved without love and concord with the Sacramentarians, but not without pure doctrine and faith. Otherwise we shall be happy to observe love and concord toward those who faithfully agree with us on all the articles of Christian doctrine.... [63]

For that blessing we pray to God.

Notes

1. The Rev. Dr. Ronald Feuerhahn is associate professor of historical theology at Concordia Seminary, St. Louis, Missouri. He holds an M.Div. from Concordia Seminary and M.Phil. and Ph.D. degrees from Cambridge University, Cambridge, England. This paper was prepared and read as part of the annual theological symposium of Concordia Seminary in September 2002.

2. Greek: πᾶν (acc. sing. neut. of πᾶς) + θεόν (acc. sing. of θεός).

3. Perhaps an extreme form of this is when people show up at church and expect the church to perform the social or even quasi-religious ceremonies of Baptism for their children, weddings for their daughters, and funerals for their fathers.

4. The Greek text reads: ῥαββί, σὺ εἶ ὁ υἱὸς τοῦ θεοῦ, σὺ βασιλεὺς εἶ τοῦ Ἰσραήλ.

5. Scripture quotations in this essay are from the RSV.

6. The Greek text reads: [καὶ] ὁ βασιλεὺς τοῦ Ἰσραήλ.

7. *Webster's Encyclopedic Unabridged Dictionary of the English Language*, (New York: Gramercy, 1989), 377.

8. F. L. Cross and E. A. Livingstone, eds., *The Oxford Dictionary of the Christian Church*, 3d ed. (Oxford: Oxford University Press, 1997), 405. Hereafter: ODCC3.

9. ODCC3, 405.

10. Erwin L. Lueker, ed., *Lutheran Cyclopedia*, 2d ed. (St. Louis: Concordia, 1975), 172.

11. Justo L. González, *The Story of Christianity*, 2 vols. (San Francisco: Harper, 1984), 1:113.

12. The title used by González, *Story of Christianity*, 1:111; and Richard A. Norris, *A History of the Christian Church*, ed. Williston Walker , 4th ed. (New York: Charles Scribner's Sons, 1985), 124.

13. ODCC3, 792.

14. González, *Story of Christianity*, 1:313.

15. ODCC3, 792ff.

16. As Kenneth Setton points out, Ossius had changed his mind in the thirty years following the Council of Nicaea; see Kenneth Meyer Setton, *Christian Attitudes towards the Emperor in the Fourth Century: Especially as Shown in Addresses to the Emperor* (New York: AMS, 1967 [c1941]), 91.

17. Citation from "Protest by Ossius of Cordova to Constantius II, c. 356; Ap. Ath., Hist. Arian, 44," cited in *Creeds, Councils, and Controversies: Documents Illustrative of the History of the Church A.D. 337–461*, ed. J. Stevenson (London: SPCK, 1966), 38.

18. ODCC3, 49.

19. Lueker, *Lutheran Cyclopedia*, 172b.

20. ODCC3, 1602.

21. "Princes were regarded as the legal successors of the Catholic bishops in their respective territories" from the Augsburg Peace of 1555 in many cases until 1918; see Julius Bodensieck, ed., *The Encyclopedia of the Lutheran Church* (Minneapolis: Augsburg, 1965), 2:277.

22. Note that the Puritans had translated "citizenship" with "commonwealth" in the KJV.

23. AC XXVIII, 12–18 (K-W, 92); note the similar language in Luther:

   God has ordained two governments among the children of Adam, the reign of God under Christ, and the reign of the world under the civil magistrate, each with its own laws and rights. The laws of the reign of the world extend no further than body and goods and the external affairs on earth. But over the soul God can and will allow no one to rule but himself alone. Therefore where the worldly government dares to give laws to the soul, it invades the reign of God, and only seduces and corrupts the soul. This we shall make so clear that our noblemen, princes, and bishops may see what fools they are if they will force people with their laws and commandments to believe this or that. . . . In matters which relate to the soul's salvation nothing should be taught and accepted but God's word" ("Temporal Authority: To What Extent It Should Be Obeyed" [1523], LW 45:81–129).

24. John Calvin, *Institutes*, 4.20.3.

25. Calvin, *Institutes*, 4.20.9.

26. Sydney E. Ahlstrom, *A Religious History of the American People* (New Haven: Yale University Press, 1972), 72.

27. Ahlstrom, *Religious History of the American People*, 148ff.

28. Ahlstrom, *Religious History of the American People*, 151.

29. Ahlstrom, *Religious History of the American People*, 83.

30. "You are the light of the world. A city set on a hill cannot be hid" (Matthew 5:14).

31. Peter J. Gomes, "A Pilgrim's Progress: The Bible as Civic Blueprint (Best Sermon in The Best Series)," *The New York Times Magazine* (18 April 1999): 102.

32. Perry Miller, *Nature's Nation* (Cambridge: Harvard University Press, 1967), 6.

33. Ahlstrom, *Religious History of the American People*, 7.

34. Ahlstrom, *Religious History of the American People*, 8.

35. Ahlstrom, *Religious History of the American People*, 9.

36. Ahlstrom, *Religious History of the American People*, 10.

37. As cited in Ahlstrom, *Religious History of the American People*, 7. E.g., Hector St. John de Crevecoeur, *Letters from an American Farmer, and Sketches of Eighteenth–Century America*, ed. Albert E. Stone (New York: American Library, 1963).

38. Hermann Sasse, *Amerikanisches Kirchentum* (Berlin-Dahlem: Wichern-Verlag, 1927), ET: "American Christianity and the Church," in *The Lonely Way*, trans. Matthew Harrison (St. Louis: Concordia, 2001), 1:23–60, here at 26.

39. Sasse, *Amerikanisches Kirchentum*, ET, 31.

40. Personal letter from Sasse to Tom Hardt (8 January 1962), from the files of the author.

41. Sasse, *Amerikanisches Kirchentum*, ET, 35.

42. ODCC3, 268

43. Sasse, *Amerikanisches Kirchentum*, ET, 36.

44. Sasse, *Amerikanisches Kirchentum*, ET, 29.

45. Ahlstrom, *Religious History of the American People*, 148ff.

46. H. Richard Niebuhr, *The Kingdom of God in America* (New York: Harper & Bros., 1937), cited by Robert N. Bellah, "The Kingdom of God in America: Language of Faith, Language of Nation, Language of Empire," in *Religion and the Public Good: A Bicentennial Forum* (Macon, Ga.: Mercer University Press, 1988), 43.

47. Thus the Yankee Stadium event of 9/23/2001 was titled by C–SPAN as the "Service for Terrorism Victims."

48. ODCC3, 1568.

49. Richard McBrien, ed., *The Harper Collins Encyclopedia of Catholicism* (San Francisco: Harper, 1995), 1:234.

50. Abdel Ross Wentz, *A Basic History of Lutheranism in America* (Philadelphia: Muhlenberg, 1958), 74.

51. Similar titles were conferred on the kings of France and Spain, *Christianissimus* (most Christian) and *Cathholicus* (Catholic). ODCC3, 463.

52. That last word, *temporal,* is the important one: In Britain, the parliament oversees the temporal affairs of the Church of England while the church's convocation (and later synod) oversees the ecclesiastical affairs. But there have been cases of notorious lapses in this arrangement, especially in the Reform Bill (1832) in which Parliament suppressed ten bishoprics in Ireland, an act that prompted the Oxford Movement (1833–1845). When the matter of a new prayer book for the Church of England came before Parliament in 1927 it was rejected by the House of Commons, even though it had been passed by the Convocations of the Church Assembly. This, too, precipitated a crisis.

53. ODCC3, 560.

54. OCDD3, 398. In actual fact it is more the appointment of the prime minister than of the monarch, as those who are familiar with the appropriate episode of "Yes, Prime Minister" will know.

55. As the Formula of Concord notes:

The law has been given to men for three reasons: (1) to maintain external discipline against unruly and disobedient men, (2) to lead men to a knowledge of their sin, (3) after they are reborn, and although the flesh still inheres in them, to give them on that account a definite rule according to which they should pattern and regulate their entire life. (FC VI [Tappert, 479–80])

Thus the phrase "first use of the Law" commonly refers to that function of God's word of law that works in the conscience of man to restrain evil in the world at large.

56. Sydney Ahlstrom identifies the American mythic theme with a *theologia gloria*, "in which patriotism and religion are inextricably entwined" (*Religious History of the American People*, 9).

57. John Williamson Nevin condemned the revivalism so prevalent in nineteenth-century America for its "Gnostic, unchurchly, Nestorian spirit" (as noted in Ahlstrom, *Religious History of the American People*, 473).

58. See Hans-Werner Gensichen, *We Condemn: How Luther and 16th Century Lutheranism Condemned False Doctrine*, trans. Herbert J. A. Bouman (St. Louis: Concordia, 1967).

59. Robert N. Bellah, "Conclusion: Competing Visions of the Role of Religion in American Society," in *Uncivil Religion: Interreligious Hostility in America*, ed. Robert N. Bellah and Frederick E. Greenspahn (New York: Crossroad, 1987), 219.

60. This adjective is used merely to indicate the popularly observed perception of this remarkable man, especially in contrast to his seemingly "dour" predecessor, Pius XII.

61. As cited by Patrick Keifert, professor at Luther Seminary, St. Paul, Minnesota, in a presentation to a Concordia Seminary student convocation, 26 January 2000.

62. LW 27:37ff.

63. LW 27:41ff.

7

Polytheism

The New Face of American Civil Religion

ALVIN J. SCHMIDT[1]

Although scholars of religion in the United States have during the last fifty years analyzed and published numerous articles and books on American civil religion, the topic or concept has not been a household word. Even in many formal religious contexts such as Bible classes, Sunday morning sermons, or congregational meetings, American church members (including members of Lutheran Church—Missouri Synod congregations) have not heard the topic discussed.

However, since the catastrophic events that occurred in the United States on September 11, 2001, and some of the formal religious activities that soon followed these events, more Christians are now hearing discussions concerning American civil religion, prompted by events such as: the interreligious assembly (Christians, Jews, and Muslims) that met for the "Day of Prayer and

Remembrance" in Washington's National Cathedral three days later on September 14; the religious gathering of Christian, Jewish, Muslim, Sikh, and Hindu representatives who met for "A Prayer for America" in Yankee Stadium on September 23; the first anniversary memorial service held in Columbia, South Carolina, to commemorate the terrorist bombings of September 11, 2001; and the memorial service conducted for space shuttle *Columbia*'s astronauts in Cleveland, Ohio, on February 8, 2003. These interreligious gatherings illustrate American civil religion in action. But still more, they reveal that the nature of American civil religion has changed from its deistic posture, which had characterized it since the mid-1700s, to a polytheistic stance.

WHAT IS AMERICAN CIVIL RELIGION?

American civil religion goes back to the Puritans, who arrived on ten ships in 1630 and established the Massachusetts Bay Colony under the leadership of John Winthrop. (This group is not to be confused with an earlier contingent of Puritans, commonly known as the Pilgrims, who came on the *Mayflower* and set up Plymouth Colony on Cape Cod in 1620.) Winthrop's new Americans saw their religious beliefs intertwined with their new country's future status. As God guided ancient Israel to its Promised Land, Canaan, so the Puritans believed He had also guided them to a Promised Land, America. Here they would establish "a city on the hill," as Winthrop, the Bay Colony's first governor, expressed it. America would be a religious commonwealth, for all (especially England) to see as a Christian model.

As American civil religion in its early years was largely confined to the Puritan Christian population, it had a decided Christian aura. By the time a century and a half passed after the Puritans had set foot on the shores of America, this civil religion had become deistic. Yet this change did not alter the early American Puritan belief, also held by many prominent and influential deistic

Americans, that their country was the Promised Land, similar to what the land of Canaan was for the ancient Israelites when they came out of Egypt. Two such influential individuals were Benjamin Franklin and Thomas Jefferson.

After the Declaration of Independence was signed by John Hancock on July 4, 1776, the Continental Congress commissioned a committee of three (John Adams, Benjamin Franklin, and Thomas Jefferson) to design the Great Seal of the United States. Franklin drew the biblical image of Moses lifting his wand and dividing the Red Sea with Pharaoh and his charioteers drowning, clearly a reference to God guiding the Puritans and other emigrants to America, the Promised Land. Somewhat similarly, Jefferson tried to depict the Israelites being led through the wilderness by a cloud during the day and by a pillar of fire at night, implying that the early Americans were the new Israelites whom God guided in their exodus from Europe to the Promised Land of America. Franklin's and Jefferson's designs, though never adopted as the Great Seal of the United States, form two examples of the civil religious heritage that was already 150 years old at the time of American independence.

While the phenomenon of self-reflective civil religion goes back historically at least to the ancient Romans, who believed their various pagan religious beliefs should serve civic objectives, it was the French philosopher Jean-Jacques Rousseau who first coined the term in 1762 when he published his book *The Social Contract*. He discussed this concept in book four, the eighth chapter titled "Civil Religion." Rousseau believed that civil religion would sanctify and legitimate France's values and practices and thereby create social cohesion between the people and the country. His discussion was clearly influenced by ancient Rome's civil religious rites. He wanted French civil religion to reflect the meaning of the Latin word *religare*, a social bond between the Roman people and the state.[2] He did not like the idea that the early Christians did not see themselves as members of the Roman state and its ties to various gods because they saw themselves as belonging to a separate spiritual kingdom, one not of this world.[3] The socioreligious bond of the Romans that Rousseau desired for the French is explained by one historian:

> In the mind of the ancient world the association between religious unity and political unity was so intimate that the concept of political unity could never have been complete unless religion was associated with it. One state, one worship, was to that world an idea as old as time.[4]

Rousseau wanted a governmental leader to establish France's civil religion. He wanted this leader to be duty-bound "to decide upon articles, not precisely as dogmas of religion, but as sentiments of sociality without which it is impossible to be a good citizen or a faithful subject."[5] But his suggested model did not materialize.

More than half a century after Rousseau's proposal, his own countryman Alexis de Tocqueville, who visited the United States in 1831, noted the following in his work *Democracy in America* (1834): "In France, I had almost always seen the spirit of religion and spirit of freedom marching in opposite directions. But in America . . . they were intimately united and they reigned in common over the same country."[6] He also observed that religion in America was "indispensable to the maintenance of [its] republican institutions."[7] Citing these and other observations regarding the role of religion *vis-a-vis* political life in the United States, "Tocqueville presented a model of American civil religion in which religious belief and morality were fused with a political system of democratic values and laws."[8] Indeed, what Rousseau wanted the state to impose on France as civil religion was by 1831 operating in America. Here, no political leader or state imposed it. Rather, it developed and functioned voluntarily and independent of the state.

When Will Herberg in *Protestant—Catholic—Jew* (1955) wrote of America fusing religion with its national purposes, he had in mind the phenomenon of civil religion, even though he did not use the term. Similarly, when Martin E. Marty in *New Shape of American Religion* (1959) discussed the American belief in a "religion-in-general," he, too, had in mind America's civil religion.[9] More recently, Robert Bellah, who brought the concept of civil religion to the attention of the academic world in 1967, defined American civil religion as consisting of "a collection of beliefs, symbols, and rituals with respect to sacred things and institutionalized in a collectivity."[10] These national beliefs, symbols, and rituals, Bellah argued, give the United States a bond of national unity.

American civil religion today has a number of key characteristics. It is a religion that uses generic terms for God: the Almighty, Creator, Providence, our Maker, Supreme Being, etc.; it does not define God; it commonly does not see Him as a God of judgment; it makes no mention of heaven and certainly not hell. It embodies a strong belief in the American way of life: democracy, freedom, equality, justice, tolerance, progress, opportunity. It has its own holy days: Memorial Day, Independence Day (July 4), Thanksgiving Day, presidential inaugurals. It has its own sayings, such as "In God We Trust" on coins and paper currency; *Annuit Coeptis*[11] (He has favored our undertaking) on the one dollar bill's backside; and the Pledge of Allegiance. It has its own doctrines, embodied in the Declaration of Independence, the Constitution, the Bill of Rights, and Lincoln's Emancipation Proclamation. It has its own saints: Washington, Jefferson, Madison, Lincoln. Finally, American civil religion has its own shrines: the Washington Monument, the Lincoln Memorial, Jefferson's Monticello, Valley Forge, Mount Rushmore, the Statue of Liberty, the Alamo, Arlington Cemetery.

In light of the above, American civil religion may be defined as the deeply held beliefs that unite Americans regarding their nation's values and practices pertaining to freedom, democracy, equality, progress, opportunity, toleration, and justice, which are portrayed by patriotic symbols in collective gatherings where they are publicly revered and honored as sacred because the values they symbolize are given by God, who is undefined, and who has chosen the United States to play a special, salutary role in human history.

AMERICAN CIVIL RELIGION BECOMES DEISTIC

With its Puritan orientation in the 1630s, American civil religion initially had a Christian aura. But, as indicated above, 150 years later it had become increasingly deistic. Then, for the following 200 years and more (from about 1750 to the 1980s), participants in American civil religious ceremonies commonly called upon "God" in deistic language that portrayed Him in anonymous, generic terms. Consistent with deism, this god was thought to have revealed himself in the laws of nature but not through Jesus Christ in biblical revelation. This god governed the world by natural laws that, one advocate argued, "are like Himself immutable . . . [and] violations of these laws, or miraculous interference in the movements of nature, must be necessarily excluded from the grand system of universal existence."[12] If Christians in civil religious ceremonies understood the anonymous or generic invocations as trinitarian, that was, of course, their prerogative. But it was likewise the prerogative of deists and other non-Christians to understand such references to the divine as totally unrelated to the Christian Trinity. The focus was not on Jesus Christ but on one divine, anonymous being. Since the 1980s, civil religion in the United States has shifted from deism to an increasingly polytheistic posture, as will be discussed below. But first it is necessary to probe further into the deistic stage of American civil religion.

THE BRITISH CONTRIBUTION
TO AMERICAN CIVIL RELIGION'S DEISM

For the most part, the deistic movement developed in England during the 1600s and early 1700s. It was a product of the Age of Enlightenment, or the "Age of Reason," as the American deist

Thomas Paine called it. This age produced several deistic writers. Lord Herbert of Cherbury (1583–1648), often called the father of British deism, wrote *De Veritate*. John Toland (1670–1732) penned *Christianity Not Mysterious*. Anthony Collins (1676–1729) authored *Discourse on the Grounds and Reasons of the Christian Religion*. Thomas Woolston (1669–1733) wrote *Discourses on the Miracles of Our Savior*, and Matthew Tindal (1657–1733) issued *Christianity as Old as Creation*. In one way or another, all of these publications questioned biblical revelation and the supernatural accounts in the Bible that comprise many of Christianity's teachings. These writers contended that only through human reason, guided by the "Book of Nature" (natural religion), can one know and understand God. Thus nature, not the Bible, was God's revelation. Given these premises, Tindal's book, *Christianity as Old as Creation*, for instance, took the next logical step by formally denying the deity of Christ.

The deistic impact of these and related writings soon traversed the Atlantic to colonial America, where it shaped the religious beliefs of many Founding Fathers. For instance, Benjamin Franklin (1706–1790), one of the signers of the Declaration of Independence and the American Constitution, became an avowed deist early in life. Thomas Jefferson (1743–1826), the primary author of the Declaration of Independence and the nation's third president, revealed his deistic convictions in the Declaration by employing the terms "Creator" and "Nature's God." It is well known that he excised all miracles in the New Testament Gospels with a scissors, producing the so-called "Jefferson Bible."

George Washington (1732–1799), head of the Continental Army, chairman of the Constitutional Convention, and the first president under the Constitution, revealed his deistic bent by frequently referring to God in generic or anonymous terms, such as "Providence," "Heaven," "Supreme Being," "Great Ruler of Nations," and so on. When Benedict Arnold's plans to deliver West Point's post and garrison to the British (plans that included the British capture of Washington himself) were averted, Washington saw it as the "interposition of Providence."[13] In his first presidential inaugural address (1789), Washington referred to God as "the invisible hand that conducts the affairs of men. . . ."[14] In this address he also spoke of "the propitious smiles of Heaven. . . ."[15] In his twenty volumes of correspondence he mentioned Jesus Christ only once, in a speech to the Delaware Indian chiefs. Paul Boller, an historian of Washington, believes an aide wrote this reference and Washington simply read it without editing it.[16] Boller adds that in all of Washington's letters to his friends and associates he never mentioned the name of Jesus Christ.[17]

Other American Founding Fathers were also known deists, such as John Adams (1735–1826), the country's second president, even though he called himself "a church-going animal," and James Madison (1753–1835), the father of the Constitution and the nation's fourth president. All of these prominent figures, as well as others, contributed to the deistic nature of American civil religion that characterized it until the twentieth century's last couple of decades.

FREEMASONRY'S CONNECTION TO DEISM IN AMERICAN CIVIL RELIGION

Before the late 1600s, Freemasonry in England consisted mostly of stonemasons, whose lodge meetings, according to its *Old Charges* (a.k.a. *Gothic Constitutions*), included trinitarian Christian prayers and required members to be loyal to the church. But in 1717 British Freemasonry reorganized itself to become a fraternity whose members no longer were operative masons, and in 1723 it revised its *Old Charges*, some of which dated back to the 1390. In the 1723 revisions, it absorbed the deistic spirit that was then in the air. Briefly put, the revised Masonic charges, which became known as *Anderson's Constitutions*, "replaced Christianity by deism," as shown by two renowned British historians of Freemasonry.[18]

Reorganized Freemasonry was nontrinitarian in orientation. It emphasized deeds, not Christian creeds. In line with this emphasis, it focused on symbolic/speculative meanings of what once were operative masonry's ancient tools. The *square*, for instance, now symbolized living one's life on the square, that is, being morally upright. The *level* symbolized equality among members. The *compass* meant circumscribing one's passions; the *white lambskin apron* conveyed purity and innocence; the *trowel* stood for cementing brotherly behavior; and so on.

By the mid-1700s deistically oriented Freemasonry was well established in colonial America, where it also had become an influential sociopolitical force. In the words of Bernard Faÿ, a French scholar of Masonry:

> Freemasonry in the colonies was the center around which were grouped all the fashionable young men . . . where social organization was still in a rudimentary state, it constituted the most important intercontinental network . . . it attracted the most prominent persons.[19]

The Masonic influence in America, especially on events that occurred from 1765 to 1800, has been largely overlooked by American historians. Thus this influence is not recorded in high school or college history books, and noting this influence often comes as news to many. In this regard, the observation of Philip Roth, a Masonic historian, is pertinent:

> One may turn in vain to the indexes of a complete library of standard works upon American history for any except the most casual reference to an institution [that is, Freemasonry] that drew together in the bonds of unity and brotherly love the leading citizens of scores of Colonial towns and villages.[20]

Still another observer of Freemasonry's influence on the United States, especially in the eighteenth century, has stated: "Freemasonry in America was in fact a kind of religion, as real as

Christianity to many, and more real to some."[21] Recent research has shown that Freemasonry itself in some ways functions as an American civil religious organization.

The longstanding presence of American civil religion owes much to the deistic influences Freemasonry has had on it. The highly influential deist Benjamin Franklin, who helped shape and direct much of the ideology and political structure of the United States government, was a staunch Freemason to the end of his 84 years of life. He was also a strong advocate of civil religion, which he called "publick religion." History, he argued, shows that public religion is beneficial to society. In this context, he even mentioned "the Excellency of the Christian Religion," which was, he said, "above all others, antient [sic] or modern."[22] However, we must remember that Franklin's understanding of the Christian religion, like that of all deists, referred only to Christianity's moral teachings, not its Christ-centered soteriological doctrines.

Parenthetically, it is interesting to note that George Washington, who, as already noted, liked to use deistic terms for God, was also a member of the Masonic lodge.[23] On September 18, 1793, even as president of the country, he participated in a Masonic cornerstone-laying of the Capitol building in Washington, D.C., and there he wore a Masonic apron.[24] Many other Founding Fathers, too numerous to mention here, were also Freemasons. They were well-represented in the signing of the Declaration of Independence in 1776 and also in formulating the federal Constitution in 1787. These two documents are the most significant pillars of the American nation.

Deistic convictions are evident in many of the thoughts and actions of the Founding Fathers. Those who were Freemasons either acquired these convictions in Masonic lodge gatherings or had them reinforced there. Those who were not Masons, such as Samuel Adams, John Adams, and others, had similar deistic beliefs through close associations with their Masonic friends as well as through reading similar literature. John Adams once said, "Many of my best friends have been Masons."[25] When he succeeded Washington as president, the religious utterances of Adams were as deistic as those of any Mason. For instance, upon being elected to the presidency, he referred to God as "Sovereign of the Universe, the Ordainer of civil government on earth. . . . "[26]

AMERICA'S PRESENT POLYTHEISTIC CIVIL RELIGION

Until the early 1980s, as indicated above, American civil religion was decidedly deistic. But as multiculturalism and its complementary force of political correctness gained ascendancy in the United States at this time, and as public officials began genuflecting before the altar of multiculturalism, American civil religion became increasingly polytheistic. In the canons of multiculturalism, not only are all cultures equal, so also are all religious beliefs. Hence, much of American civil religion now resembles the polytheistic civil religion of the pagan Roman Empire. Today the different pagan gods of Hindus, Sikhs, Buddhists, and other pagan groups are given equal honor and recognition in numerous American civil religious ceremonies.

The polytheistic nature of American civil religion today is largely the product of contemporary multiculturalism. However, precedent for it was set early on, with Virginia's Act for Religious Freedom of 1786. In draft form this act attempted to say that religious coercion was contrary to the teachings of Jesus Christ. According to Thomas Jefferson, this reference to Christ was rejected in deference to Jews, infidels, and Hindus.[27] Thus the name of Jesus Christ was omitted, even though the proposed draft had not assigned any divine status to Him. The mere mention of Christ's name proved unacceptable to Virginia's deistically influenced legislators. Deism, together with the desire not to offend infidels or Hindus (polytheists), had its way with them. But the act in its final form did more than avoid offending a polytheistic group. It also opened the door to honoring multiple gods in America's civil religious ceremonies.

It would be interesting to research the degree of influence exerted by those who backed Virginia's Act for Religious Freedom of 1786 on the United States Constitution of 1787. Notably, the Constitution does not mention God at all, unlike the Declaration of Independence that uses deistic terms in reference to God. Further, in Article VI, the Constitution prohibits religious tests for public officeholders. Was the Constitution in effect a second hand extended in openness to polytheists, present or future?

At any rate, Virginia's course of action in 1786 is not surprising in light of Freemasonry's influence on the formation of early American sociopolitical values. For when Freemasonry revised its constitutions in 1723 and became deistic, it also welcomed members from polytheistic religions. To this day, Freemasonry (except on the Continent) requires what it calls the "Volume of the Sacred Law" (VSL) to be placed on a lodge's altar during its sessions. In the United States, Canada, England, and Australia the VSL is commonly the Bible. In Muslim countries it is the Qur'an, in a Mormon lodge it is the Book of Mormon, and in India it is the Bhagavad-Gita of the Hindus, etc.

Although the United States formally does not have a pantheon of gods as did ancient Rome, it does have a modern parallel in many of its civil religious activities, such as when Christians, Jews, Muslims, Hindus, Sikhs, Buddhists, and others gather jointly to call upon different, even multiple, gods to protect America's national values, the American Way of Life. Such assemblies demonstrate that American civil religion is no longer the belief in a god-in-general but a syncretistic belief in *many gods-in-general.*

TWO MISSING INGREDIENTS:
UNCONDITIONAL GOSPEL AND *SOLUS CHRISTUS*

As already noted, a major shift occurred in American civil religion within a century and a half after Puritan Christians laid its foundation in the 1630s. By about the mid-eighteenth century, the initial Christian orientation became deistic. How did this happen? Any attempt to answer such a question in limited space is obviously fraught with the danger of oversimplification. I shall attempt to provide a brief answer, nevertheless, because this answer can be instructive for us as we face polytheistic civil religion today.

Beside factors such as the influence of deism in America, particularly in the form of Freemasonry, changes occurred among America's Puritans themselves that eventually complemented a deistic outlook. The preaching and teaching prevalent among the Puritans from 1630 to the mid-1700s increasingly urged members to fulfill and uphold their Christian moral duties and responsibilities by performing good deeds. Although God's grace was not totally ignored, it is quite clear in Puritan sermons that man was urged to do good works to give evidence of his salvation, rather than doing them in appreciation for salvation. It made little difference whether the sermons came from John Winthrop (1588–1649), John Cotton (1584–1652), Thomas Shepard (1605–1649), Increase Mather (1639–1723), Cotton Mather (1663–1728), or others. All of them exhorted hearers to live a God-pleasing life, to keep God's covenant intact. In other words, while there was considerable variation among preachers of the Puritan covenant theology, they had at least this much in common: In terms of the distinction between Law and Gospel, their sermons typically contained much Law with little or no unconditional Gospel message to motivate people to bring forth the works expected of them.

Closely related to this lack of clear Gospel motivation, one finds no sermon references to the biblical teaching of *solus Christus,* namely, that God can only be found in Jesus Christ and that there is no salvation outside of Him. "Neither the human person of Jesus nor the incarnate Logos nor the mystery of participation in the death and resurrection of Christ [was] a theme of lively interest in the Federal [covenant] Theology."[28] Here the "Gospel-Covenant" theology of Peter Bulkeley (1583–1659) can be cited as an example. One observer noted that Bulkelely's version of Puritan theology did in effect "diminish Christ as the sole agent of redemption by reinstating the exemplarity of Abraham."[29]

As the sermons of Puritan Congregationalists strongly urged people to exercise their duties and responsibilities without an unconditional Gospel message to motivate them, it is not difficult to see how the emphasis on "deeds, rather than creeds" (a popular phrase of the deists), gained ascendancy. Sermons by Presbyterians and Episcopalians also strongly emphasized deeds with either weak or no Gospel motivation. In a spiritual environment where human deeds receive the main emphasis, Christ's redemptive act of salvation is not the motivating force to pursue them, and *solus Christus* is not accented, it is not difficult to see why morally-minded individuals opted for a deistic brand of theology compatible with the religious philosophy of Freemasonry. In fact, by the early 1800s many congregations with Puritan Congregationalist roots, "particularly in Boston and its environs, became Unitarian."[30] The eighteenth-century Puritans (Congregationalists), Episcopalians, and Presbyterians furnished many of the influential Founding Fathers who shaped the Declaration of Independence and the Constitution. These men not only formulated the country's major documents, but they also provided the deistic philosophy that for the next two hundred years would characterize American civil religion.

Two centuries later, in late twentieth-century America's environment of multiculturalism and political correctness, there has been virtually no opposition to the move from a deistically oriented civil religion to one that is now polytheistic. In this respect, the recent shift resembles the earlier move to deism. The relatively longstanding practice of preaching a weak or shrouded Gospel, together with the absence of *solus Christus*, facilitated the shift to deism in America's civil religion in the eighteenth century. More recently, it has made possible an unopposed transition to polytheism (along with many of its pagan elements) in a nation that does not seem to realize or care that polytheism brings with it paganism.

EQUATING FAITH WITH RELIGION: A POLYTHEISTIC CIVIL RELIGIOUS PHENOMENON

For some time Americans, as well as many others, have been equating faith with religion, regardless of whether that religion is Christian or not. Thus we hear people speak about "the Muslim faith," "the Hindu faith," "the Buddhist faith," and, of course, "the Christian faith." Equating faith with religion has even become a part of today's political language. President George W. Bush speaks of "faith-based initiative" programs.

The equation of faith with religion slights Christianity. First, it ignores the important fact that the use of the word *faith* in the religious sense is of Christian origin. Really, it is a Christian innovation. Although the English word *faith* translates the Greek word *pistis* and the Latin *fide*, neither of these words had any religious connotations among the pagan Greeks or Romans. As one scholar has observed, " 'Faith' as a central category of Greek religious language did not exist."[31] Neither did the Greeks or Romans use "faith" as a term for a body of religious knowledge or truth, as the New Testament does in Acts 6:7; Galatians 1:23; 1 Timothy 4:1, 6; Titus 1:4; and Jude 3. Nor did they use the word *faith* as a synonym for religion, as many Christians do today when, for instance, they speak of "the Muslim faith" or "the Hindu faith."

Second, such speech slights Christianity by misrepresenting it. It implies that Christianity is like non-Christian religions: namely, that its teachings, like theirs, are also based only on "faith" without any factual foundation. This is false! Christianity is the only religion whose faith is linked to historical facts. For example, faith in the physical resurrection of Jesus Christ rests upon the fact that He did indeed rise from the dead, a phenomenon that happened in real history, not in the faith of His disciples. It is not the faith of Christians that makes Christ's resurrection true and valid, but rather it is His physical resurrection that makes their faith true and valid. In short, the Christian concept of faith is not faith in faith itself. Christians do not have a faith that stands independent of any historical facts or referents. Unfortunately, the latter is how our society, including many religious leaders, speak of faith today. Believing in something for which there is no evidence is not faith. In Christian theology it is no faith at all.

The classical Greeks saw faith as "the lowest grade of cognition: it was the state of mind of the uneducated, who believe[d] things on hearsay without being able to give reasons for their belief."[32] But that is not how the New Testament speaks of faith. For instance, St. Paul told skeptics that if they did not believe Christ had risen from the dead, they could ask some 500 people who had seen Him after His resurrection. Paul also stated that if Christ had not risen, the faith of Christians was empty (1 Corinthians 15:6, 14). Further, Christ did not tell doubting Thomas to accept His resurrection on mere faith, without evidence. Instead, He let Thomas see and touch His crucifixion wounds. That experience moved Thomas to say, "My Lord and my God!" (John 20:28).[33] It produced the greatest confession of faith recorded in the entire Bible, and it demonstrates again that the Christian faith is based on real historical facts.

Christians have from the beginning been urged to give sound reasons for their faith. St. Peter told first-century Christians: "But in your hearts regard Christ the Lord as holy, always being prepared to make a defense to anyone who asks you for a reason for the hope that is in you" (1 Peter 3:15). Such a concept of faith was unimaginable to the ancient Greeks, and it is absent from all non-Christian religions. Thus to use the term "faith" in reference to other religions not only slights Christianity, it also compliments and lends support to those religions! Recognizing the powerful effect of language, Christians need to make a deliberate, conscious, and consistent effort to cease and desist using the term "faith" when referring to any non-Christian religious group. Instead, they should say "the Buddhist religion," "the Hindu religion," etc. Similarly, Christians also should not use the term "interfaith" when referring to a civil religious event in which one or more non-Christian religions are represented.

An Example for Christians Today

By the time Emperor Constantine legalized Christianity in A.D. 313, the early Christians had for 300 years spurned all polytheistic civil religious activities of ancient Rome, even though the pagan Romans expected them to take part. Their example can be helpful for American Christians who are urged by many in today's multiculturalist environment to participate in America's polytheistic civil religious events. We do well to examine further the early Christians' refusal to participate in Rome's civil religious activities.

They were not moved by the Roman notion that the state's religious values and its people formed a common bond, each reinforcing the other. Instead, they saw themselves as the *ecclesia* ("called-out" ones), a people whom God Himself "called . . . out of darkness into His marvelous light" (1 Peter 2:9). Early Christians also believed that if they honored Rome's many gods, they would be engaged in idolatry and thus deny the true God: Father, Son, and Holy Spirit. They refused to call the emperor "Lord," which the Romans saw as a civil religious duty. The Christian rejection of these civil religious practices angered the Romans, who therefore saw Christians as exclusivists, even as atheists.[34]

A common civil religious ritual among the Romans consisted of performing libations, that is, pouring or sprinkling wine, oil, or some other liquid substance on a deified object or statue. The latter was frequently a replica of the emperor, whom the Romans commonly saw as *deus* (god). Nor did the Christians participate in offering firstfruits, man-made food articles, or frankincense, which were either burned on altars or placed on sacrificial tables. Most of the complying Roman populace performed these civil religious rituals and activities perfunctorily. Personal devotion or commitment in religious activities was not necessary. Still, this did not make them acceptable to the Christians. Thus Justin Martyr (ca. A.D. 100–166), an early Christian apologist martyred under Emperor Marcus Aurelius, informs us that Romans often accused Christians of being atheists for refusing to participate in Rome's civil religious practices. Justin wrote: "And neither do we honor with many sacrifices and garlands of flowers deities as men have formed and set in shrines and called gods" (*First Apology*, 9). In the early part of the fourth century, another prominent church father, Lactantius (d. A.D. 330), reported that Emperor Galerius demanded Christians to make offerings of incense to pagan gods on various altars and perform sacrifices as well. When they refused, they were severely persecuted by imprisonment, torture, and often death (*Of the Manner in Which the Persecutors Died*, 15).

Although Christians were persecuted at times for rejecting Rome's civil religious practices, their noncompliant behavior did not harm Christianity's long-term influence. In time, their firm faith and conviction had profoundly positive effects on many aspects of life within the Roman world. Keith Hopkins, though an atheist, says it well: "Christianity subverted the whole priestly calendar of civic rituals and public festivals on which Roman rule in the provinces rested. Christianity was a revolutionary movement."[35]

The uncompromising stance of the early Christians for three hundred years had other powerful effects, reminiscent of Jason and his fellow Christians who, in the middle of the first century in Thessalonica, were accused of having "turned the world upside down" (Acts 17:6). Thus by the mid-fourth century (one generation after Christianity became a legal religion) many pagan laws and practices were turned upside down by emperors who now were Christians. Constantine the Great outlawed branding the faces of criminals, banned crucifixion as a form of execution, and ordered speedy trials for the accused. His son Constantius ordered the segregation of male and female prisoners. Emperor Valentinian in A.D. 374 outlawed Rome's widely accepted and legal practice of abortion, infanticide, and child abandonment. By the latter part of the fourth century Theodosius I outlawed the inhumanly cruel gladiator contests in the East, and in A.D. 404 Emperor Honorius outlawed them in the West. Many other wholesome changes, effected by the influence of Christians, could be cited.

CONCLUSION

Because American civil religious events are either deistic or increasingly polytheistic, may faithful, biblically minded Christians participate in them? Often, this question has not even been asked. The very nature of American civil religion, so closely associated with patriotism, makes the question itself seem almost un-American.

If the question is asked, sometimes American Christians show how little they understand the nature of American civil religion. When some Christians hear that it is not God-pleasing to participate in American civil religious exercises, they wonder: "What is wrong with Christians praying for our nation with individuals who are Muslims, Hindus, Sikhs, Buddhists, or Jews? After all, they all are praying, are they not? How can that be wrong?"

Why do well-meaning Christians ask such questions? At least four reasons come to mind. First, Christians often have not been taught that praying with non-Christians in civil religious activities is biblically prohibited. For instance, St. Paul cautioned the Corinthian Christians: "Do not be unequally yoked with unbelievers . . . [and] what agreement has the temple of God with idols?" (2 Corinthians 6:14, 16).

Second, many Christians have not been adequately reminded that such interreligious prayers violate the First Commandment, which prohibits honoring gods of other religions (Exodus 20:3).

Third, many American Christians unfortunately have not been urged to follow the example of the early Christians, who refused to participate in ancient Rome's civil religious activities, even though they were often persecuted by the Romans for their noncomplying stance. Keith Hopkins portrays an imaginary, but historically realistic, third-century exchange between Macarius (a Christian) and Celsus (a pagan skeptic). Celsus asks Macarius:

> Why can't you [Christians] compromise? he said. After all, different peoples all over the world call their Gods by different names. . . . Couldn't you just participate in our public festivals, for the sake of form . . . and perform public duties for the common good? Actually, I personally know of some quite respectable Christians who do just that, however much it goes against their highest ideals.[36]

The compromising behavior by some weak Christians, described here by Celsus, unfortunately depicts many American Christians today, some of whom on various occasions participate in either deistic or polytheistic civil religious activities. Had the early Christians behaved similarly in connection with Rome's civil religious customs, how long would Christianity have survived?

There is a fourth likely reason many Christians wonder why it is not God-pleasing to participate in American civil religious events with non-Christians. It pertains to their not having been catechized that they should not refer to non-Christian religions as "faith groups." To ascribe the word "faith" to non-Christian religions unwittingly gives support to America's current polytheistic civil religion. To use such language, as noted earlier, implies that non-Christian religions are as valid and God-pleasing as Christianity. It overlooks the words of St. Peter: "And there is salvation in no one else, for there is no other name under heaven given among men by which we must be saved" (Acts 4:12). Thus today's Christians must break away from their culture's way of speaking by no longer referring to non-Christian religions as "faith groups." To say, for example, that Muslims belong to the "Islamic religion" rather than to the "Islamic faith" may not be judged politically correct in today's American culture, but Christians need to remember that it is biblically and theologically correct.

Recently, some have argued for participation in civil religious activities because they are performed under civic, not ecclesiastical, auspices. Such activities, the contention runs, are outside the context of worship and therefore biblically permissible. This argument conveys a faulty understanding of the nature of American civil religion, which clearly involves worship. Webster's dictionary defines worship as an activity in which people "adore or pay divine honors to a deity." When civil religious events invoke an anonymous god-in-general (deism) or anonymous gods-in-general (polytheism), these are acts of worship, even in a civic setting. Further, the argument also overlooks the fact that when St. Paul told the Corinthians not to be unequally joined with unbelievers and when Moses told the Israelites they were not to revere gods of other religions, no distinction was made relative to the context or setting of such behavior. The context, civil or otherwise, was irrelevant.

People want to be liked and publicly accepted. Understandably, then, many Christians find it difficult to decline participation in civil religious events. To do so often means that others will see them as narrow-minded, or worse, even as bigoted. When such likely responses occur, Christians need to remember the words of St. Paul, Moses, and the stalwart behavior of the early Christians, along with the words of Jesus. He said: "Woe to you, when all people speak well of you" (Luke 6:26). Christians also need to recall that God does not want them to conform to this world (Romans 12:2). To be sure, they will often be disliked, even hated, for not conforming to the standards of the world, including the standards of America's civil religion. Christ said: "You are not of the world, but I chose you out of the world, therefore the world hates you" (John 15:19). Finally, contemporary Christians must not forget that God in time blessed the uncompromising behavior of the early Christians, as noted above with the positive changes that transpired after A.D. 313. Their behavior is an excellent model for faithful Christians to emulate today, even though the world makes such Christian behavior difficult, even as it did in the days of the Romans. May God bless all who seek to emulate their early Christian ancestors.

Notes

1. The Rev. Dr. Alvin J. Schmidt is professor emeritus of sociology at Illinois College, Jacksonville, Illinois. He holds an M.Div. from Concordia Theological Seminary and M.A. and Ph.D. degrees in sociology from the University of Nebraska.

2. Recently, Robert Kolb has argued that the English word *religion* is derived from the *religere* (to regard with awe), not *religare* (to bind together). However, he still says religion "indeed does function as that which binds together all aspects of life." See his "Nothing But Christ Crucified: The Autobiography of a Cross-Cultural Communicator," in *The Theology of the Cross for the 21st Century*, ed. Alberto L. Garcia and A. R. Victor Raj (St. Louis: Concordia, 2002), 53.

3. Jean–Jacques Rousseau, *The Social Contract or The Principles of Political Rights* (New York: G. P. Putnam's Sons, 1893), 206.

4. G. P. Grundy, *A History of the Greek and Roman World* (London: Methuen, 1925), 484.

5. Rousseau, *Social Contract*, 218.

6. Alexis de Tocqueville, *Democracy in America,* trans. Phillips Bradley (New York: Vintage Books, 1945), 1:319.

7. de Tocqueville, *Democracy in America*, 1:316.

8. Gail Gehrig, *American Civil Religion: An Assessment* (Storrs, Conn.: Society for the Scientific Study of Religion, 1979), 6.

9. See the essay in this book by Ken Schurb.

10. Robert Bellah, "Civil Religion in America," *Daedalus* (Winter 1967): 8.

11. This Latin phrase comes from Virgil's *Aeneid*, 9:625, which reads: "*Juppiter omnipotes, audacibus annue coeptis*" ("Almighty Jupiter favor [my] audacious undertakings"), according to Gaillard Hunt, *The Seal of the United States: How It Was Developed and Adopted* (Washington, D.C.: Department of State, [1892] 1909), 20–21. Regarding this wording, Richard S. Patterson and Richardson Dougall say that Charles Thomson (one of the committee members to design the Great Seal) "changed . . . *annue*, and imperative, to *annuit*, the third person singular form of the same verb in either the present tense of the perfect tense. In the motto *Annuit Coeptis* the subject of the verb must be supplied, and the translator must choose the tense. . . . " And they further say: "Hunt suggested that the missing subject was in effect the eye at the apex of the pyramid . . and translated the motto—in the present tense—as 'it (the Eye of Providence) is favorable to our undertakings.' " See Patterson and Dougall, *The Eagle and the Shield: A History of the Great Seal of the United States* (Washington, D. C.: Department of State, 1976), 89. Thus, the words *annuit coeptis* are commonly interpreted as God having favored the American undertaking, that is, the creation of a new nation, the United States of America.

12. Elihu Palmer, *Principles of Nature or A Development of the Moral Causes of Happiness and Misery among the Human Species* (New York: s. n., 1806), cited in Kerry S. Walters, *The American Deists: Voices of Reason and Dissent in the Early Republic* (Lawrence: University Press of Kansas, 1992), 4.

13. George Washington, "To Lieutenant Colonel John Laurens," in *The Writings of George Washington from the Original Manuscript Sources, 1745–1799,* ed. John C. Fitzpatrick (Washington, D.C.: United States Government Printing Office, 1937), 20:173.

14. George Washington, "The First Inaugural Address," in *Writings of George Washington*, 30:293.

15. Washington, "First Inaugural Address," 30:294.

16. Paul F. Boller, *George Washington and Religion* (Dallas: Southern Methodist University Press, 1963), 68.

17. Boller, *George Washington and Religion*, 76.

18. Douglas Knoop and G.P. Jones, *The Genesis of Freemasonry* (Manchester, England: Manchester University Press, 1949), 257.

19. Bernard Faÿ, *George Washington: Republican Aristocrat* (Boston: Houghton Mifflin, 1931), 64.

20. Philip Roth, *Freemasonry in the Formation of Our Government* (Washington, D.C.: Masonic Service Association, 1924), 7–8.

21. Alan Gowan, "Freemasonry and the Neoclassic Style in America," *Antiques* (1952): 172.

22. Benjamin Franklin, "Proposals Relating to the Education of Youth in Pennsylvania," in *Benjamin Franklin on Education*, ed. John Hardin Best (New York: Teachers College Press, 1962), 143.

23. *Editor's Note*: Washington was initiated into Freemasonry at the age of 20 on 4 November 1752 and elevated to the order of Master Mason in 1753. It often comes as a surprise to many people to learn that the Washington, D.C. metropolitan area actually has *two* Washington monuments. The government's 555-foot tribute to the first president is well-known, but just across the river in Alexandria, Virginia, there stands another tribute, the 333-foot George Washington Masonic National Memorial. This memorial, the only nationwide project of American Freemasonry, recognizes and honors Washington as the most important figure in American Freemasonry. His importance to contemporary Freemasons is summarized in this paragraph from a recent article in *The Messenger*, the newsletter of the George Washington Masonic National Memorial:

    We as Master Masons are even further compelled to honor and to emulate our dear departed Brother. The ideals of Masonry, which attracted him to the craft, had a profound impact on his life. His exposure to Masonic philosophy helped frame his ideas of life, both personal and professional. He took its teachings seriously, its apron and trowel, all its symbolism and ritual. Eventually he would become the best known and respected Mason in America. He would bring to the Fraternity unparalleled dignity and prestige. (James Parrish Hodges, "Washington and Freemasonry," *The Messenger* 9, no.1 [2003]: 4)

24. Philip A. Roth, *Masonry in the Formation of Our Government, 1761–1799* (Milwaukee: Masonic Service Bureau, 1927), 46.

25. John Adams, "Address: To the Grand Lodge of the Commonwealth of Massachusetts," in *Proceedings of the Most Worshipful Grand Lodge of Ancient and Accepted Masons of the Commonwealth of Massachusetts, 1798*, 134.

26. John Adams, quoted in Edward Stanwood, *A History of Presidential Elections* (Boston, 1888), 29.

27. P. L. Ford, ed., *The Writings of Thomas Jefferson* (New York: G.P. Putnam's Sons, 1892), 1:62.

28. John Coolidge, *The Pauline Renaissance in England: Puritanism and the Bible* (Oxford: Clarendon Press, 1970), 129.

29. Janice Knight, *Orthodoxies in Massachusetts: Rereading American Puritanism* (Cambridge: Harvard University Press, 1994), 110.

30. J. William T. Youngs, *The Congregationalists* (Westport, Conn.: Greenwood Press, 1990), 7.

31. Dieter Lührmann, "Faith," in *The Anchor Bible Dictionary*, ed. David Noel Freedman (New York: Doubleday, 1992), 2:751.

32. E. R. Dodds, *Pagan and Christian in an Age of Anxiety: Some Aspects of Religious Experience From Marcus Aurelius to Constantine* (Cambridge, England: Cambridge University Press, 1965), 121.

33. Scripture quotations in this essay are from the ESV.

34. Alvin J. Schmidt, *Under the Influence: How Christianity Transformed Civilization* (Grand Rapids: Zondervan, 2001), 25.

35. Keith Hopkins, *A World Full of Gods: The Strange Triumph of Christianity* (London: Penguin, 1999), 76.

36. Hopkins, *World Full of Gods*, 210.

8

The Church in the Public Square in a Pluralistic Society

DAVID L. ADAMS[1]

C ivil religion in America exerts a significant force on our national religious consciousness, yet historic Christian confessions in America have not paid sufficient attention to it. Church bodies (including The Lutheran Church—Missouri Synod) have consequently failed to recognize it as a key element of the cultural and spiritual context in which we operate, to our own detriment and the detriment of our ministries.

Drawing on my experience of having served from 1996 until 2000 as executive director of the LCMS Office of Government Information in Washington, D.C., and reflecting on the issues that I encountered in the process of working "in the public square" on behalf of the church, I offer here not so much a systematic treatment of the theological and sociological issues before the church, but rather a sort of "report from the front" on what the church can and must understand about its encounter with civil religion in contemporary American society. To put civil religion and its impact on the table for our consideration, I present this topic in the form of ten theses.

THESIS 1

American Civil Religion Is the State Religion of the United States of America.

If asked, most Americans would say that we have no state religion, even that the First Amendment of the federal Constitution prohibits it. While this statement may be technically, legally, and constitutionally correct, it ignores that fact that here in America we have developed a national religious ideology that performs every function for our society that a formally recognized state religion serves in other nations. Historically, state religions perform four such functions:

- to secure the blessings of God for the state and/or society;

- to contribute to the coherence of the society by establishing a fundamental aspect of the identity that connects the individual to the community;

- to provide the society with a unifying rallying point in times of national crisis; and

- to provide a least common denominator for the national ideological and moral discourse.

Of these four, American civil religion performs the first two only to a limited degree, and the second two rather more fully.[2]

Most basically, American civil religion supplies the "god" element of the traditional American trinity of "god, mother, and apple pie." As we saw powerfully demonstrated in September 2001, American civil religion serves the interests of the state most powerfully by providing our nation with a socially unifying rallying point in times of national crisis and a presumed least common denominator for our national social discourse.

American civil religion differs from other state religions in only two significant respects. First, it is not vested in an external institution. Second, it lacks a formal clergy, canon, and *corpus doctrinae*. In fact, each of these apparent shortcomings forms an *essential element* of our national religious faith.

Part of the genius of American civil religion is that it is not vested in an institution. Institutions provide definition and control. American civil religion operates not on institutional power but on consensus and social pressure, and it is all the more forceful as a result. Moreover, one may oppose institutions on the grounds of conscience. Opposing American civil religion somewhat resembles shadowboxing: You can take your best shot, but you can never quite make contact.

Similarly, the lack of a formal clergy, canon, and body of doctrine are essential elements of our national faith. The clergy of American civil religion are rather like the Old Testament judges. They are charismatic leaders (in our case, usually politicians or entertainers) who arise in time of national crisis and serve *pro tempore* before returning to their "day jobs" when the crisis is past. And just as the U. S. Constitution says whatever the nine justices of the Supreme Court say that it says at any given moment, so also the canons and doctrines of American civil religion are defined afresh moment by moment in the councils of our public consciousness: at one moment Christian, at another deistic, at yet another New Age personal spirituality. Civil religion is always becoming whatever it needs to be to maintain its function.

THESIS 2

American Civil Religion Is Now Irreducibly Polytheistic.

The great religion of the ancient world was that of the Sumerians. It provided the foundation of all that we think of today as ancient mythology. Moving westward from its roots in what is today southeastern Iran, Sumerian religion was borrowed and modified in turn by the Akkadians, the Babylonians, the Assyrians, the Arameans, the Canaanites, the Hittites, the Greeks, and the Romans.[3] The names of the gods changed and the details of the myths were modified over time, but the essentials remained the same. Moving eastward, Sumerian religion provided the ancient background for what eventually developed into Hinduism. Wherever it went in the ancient world, this religion spread through its chief operational principle: inclusion.[4] All the gods of all the nations were either incorporated into its pantheon or equated with one or another of the gods already there. Enlil becomes El becomes Zeus becomes Jupiter.

I am not suggesting that there is really a direct link between Sumerian religion and American civil religion. Yet they share a common material principle, the principle of *inclusion*. At various times and places in our past, American civil religion has been in turn Calvinistic, Anglican, Methodistic, or deistic. As America has become more culturally diverse and more *pluralistic*, American civil religion has in turn become increasingly *polytheistic*. Today and in the future, barring some tidal shift that would make America more culturally uniform, American civil religion is and will continue to be increasingly polytheistic to the point that we must recognize that the "god" in whom our money says we trust and to whom we appeal to "bless America" will be defined by each speaker and heard by each listener in his own way.

The principle of inclusion stands in stark contrast to the scandal of particularity that shapes the historic Christian confession. Historic Christianity, with its insistence that there is but one God and one way that a fallen humanity may be restored to God through Jesus Christ alone, is out of sync with American civil religion and will be increasingly so. We ignore this fact at the peril of our witness to the divine truth. Only the most utterly naive Christian can invoke *god* in the public square while assuming that everyone else means by that term precisely what we mean.

Indeed, we must go one step further and recognize that in American civil religion today the same is virtually true of the name *Jesus* also. At the risk of seeming impious, we must recognize that even the Doobie Brothers could confess that "Jesus is just alright with me." When we use the term *god* and the name *Jesus*, we invest those terms with all the proper biblical content. Those around us in the culture do not. We would be foolish to believe that we are giving a Christian witness just because we use the terms *god* and *Jesus* in an orthodox way. When speaking in the public square, we must explicitly express the particularity of the Gospel message in such a way that it continues to scandalize American civil religion.

THESIS 3

American Civil Religious Events
Bridge the Gap between Worship and Civic Events.

Much of the discussion about the participation of Christian clergy in events held in the public square that have a religious content proceeds from the frightfully simplistic presupposition that any given event can be characterized either as a *civic event* or as a heterodox or polydox[5] *worship service*. This facile distinction ignores the fact that these are not the only alternatives.

Between the worship service (which we recognize by the elements of invocation, confession and absolution, proclamation, celebration, intercession, and benediction) and the civic event (the inauguration of a president, the meeting of a school board, and so forth) there stands another kind of event, a *civil religious event*. The civil religious event is neither fish nor fowl, but in certain respects both fish and fowl. That is, it has some aspects of a worship service and other aspects of a civic event.

Perhaps it will be useful to compare these types of events on the basis of the following criteria: the community that participates in the event, the substance of the event (i.e., what actually takes place there), the goal of the event (i.e., the intention or expectation of either the organizers or the majority of the participants), and the realm into which the event belongs.

The Worship Service

We begin with what we know very well: the worship service.

	Worship Service
Community	Confessing body
Substance	Prayer, praise, adoration, etc.
Goal	Receive divine gifts, proclaim the Gospel, etc.
Realm	The church

Here the community of participants is primarily that of the confessing body, those engaged in worshiping a god or gods. In many instances, visitors or outsiders may be present along with the confessing body, but the boundaries of the primary community conducting the event remain clear.[6]

The substance comprising the event of religious worship includes such activities as prayer, praise, adoration, thanksgiving, and so forth. Lutherans would emphasize other elements as well, especially the reception of the Sacraments and the proclamation of the Word. While all of these elements comprise corporate worship among Christians, they need not all be present for there to be a worship service.

The intention or goal of the service is also important. For Christians, proclaiming God's Word and receiving and acknowledging His gifts are among the goals of worship. Particular services may or may not pursue all possible goals, however, and other goals may be more important in different religious traditions.

Finally, the realm to which the worship service belongs is that of the church. *Realm* is defined in terms of the traditional Lutheran understanding that God operates in two realms: The church, which has as its sphere the proclamation of the Gospel and the care of the spiritual life of Christians, and the civil authority, which has as its sphere the external life of man, the maintenance of good order, the preservation of life, and the protection of property.

The Civic Event

In addition to the worship service, we readily recognize the civic event.

	Worship Service	Civic Event
Community	Confessing body	The public
Substance	Prayer, praise, adoration, etc.	Public business
Goal	Receive divine gifts, proclaim the Gospel, etc.	Advancing the public good
Realm	The church	The state

The community engaged in the civic event is, at least potentially, the entire public of that community. Civic events are, by their nature, intended to engage the entire community. And while it is hardly ever the case that the entire populace is actually present at a civic event, even those physically absent are understood to be in some way included (morally or by representation) in the event.

The substance of the community event is the conduct of community business. This may be the coronation of a king or the inauguration of a president, or it may be the meeting of a parliament, town council, school board, or any other corporate community event (such as an athletic contest).

The goal of the civic event is the promotion of the community good. This goal is necessarily vague. Communities conceive of what constitutes their good in many different ways. The key here is that the goal of the event is self-referential. The event meets the needs of the community, however those needs are defined by the community itself.

Finally, the realm of the event is the state, not the church.

The Civil Religious Event

As long as these two realms, the church and the state, were related to each other through the mechanism of the established (or state) church, these two categories could help people sort through the issues that arose. By prohibiting the establishment of a national church, the U. S. Constitution has unwittingly introduced something new into this picture. While prohibiting the establishment of a legally favored church or state church, it cannot eliminate—indeed, it most certainly *has not* eliminated—the confluence of social and spiritual forces that give rise to state churches in the first place. To fill this void and provide for those socially and psychologically necessary roles of a unifying rallying point in times of national crisis and a presumed least common denominator for our national social discourse, American society has generated a form of civil religion. The outward public expression of this civil religion is an event that is part religious service and part civic event: the *civil religious event.*

	Worship Service	Civil Religious Event	Civic Event
Community	Confessing body	The public	The public
Substance	Prayer, praise, adoration, etc.	Discourse from, to, or about God	Public business
Goal	Receive divine gifts, proclaim the Gospel, etc.	Advancing the public good	Advancing the public good
Realm	The church	Civil religion	The state

Like the civic event, the civil religious event is aimed at the entire community. While in some communities the population may be predominantly Christian or even predominantly belong to a single denomination or church, still the event itself is consciously defined as an event for the entire community rather than for any particular religious group that is but a part of the whole.

The substance of the civil religious event is any form of discourse from, to, or about the gods. Such events are commonly promoted as memorial services, prayer services, or thanksgiving services. They often lack the more formal structure associated with traditional worship services and they may blend elements from a variety of religious traditions. American civil religious events are not, strictly speaking, worship services. Nor are they, strictly speaking, civic events. They are clearly *religious* events, however. They deal with the divine realm, even if from a civil perspective. Whenever people gather in the public square for the purpose of discourse with or about God or the gods, there is a *civil religious* event, not simply a civic event.

The goal of a civil religious event is to advance the community good, however that good is defined by the community. Most often the goal is to promote societal unity and/or cooperation in times of disaster, express a shared sympathy in time of loss, promote a corporate psychological or spiritual healing, or seek some community good from the gods. Such events are a part of the expression of American civil religion. In our society they perform the same function that public services of the state religion perform in other societies.

Determining the realm of the civil religious event is a bit difficult. It is not the church, properly speaking, for the event's community and goals are civic. Nor is the state the realm, properly speaking. The activities done at the event are essentially religious in nature, and they give the event an undeniable religious substance. Civil religious events force us to acknowledge an additional realm that is at the same time *civil* (or *civic*) and *religious*.

THESIS 4
American Civil Religious Events
Encompass a Spectrum of Activities.

This "third category" of event, the civil religious event, is not a monolithic category. It might be considered a waypoint on a spectrum of activities between civil events and worship services. More to the point, civil religious events contain a spectrum of activities, some of which are more religious and others more civil.

Indeed, all civil religious events operate on more than one level simultaneously. On one level they exist to serve the needs of the community, thus they are always *civil*. On another level they express the beliefs of the participants with regard to the existence and nature of god and the meaning of human life, and therefore they are always *religious*. The exact nature of the civil religious event can change dramatically both as the balance between these two aspects changes and as the religious content shifts from more homogeneous to more diverse (depending upon the religion of the organizers and participants within the community). This is evident when we examine the above criteria in greater detail.

The Community

With respect to the community engaged in these events, we must recognize "the public" that engages in a civil religious event is seldom coextensive with "the public" that engages in other civic events. We see this tendency at work even within civic events. For example, if we were to compare a school board meeting with a meeting of the local health authority, we would likely find that the school board meeting is quite likely to have a higher percentage of attendees with children in school than the health authority, for the parents of school-age children are generally more interested in the operation of the schools than those who do not have school-aged children. In the same way, in a civil religious event the members of a community who are concerned with spiritual life, their own and that of the community as a whole, are likely to be represented in higher percentages than they comprise in the general population.

Worship Service	Civil Religious Event	Civic Event
Confessing body	The public	The public

The more circumscribed and, especially, the more homogeneous the participating public in a civil religious event is, the more a civil religious event becomes like a worship service.

The Substance

Here, too, the breadth of the spectrum helps define the nature of the event. The greater the number of different elements common to worship services and the more prominent these elements are in the event, the less a civil religious event resembles a civic event and the more it becomes like a worship service. More specific activities can further shape the nature of the event. For example, the incorporation of a number of rites or ceremonies specifically associated with one particular religious group would move the event in the direction of being a worship service of a particular confession.

Worship Service	Civil Religious Event	Civic Event
Prayer, praise, adoration, etc.	Discourse from, to, or about God	Public business

The increasingly polytheistic nature of American civil religion has produced two tendencies. One tendency is for expressions and activities in civil religious services to be limited to some least common denominator that is thought to be inoffensive to all participants. In these cases participants are sometimes explicitly told that they are expected to restrict their expressions, but more often this expectation goes unexpressed because organizers assume that a general social principle of *tolerance* will make it obvious to everyone. For example, Christians are sometimes told that prayers in civil religious events should be offered to god, but not to the triune God, and not "in Jesus' name," for such expressions would be offensive to adherents of other religions. At other times this expectation is taken for granted, and it is assumed by the organizers that Christians will omit from their prayers any such scandalous notions.

The other tendency is to incorporate increasingly polydox practices. Although such practices may be unacceptable to one of the participating groups within the circles of their own religious belief and practice, they are expected to tolerate participation in them in civil religious events under the compelling social rubric of tolerance.

The Goal

As with community and substance, civil religious events reflect a range of possible goals, stretching between the strictly civic event and the worship service. Yet as in civic events, the *overall* goal of the civil religious event is to advance some community good.

Worship Service	Civil Religious Event	Civic Event
Receive divine gifts, proclaim the Gospel, etc.	Advancing the public good	Advancing the public good

Generally, the community good promoted by a civil religious event is defined in relation to one of the functions of a state religion: the securing of divine blessing, the promotion of civil unity, the provision of a unifying rallying point in times of national crisis, or the promotion of a least common denominator for the national ideological and moral discourse. These goals are expressly *civil* in nature, and it is inevitable that the state will use the religious expressions articulated within civil religious events to promote its own ends.

The Realm

In the past, faithful articulation of the teachings of the Scriptures and the Lutheran Confessions has obligated The Lutheran Church—Missouri Synod to define the criteria by which the Synod and its members may and should interact with the state, on one hand, and with other churches, on the other. In this the Synod has not been alone: other churches have adopted similar guidelines. However, the appreciation of the role of civil religion in contemporary American culture adds an additional layer of complexity to these issues, and forces the church to articulate an additional set of relationships, that with the realm of civil religion.

Worship Service	**Civil Religious Event**	**Civic Event**
The church	Civil religion	The state

Civil religion, and civil religious events, include a spectrum of possibilities. These range from the nearly civil or secular to the clearly religious and even ecclesiastical. In certain contexts civil religion may take on a more explicitly Christian, even Lutheran, form. In other contexts it may be more non-Christian, even aggressively anti-Christian.

Civil religious events thus constitute a spectrum that operates on more than one plane simultaneously: the plane of religious diversity and the plane that represents the spectrum between the strictly civic and strictly religious events. To evaluate such events, the church must think on two planes at the same time.

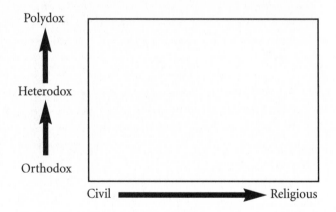

In this diagram, the horizontal axis represents the degree to which an event is religious in nature. The vertical axis represents the degree of religious diversity in the event.[7] The location of the event within the matrix thus created depends upon the relative position of the event on each of these axes. The point of origin in the matrix represents the point at which one scale makes the other irrelevant. If an event is purely civil, it does not matter how diverse the religious views of the participants. If the participants are entirely orthodox Lutherans, it does not matter how civil or religious the event. As one moves outward in either direction from the point of origin, the nature of the event changes and participation in the event becomes increasingly problematic for the pastor or church leader.

From the discussion thus far it should be manifest that the diverse, often conflicting, interests and agendas of those who organize and/or participate in civil religious events are likely to create problems for the pastor or church official who must evaluate whether or not to participate in them. Participation in civil religious events is likely to place the pastor or church official in a situation where he must either risk offending other participants or compromising his own confession. However, the wide range of possibilities within the spectrum of civil religious events makes it impossible to specify one simple answer that will suffice in every circumstance. In such an environment we may, however, provide some guidance for the pastor or church leader by indicating the kind of issues involved in making a decision whether or not to participate, depending on where the event falls in the matrix described above. We may also provide some boundaries beyond which one may not go without transgressing. The following theses attempt to provide such guidance.

Having established the existence and nature of the spectrum of activities that we might refer to under the rubric *civil religious event*, the question arises whether, and how, the church is to relate to such events. Before answering that question more fully, though, it is necessary to understand the need for the church to be engaged with the culture in which it is planted and the nature of the engagement to which the Gospel compels us. The next two theses address this issue.

THESIS 5

Both the Mission of the Church and the Obligation to Work for the Welfare of Our Neighbor Require the Church to Be Engaged with the Broader Society.

In sending the church into the world with the mission of making disciples, Jesus thrusts His people into an engagement with states and cultures "to the ends of the earth." To proclaim the Gospel to those who do not know the revelation of God in Jesus Christ, the church must be among unbelievers. To witness to truth in the midst of falsehood, the faithful must interact with misbelievers. The Great Commission obligates the church to be *in* the world without being *of* the world to witness *to* the world. The love of Christ for the lost compels us to seek out every opportunity to bear witness to the truth of God in Jesus Christ. Withdrawal into a safe corner can never be an option for the people of God.

Moreover, as Christians live in the world, we are compelled by both the positive implications of the commandments of the Second Table of the Law and the example of Christ to care for our neighbors in need. The church's engagement with the world can never be conceived of in such a way that separates witness to the Gospel from genuine care for those in need. The love of God in Christ constrains us to care both for our fellow Christians and for those who do not know Him, even those who would persecute Him and His people. This, too, drives us into engagement with society.

THESIS 6

The Limits and Form of the Church's Engagement with the World Are Shaped by the Mission Imperative and the Necessity of Faithfulness to the Teachings of God's Word.

Being sent by Christ into the world compels the church to be engaged with the societies within which it is planted. Yet this fact does not mean that engagement is an end in itself. For the church, engagement with society is always a means to serve a greater end: faithfulness in and to the Gospel. The church engages the surrounding culture to make disciples and live discipled lives. Its interaction with culture is thus shaped by its evangelical mission and by the call to be faithful, even unto death, to God's Word and to the way of the cross. Just as we err if we think that the "spiritual" mission of the church (i.e., the redemption of lost souls) relieves us of the need to interact with the culture in which we live and work, so we also err if we allow the desire to interact with the culture to become the driving force that shapes the church's activity and message.

Therefore, we understand the compulsion to engagement as a kind of general "policy statement." It does not mean that every Christian or pastor must engage with each aspect of society at every point. There are always limits to any general policy.[8] Our first obligation is to remain faithful to the teachings of Christ and His Word. The mission and ministry of the people of God compel our engagement with the world, but they also compel us to manage our engagement with the culture in ways that are consistent with our obligation to faithfulness. As a result, the church must manage its interaction with the culture in such a way that this interaction primarily serves, and does not conflict with, the mission of the church to make disciples for Christ, and secondarily serves the needs of society insofar as these do not conflict with the needs and mission of the church.[9]

In light of our obligation to faithful engagement, we consider principles to guide a pastor or church leader in determining whether or not to participate in a given civil religious event. This largely depends on the exact nature of the specific event. As noted above, such events vary on two scales at the same time, and thus they may differ widely from one another. In general, however, most events will fall into one of three major categories.

1. In certain communities and in some instances, a particular civil religious event may be little different in practice from a

Christian worship service involving members of a variety of churches within the community.

2. In other instances civil religious events may be polytheistic in nature, involving worship acts by a variety of religious groups directed toward the worship of different gods.

3. Still other civil religious events may be little more than public rallies with a thin coating of ill-defined religious veneer.

The next three theses explore principles for evaluating these three categories of events.

THESIS 7

To the Extent That a Civil Religious Event Is an Event Involving Christians of Different Confessions, Participation in the Event Must Be Governed by the Same Principles That Govern Our Interaction with Other Christian Church Bodies.

The Lutheran Church—Missouri Synod has adopted a biblical position on participation in heterodox religious activities that obligates its pastors and teachers, as a condition of membership in the Synod, to renounce unionism and syncretism of every description.[10] Where a civil religious event is most like a worship service involving Christians from different confessions, our participation in this event must be governed by this position. In addition to our conviction that this teaching is based on the clear Word of God,[11] we make this commitment on the basis of two important theological principles:

First, our commitment to the principle of Sola Scriptura *entails the view that the proclamation of the Gospel cannot stand on obscurity or intentional deception with regard to teaching.*

If we genuinely believe that God has revealed His teaching in His Word for the guidance of faith and life in His church, then we are obligated to seek to find that truth and, having found it, to live by it. At the same time Christ compels us to love and to work for the true unity of the church. But we cannot achieve the latter at the expense of the former. While we do understand that life in a fallen world has ragged edges and gray areas, we may neither take comfort in ambiguity nor seek it out as a cover for disagreement. To do so is to deceive ourselves and to lie to the world. God is not the father of such deeds.

Second, we believe on the basis of Scripture that coming together as a community to worship God and receive His gifts in the sacraments is the highest expression of the unity of Christian confession, not an instrument to be used to achieve such unity.

It is commonplace today, both within the liberal ecumenical movement and within more conservative evangelicalism, to treat worship as a means to achieve unity rather than as a fruit of unity. Such a view reflects an overly individualistic understanding of the relationship between the believer and the community of faith as it stands before God in worship. We believe that such an understanding is at odds with both the scriptural teaching and historic Christian practice regarding worship.

We further recognize that *perfect* unity may never be achievable in a fallen world and that confessing Lutherans have not required perfect agreement as a condition of joint worship. The question then arises, "Where do we draw the line? How much agreement is enough?" We have answered that question by assembling in the *Book of Concord* documents that we believe articulate appropriate boundaries for agreement before joint worship is appropriate.

We also recognize that Christians interact in many ways besides corporate worship. Many of those interactions do not employ ambiguity to compromise the truth and do not obligate us to confess a unity that does not exist in fact. Where it is possible for Christians to work together toward a common end without giving such false impressions we ought to do so.[12] To the extent that participation by church leaders and pastors in civil events does not employ ambiguity to disguise differences in teaching and does not create a situation in which participants or observers are likely to be led to believe in a false unity, such participation *may* be appropriate.

THESIS 8

To the Extent That a Civil Religious Event Involves Participants from Non-Christian Religions, Participation in the Event Must Be Shaped by the Requirements of God's First Commandment.

We recognized above that as the United States has become increasingly culturally diverse and pluralistic, its civil religion has become increasingly polytheistic. Because civil religious events are a fundamental expression of American civil religion, they have become increasingly *polydox* in nature. Insofar as such events involve participants engaged in worshiping different gods, the participation of the Christian pastor or church leader must be guided by the First Commandment.

Of course, a Christian who engages in the direct worship of a god other than Yahweh, whether in private devotions, in corporate worship, or in a civil religious event violates the First Commandment. Shadrach, Meshach, and Abednego understood this point clearly, as their refusal to worship the golden image in accordance with the king's commands indicates (Daniel 3). This is generally understood today in our Synod as well. If any Christian performs such an act, even in the context of a civil religious event, he is clearly violating the First Commandment.

It is a much more subtle question to ask whether a Christian who worships the true God in the context of those engaged in worshiping other gods also violates the First Commandment. In this respect we often fail to appreciate the full import of the First Commandment by translating the text (Exodus 20:3) as "You shall have no other gods *before* Me" (*emphasis added*).[13] The wording of the Hebrew text is rather more precise. God says that we must not have other gods "before My [i.e., His] face" or "in My [i.e., His] presence." The point here is that Yahweh is not claiming the right to be *first* in our affections (as "before" can easily be misunderstood to mean). He is prohibiting us from allowing any other god into His presence. Yahweh does not want to be our *first* god or to be first in our life; He must be our *only* god. The First Commandment is a demand for a radical and absolute exclusivity in our relationship with the realm of divine beings.[14]

We can see the effects of failing to keep this commandment by tolerating other gods in Yahweh's presence in the example of King Solomon, who was guilty of unfaithfulness in his relationship with Yahweh during the latter years of his life (1 Kings 11). He began to sin by tolerating the worship of other gods by his foreign wives. Over time, his wives influenced him so he turned away from Yahweh and worshiped the false gods. Solomon began by violating the First Commandment indirectly and ended by violating it directly. Indeed, the repeated judgment against the kings of Judah that followed Solomon was not that so many of them worshiped false gods themselves but that nearly all of them *tolerated* the worship of false gods by failing to tear down the high places, etc. Their toleration of the worship of other gods in the presence of Yahweh was itself a sin.

Today our American cultural conditioning toward tolerance flies in the face of God's demand for a radically exclusive relationship with us whenever that cultural conditioning leads us to tolerate the worship of false gods in the presence of Yahweh. As Americans we may (and do) have to tolerate the worship of other gods within civil society, but as Christians we violate the First Commandment any time we tolerate or encourage the worship of other gods in the presence of Yahweh.

The only possible conclusion upon reading the Word of God is that the people of God must not be a party to any activity that encourages or promotes the worship of other gods. Thus it *is* possible to sin against the First Commandment by tolerating the worship of other gods in the context of worshiping Yahweh.

The most common way in which we violate the First Commandment in this regard is to engage in the worship of Yahweh in the context of the worship of other gods in such a way that the worship of the false god and the worship of Yahweh may be confused or mixed. We recognize that a speaker cannot control the way that a hearer interprets his words. Nonetheless, in situations where it is likely that an audience, by virtue of its religiously diverse composition, may equate or confuse the worship of Yahweh with the worship of another god, the Christian speaker has an obligation to articulate the scandal of particularity with unremitting clarity. As civil religious events become increasingly polydox, the Christian pastor or church leader is obligated to do everything within his power to prevent those who may hear his words from thinking that the worship of Yahweh is the same as the worship of other gods.

In this respect it is not sufficient to begin with a statement such as, "We Christians believe that . . . " or any other form of words suggesting either that the speaker simply articulates the "Christian version" of religious truth or that there may be other equally valid non-Christian perspectives. This is the most common mistake made by Christian speakers talking about God in the public square. The assumption that Christian teaching is only one of many equally valid religious perspectives has become a common view among non-Christians in American society. We must therefore be especially careful to avoid this type of error. While it might seem on the surface to be an orthodox expression of faith, it can easily lead the hearer to a false conclusion.

In this context the distinction also arises between praying "with" some group and praying "among" its members. There is clearly a difference between these two. Praying "with" those who believe in other gods (i.e., joining with them as they pray to other gods) is, as we have said, a direct violation of the First Commandment. Praying to the true God in the midst of (i.e., "among") those praying to false gods *may or may not* be a violation of the First Commandment. Praying an otherwise orthodox prayer "among" believers in other gods can violate the First Commandment *if it is done in such a way that it confuses the worship of Yahweh with the worship of another god.* In other words, while the distinction between praying "with" and praying "among" people is useful, it cannot be determinative. The determining factor is whether the worship of Yahweh is confused or mixed with the worship of other gods.

Consider a parallel case from the Old Testament: Elijah at Mt. Carmel (1 Kings 18). Here *at a time of national crisis and within the confines of a single event,* the prophets of Baal pray to their god and Elijah prays to Yahweh. Elijah prays "among" the prophets of Baal. He does not sin in this instance because he does not allow the worship of Yahweh to be confused with the worship of Baal. Rather, he distinguishes the two by demonstrating that Yahweh alone is the true God and by praying for the defeat of Baal and his prophets.

The only certain way to avoid violating the First Commandment in a polydox civil religious event is to do as Elijah did: Distinguish clearly the worship of Yahweh from the worship of all other gods, and leave no reasonable room for doubt among the hearers that we proclaim that Yahweh alone is God, and that mankind can be restored to Him only by the death and resurrection of Yahweh incarnate, Jesus Christ. Any message that lacks this degree of clarity will likely give the impression that the worship of Yahweh and the worship of other gods amounts to the same thing.

As a practical matter, the Christian pastor or church leader is faced with one of three options when asked to participate in civil religious events in which the public worship of, or prayer to, other gods is involved: (1) Offend the others present by witnessing to the exclusive claims of Yahweh and the Christian faith; (2) offend God by participating in an event in which we bear false witness regarding who the true God is; or (3) decline to participate.

To summarize, then, in relation to polydox civil religious events we may violate the First Commandment in one of two ways: *directly* when we ourselves engage in the worship of other gods or *indirectly* when we allow the worship of Yahweh to be confused or mixed with the worship of other gods. At civic religious services, which are by nature increasingly polytheistic in the modern American context, the Christian pastor will always risk either offending his hearers (by proclaiming the scandal of particularity) or violating the First Commandment (through contributing by his lack of clarity to the confusion or mixture of the worship of Yahweh with the worship of other gods).

THESIS 9

To the Extent That a Civil Religious Event Is Primarily Civil in Nature, Participation in the Event Must Be Shaped by an Appreciation of the Tension between the Interests of the Church and of the State.

In addition to the kinds of civil religious events described in the two previous theses (events that are essentially or predominantly religious in nature, whether heterodox or polydox), there are other civil religious events that are predominantly *civil* in nature. While these have some religious content, that content is typically either so ambiguous as to be meaningless or so minor as to not give a false impression as to the degree of unity among people of faith or to confuse the worship of Yahweh with that of another god.[15]

When considering whether to participate in such an event, a Christian pastor or church leader still has to consider the extent to which he is being used by the civil realm to promote interests other than those of the Gospel. In the public square, everyone has an agenda. Those who organize civil religious events seldom do so for the sake of the Gospel or to advance the ministry of the church.[16] Such events are held to serve some civic need. This by itself does not necessarily preclude a Christian pastor or church leader from participating in them, unless the civic need conflicts with the need of the church.[17]

Furthermore, the Christian pastor or church leader needs to be particularly careful about participating in civic events (whether civil religious events or purely civic events) that would tend to identify the interests of the church with the interests of one particular political party or candidate. While it frequently happens that a party or a candidate promotes a policy that is more consistent with Christian teaching than that of another, any public expression of support for a political party or candidate is likely to be problematic. There are three reasons for this.

First, the United States tax code prohibits churches and other tax-exempt organizations from directly supporting candidates.

More important, politics is a hard business that frequently requires compromise. It sometimes happens that churches support candidates, parties, or (especially) legislation on the grounds that it reflects a Christian perspective on an issue only to find later that the situation, and hence the position of the party or candidate or the nature of the legislation, changes in an undesirable direction as the political process advances. Alternately, churches may support one party or candidate because of a stance on one particular issue only to find later that their stance on another issue conflicts with Christian teaching.

Most important of all, direct engagement in the political process by supporting (or giving the impression of support for) a candidate or party always runs the risk of politicizing the church, of distracting it from its primary mission, and of dividing the church over an issue that is not directly related to the Gospel.

Thus even though Christian pastors and church leaders may be free to participate in civic events and even perhaps civil religious events that are primarily civic in nature, they ought not do so without carefully examining the motivations and intentions of the organizers and other participants. Especially should they consider whether participating in the event would be likely to place them in compromising positions or run the risk of creating controversy in the church over an issue not directly related to the Gospel.

Our final thesis addresses the question of how we relate to one another when we disagree over whether it is appropriate to participate in a given civil religious event. Here we emphasize that each party has an obligation to the whole church and its mission.

THESIS 10

Sometimes It Is Necessary to Restrict Our Own Freedom as Christians for the Sake of Others, at Other Times to Forgive Those Who Err, and Sometimes to Do Both for the Sake of the Unity of the Church and the Mission of the Gospel.

Given the complex factors involved, Christians of sincere faith and good intention will from time to time disagree in their evaluation of these events. While there are some events in which a pastor or church leader may participate in good conscience, either because they are clearly civil in nature or because they involve only orthodox participation, there are also other events the pastor or church leader must avoid because of their polydox religious nature.[18] On the borders of these clear cases there will inevitably be disagreements.

But, as noted above, Christians should not take comfort in nor seek out ambiguity. Our belief in the objective truth of God's revealed Word compels us to seek the truth. Then, having found it, we make it the basis of our practice. At the same time, the recognition that difficult areas exist compels us to two other principles: the willing self-limitation of Christian freedom for the sake of the Gospel and the willingness in Christ to forgive those with whom we disagree.

Self-limitation is biblical. In Romans 14 and 1 Corinthians 8 the apostle Paul discusses the proper attitude of the Christian in situations where brothers disagree over how to apply the Word of God in difficult real-life issues.[19] In each instance he reaches the same conclusion: Those who believe that they are free to act more broadly are encouraged to restrict their freedom for the sake of the Gospel, the brother, and the church.

Applying this teaching to the question of participation in civil religious events, we can only conclude that when an event falls into a gray area, a pastor or church official would be well-advised to abstain from participating in the event if there is any significant likelihood that his participation would produce conflict or schism within the body of Christ. Our church body and others were formed to confess Christ with a single voice to the world while we work together to fulfill Christ's commission to go and make disciples to the ends of the earth. One can only justify endangering the Synod's unity in this mission when the alternative would be to compromise the Gospel itself. Thus our commitment to the common mission of the Synod and to one another as brothers in Christ should move us to exercise restraint even, and especially, when we believe that our case falls into one of life's gray areas. This is the mature, spiritual course of action to which God, through the apostle Paul, calls us.

These same motivations—our commitment to our common mission and to one another as brothers in Christ—should move us to be generous in forgiving one another when we believe that someone has erred in this regard. We must reprove and correct one another when we believe that our brother has erred (2 Timothy 4:2). Yet we must also reaffirm our love and forgiveness for our errant brother who repents (2 Corinthians 2:7–8).

Both our willingness to limit our freedom in Christ and our willingness to forgive our brother who errs ought to be rooted in the awareness that Satan uses divisions within the church to impede the preaching of Jesus Christ. Schism is a bad thing, not because we ought to try to get along with one another as a good social principle but because schism is almost always to Satan's advantage. As J. R. R. Tolkien once wrote in *The Lord of the Rings* (a line unfortunately omitted from the movie): "Indeed in nothing is the power of the Dark Lord more clearly shown than in the estrangement that divides all those who still oppose him."[20]

St. Paul says much the same thing—if with less poetic force, then with the added authority of the Holy Spirit:

> Anyone whom you forgive, I also forgive. What I have for-
> given, if I have forgiven anything, has been for your sake
> in the presence of Christ, so that we would not be outwit-
> ted by Satan; for we are not ignorant of his designs.
> (2 Corinthians 2:10–11)

CONCLUSION

The mission for which Christ sends His church into the world compels the church to engage the society in which we live and the various religions we find here. This engagement occurs both on the personal and corporate levels. As we live in mission in a pluralistic (and increasingly polytheistic) world, we must become savvy enough to recognize that not all religious activity around us will fall into the neat categories generated in the past. We must address these new developments with a zeal for right teaching and witness tempered by love for one another in Christ and genuine care for our neighbor.

Too often we have allowed language to divide us. I sometimes think that if John Gray were to write a book about our Synod he would name it *Evangelists Are from Venus, Confessionalists Are from Mars.* We sometimes speak and act in such a way that we give the impression among ourselves and to others that confessional faith-fulness and evangelical mission are mutually exclusive propositions and that we must choose one or the other to be confessional and put orthodoxy first or to be evangelical and put Jesus first.

As a corrective to this misrepresentation, we must always remember that Christ gave His church *one* mission: to make disci-ples to the ends of the earth. This disciple-making entails both the proclamation of the Gospel (i.e., baptizing them) and confession of the right teachings of God's Word (i.e., teaching them to obey all that Jesus commanded). If we are faithfully to fulfill our calling to be the church in the world, we cannot allow these two (evangelization and confession) to be depicted as if they were in conflict with each other. There is no fulfilling our mission without both. To be the church in the public square in a pluralistic and polytheistic culture, we must embrace both aspects of this one Christ-given mission.

Notes

1. The Rev. Dr. David L. Adams is associate professor of exegetical theology at Concordia Seminary, St. Louis, Missouri. He holds M. Div. and S.T.M.degrees from Concordia Seminary, and a Ph.D. in Old Testament theology from Cambridge University. This essay is a revised and edited version of an essay originally prepared and presented in an abbreviated form at a meeting of the Council of Presidents and the faculties of the two seminaries of The Lutheran Church—Missouri Synod on 1 March 2002. The full version of that essay was published under the same title in the *Concordia Journal* (October 2002): 364–90. The version printed here omits the first part of the full presentation, which treats aspects of the church's work in the public square that are less relevant to the discussion of civil religion.

2. When evangelical Christians frequently quote 2 Chronicles 7:14, they reflect the first of these goals, at least so far as they are concerned. But such a quotation probably does not reflect the common expectation within American civil religion generally. A clearer example of the first function of civil religion may be shown in the impulse to sing "God Bless America" in response to civil crises. The second of these functions has been somewhat displaced in American thought by the substitution of democracy for religion as the unifying ideology of our society.

3. The exact nature of the relationship between Mesopotamian (i.e., Sumerian) religion and that of ancient Egypt remains a matter of scholarly debate, but most experts in the field would at the very least acknowledge some measure of influence by Mesopotamian religion upon the development of Egyptian religion.

4. The two chief *theological principles* of Mesopotamian religion were (1) the continuity of the divine realm and the material realm; and (2) the circularity of time. These two fundamental theological elements appear in all of the progeny of the Mesopotamian faith. As it spread,

246

however, the chief operational principle of *inclusion* allowed Sumerian/Mesopotamian religion to embrace and incorporate the different religious ideas and local deities that it encountered within the various cultures with which it came into contact.

5. Throughout this essay the term *heterodox* is employed to refer to those activities that involve different confessions within visible Christendom (e.g., Lutherans, Catholics, and Baptists) worshiping together. The term *polydox* is used to refer to those activities that involve groupings of people (e.g., Christians, Muslims, and Hindus) worshiping a variety of gods together.

6. This fact should help us sort out our own worship issues. Too often today we are inclined to focus on outsiders or visitors as though they constituted the primary community of the event.

7. One could generalize this chart by placing the term *homogeneous* at the bottom of the scale and *heterogeneous* at the top of the scale. But religious diversity includes both diversity within the Christian faith and also diversity between Christianity and various religions. I have therefore employed a more specific standard of measure. Here, from the Lutheran perspective, *orthodox* specifically means in agreement with the Lutheran Confessions, and *heterodox* and *polydox* are used as previously defined.

8. For example, the general policy stated by the commandments in the Second Table of the Law is that Christians should do good to their neighbors. But the command to do good is not without limitation. We may not violate one commandment to fulfill another. The first ethical requirement is to do no evil and then to do as much good as possible without violating another commandment in the process. Otherwise the end of doing good would justify every means.

9. The church and the society in which it exists may share some common interests and needs, and so they may indeed become "fellow travelers" for a time. The Christian ethic of service to the neighbor will frequently engage individual believers, if not the whole church, in activities that serve the interests of society. In the United States, for example, Christian pastors regularly perform wedding ceremonies. On one hand, these ceremonies are worship services in which we give thanks to God for the blessings of marriage and pray His blessing upon the couple being joined in this divine institution. On the other hand, the pastor at the same time acts as a civil magistrate in performing an entirely civil function, that of certifying that the marriage relationship as established within the laws framed by the society and registering this civil act with the state according to its regulations. Pastors may perform this dual (ecclesiastical and civil) function with-

out compromise to faith because in this instance the need of the state to promote the common good of marriage in an orderly manner corresponds with the mission of the church to make disciples by nurturing families within God's order for human relationships. If these two interests were to come into conflict, as for example in the case of performing same-sex marriages, the Christian pastor would be obligated to refuse to function as an agent of the state in performing such acts and registering such relationships.

10. See Article VI of the Constitution of The Lutheran Church—Missouri Synod, which all members of the Synod (congregations, their pastors, and other rostered church workers) pledge to uphold (*Handbook of The Lutheran Church—Missouri Synod*, 2001 ed., [St. Louis: The Lutheran Church—Missouri Synod, 2001], 8).

11. It is not possible here to undertake an examination of the exegesis behind this position and the history of its development, nor am I attempting to do so. I here simply observe the fact that this *is* the position of the Synod and every pastor, congregation, and rostered church worker of the Synod has sworn an oath before God and the church to uphold this position, which prohibits not only the kind of unionism and syncretism current in the historical context in which the statement originated but also unionism and syncretism of every description.

12. Such activities are sometimes characterized in theology as "cooperation in externals" (*cooperatio in externis*). Here the term *externals* refers to those matters that do not entail the Gospel and its related articles.

13. Scripture quotations in this essay are from the ESV.

14. *Editor's Note*: For a fuller discussion of the significance of the First Commandment and the First Table of the Torah, see the essay "The Anonymous God" elsewhere in this volume.

15. The singing of "God Bless America" by an assembly might be an example that meets both of these criteria.

16. Indeed, for a government official or entity to organize a civil religious event for such purposes would likely be held by the courts to be an action in violation of the First Amendment.

17. As an example, a church or a group of pastors may be asked to participate in a rally in support of a blood drive. Although the blood drive does not promote the cause of the Gospel, encouraging people to give blood to help their neighbors is consistent with Christian teaching and should generally be encouraged. As this does not conflict with the mission of the church, one may participate without giving offense. By

contrast, consider a rally in support of marriage. If a pastor were to agree to participate without finding out who is sponsoring the event and who the other participants were, he might find himself on the podium with a gay or lesbian group promoting same-sex marriage. In this case, while marriage is a civic good that is consistent with the teachings of Christ, the union of same-sex couples in a form of marriage is not. In such a case the pastor might discover that he is being used to promote an issue or position that comes in to conflict with the mission of the church.

18. Unless, like Elijah on Mt. Carmel, he chose to participate by proclaiming the Gospel's scandal of particularity with such clarity and power that the other participants would clearly be offended.

19. Each of these cases involves the freedom of the Christian to enjoy God's good creation by eating meat when other Christians might be scandalized by his actions.

20. Haldir to the fellowship, in the chapter "Lothlorien" in *The Fellowship of the Ring*.

AFTERWORD

Quo Vadis?

DAVID L. ADAMS

As the essays that comprise this volume have demonstrated, the issues that face Christianity in our generation are not new. The church in every generation has faced the formidable task of communicating the message of Jesus Christ in a complex and changing cultural environment. From the time of the early church, through the Middle Ages and the Reformation, down to the establishment of new church structures in the new American republic, Christians have struggled, and not always successfully, with the problem of how to carry out the God-given task of making disciples *in* the world without becoming *of* the world. Our age may be different, but it is not fundamentally so.

We ought not pretend that this task is easy nor fear that it is impossible. God has given to His church all the tools necessary for this task and promised her His own presence. As Dr. Okamoto reminds us in his essay, God is God; His Word and His presence vouchsafe His final victory. God neither asks nor expects us to be victorious. He does not measure our success by the human standards of the numbers in our churches or the influence that we exert upon the civil order among those who reject Him. The measure of our success is simple to understand, even if it is sometimes a struggle to implement: the faithful confession of Christ.

The faithful confession of Christ includes not only talking about Jesus and telling others of His saving work but also of learning to live as His disciples. And this does present us with a challenge. Several years ago I was invited to deliver the The Martin and Regina Maehr Lecture at Concordia University, Seward, Nebraska, on the subject of the challenges facing the church in the world in the twenty-first century.[1] In that lecture I identifed two related challenges facing all churches in America, and The Lutheran Church—Missouri Synod in particular: the challenge to the church from within to cultivate its identity and maintain its theological integrity, and the challenge from without to remain engaged in the culture to which Christ has sent us without being absorbed by it. In that essay I suggested that to meet these challenges, Christians had to relearn what it means to live, in the words of the King James translation of Exodus 2:22 (and 18:3), as "strangers in a strange land."

This theme recurs time and again in the Bible, in Israel's experience of life in exile (cf. Psalm 137), in the prayer of Jesus as His earthly ministry was drawing to an end (cf. John 17), and in the apostolic church's understanding of the nature of Christian citizenship (cf. Hebrews 11). Nor was this sense of being "called out" lost on the early church, as Alvin Schmidt points out in his essay. The second-century *Epistle to Diognetus* puts it well:

> For Christians are not distinguished from the rest of mankind either in locality or in speech or in customs. For they dwell not somewhere in cities of their own, neither do they use some different language, nor practice an extraordinary kind of life. . . . But while they dwell in cities of Greeks and barbarians as the lot of each is cast, and follow the native customs in dress and food and the other arrange-

ments of life, yet the constitution of their own citizenship, which they set forth, is marvelous, and confessedly contradicts expectation. They dwell in their own countries, but only as sojourners; they bear their share in all things as citizens, and they endure all hardships as strangers. Every foreign country is a fatherland to them, and every fatherland is a foreign country.[2]

Perhaps it was easier in those first generations after Christ to live this way, in the immediate expectation of Christ's second coming. I don't know. I wasn't there, and I did not have to face the challenges that they faced. I do know that as the centuries have rolled on we have been tempted to lose sight of His imminent return and have taken to ourselves the words of the Hebrews in exile: "He has sent this message to us in Babylon: 'It will be a long time. Therefore build houses and settle down; plant gardens and eat what they produce'" (Jeremiah 29:28).[3]

There is a genuine tension here. On one hand God acknowledges that His people live in the world and their welfare is tied to the welfare of the lands to which He has sent them.[4] At the same time we are reminded never to loose sight of the fact that our ultimate citizenship lies in another land:

> Therefore prophesy and say to them: "This is what the Sovereign LORD says: O My people, I am going to open your graves and bring you up from them; I will bring you back to the land of Israel. Then you, My people, will know that I am the LORD, when I open your graves and bring you up from them. I will put My Spirit in you and you will live, and I will settle you in your own land. Then you will know that I the LORD have spoken, and I have done it, declares the LORD." (Ezekiel 37:12–14)

and:

> All these people were still living by faith when they died. They did not receive the things promised; they only saw them and welcomed them from a distance. And they

> admitted that they were aliens and strangers on earth. People who say such things show that they are looking for a country of their own. (Hebrews 11:13–14)

And so the life of the church in the world has an eschatological dimension that reflects the "now/not yet" nature of the unveiling of God's kingdom.

There is, of course, one major difference between the church and ancient Israel in this respect: We are not exiles here, expelled from the land for our sins and biding our time until our 70 years have passed. We are missionaries, sent out with the mission of making disciples in the name of Jesus. It is this difference that, in the end, shapes our understanding of what it means to be *in* the world but not *of* the world.

This same difference also shapes the world's response to our mission. If the Word of God is to be believed, we should expect to be met with hostility by those who will not receive Christ in faith. One morning a few years ago I was sitting in a conference room in one of the congressional office buildings in Washington D. C. Gathered for the breakfast meeting that day was a small group of half-a-dozen or so who were working to craft legislation that would make the U. S. government more responsive to the problem of religious persecution, especially the persecution of Christians, around the world. On this particular morning the group was listening to the concerns of a certain member of Congress who was not entirely sympathetic to their cause. The young female staff member who was representing the congressman at the meeting was saying that *really* the problem was caused by Christians themselves. If Christians in other countries would just be content to believe what they believed and would stop trying to persuade others to believe it, then they would not bring so much persecution upon themselves. She was, of course, quite right. Christians who live in cultures that are hostile to Christ and inimical to the proclamation of the message of Jesus *do* bring persecution upon themselves by their willingness, even their determination, to risk the hostility of the state or of the surrounding culture for the sake of the preaching of Christ. What she failed to understand, and what most people who stand outside of historic Christianity fail to understand, is that the impulse to confess Christ—to publicly proclaim that Jesus Christ is God, that His death and resurrection provide the only way for humanity to be reconciled to God, that we are to teach and to live in accordance with His teachings, and that we are to attempt to persuade others of these truths—is an intrinsic and fundamental part of the Christian faith. It is our mission. It is what we are here for. We cannot do otherwise. The very essence of the Christian faith compels Christians to bear witness to Christ and His teaching in every circumstance, regardless of the consequences. That is why Jesus said that it is inevitable that the world will persecute those who follow Him.[5]

The modern, especially Western, world simply does not understand this aspect of historic Christianity. Our age has become so imbued with the personalization and the internalization of religion that the confessional impulse of Christianity is for the most part incomprehensible to the modern mind. Modernity is, by its very nature, offended by what Christian theologians sometimes call the *scandal of particularity* and the exclusive claims of Christ and His followers. Modernity is, as Ken Schurb noted was the case with Sidney Mead, "scandalized by particularity," especially the particularity of the incarnation and of the cross. Modernity cannot understand why Christians are unable to be content to believe in their hearts whatever they choose to believe and to sit by silently while others do the same.

Confessing Christ and His teachings is what Christians do in the crucible of the world. This aspect of Christian discipleship inevitably brings Christians into conflict with non-Christians and with anti-Christians. In this conflict, the culture around us attempts to pressure the church to compromise in one or more of the following ways: to compromise on who God is,[6] to compromise on who Jesus is,[7] to compromise on what the Gospel is,[8] to compromise on what Jesus' teaching is,[9] or to compromise on the mission of the church.[10] How the church responds to this conflict, whether by maintaining a true and full confession of its faith or by giving in to compromise, is the measure of the faithfulness of the church in every age and in every culture.

In America at the beginning of the twenty-first century, civil religion is one instrument by which the world seeks our compromise. It asks us to accept this least common denominator, at least in our engagement in the public square, and offers us peace and toleration in exchange. And for the sake of peace and the approval of the public we are sometimes tempted to take this compromise, to cut corners, forgetting that every corner we cut changes the shape of our message.

As the preceeding essays have shown, the promotion of American civil religion by the broader society challenges certain aspects of biblical Christianity. It may be useful to conclude this volume with a brief summary of these challenges that confront every pastor and every Christian who takes seriously his missionary calling in our day.

CHALLENGE NO. 1:
CONFRONTING THE FALSE SENSE OF SECURITY

The chief spiritual danger of American civil religion is the sense of being right before God that it may promote among those who do not know Christ. Fallen man is always tempted to think that his condition before God is better than it actually is. Far from embracing the Word of God that convicts us of our sins, we avoid and neglect it. Civil religion, with its many outward expressions of piety, reinforces in the lost the sense that they are right before God by defining religion in terms of general morality and civic duty. For civic ends, it promotes the notion that those who do good deeds are rewarded by God and those who do bad deeds are punished by Him. This civil righteousness is at odds with the righteousness that comes by faith in Jesus Christ, for it regards Christ's salvation through Christ alone as unnecessary.

By constantly telling people that religion consists of a general and vague morality, civil religion undermines the preaching of God's Law and thereby undermines the preaching of the Gospel as well. It leads, as several of our essayists have reminded us, to a theology of glory and turns away from the theology of the cross. For preachers, the temptation is to give way to this cultural pressure and reduce the Gospel to what Dietrich Bonhoeffer called *cheap grace*, which he defined as the "forgiveness of sins proclaimed as a general truth, the love of God taught as the Christian 'conception' of God."[11] Such a gospel, disconnected from the Law and proclaimed to those who have not repented, is no gospel at all. "Cheap grace is the grace we bestow on ourselves," Bonhoeffer wrote.[12] Had he been writing of civil religion, he might have said that cheap grace is the grace that society bestows upon us for being decent citizens. It is this false grace, this false sense that we are right before God because we are generally good citizens and good people that biblical Christianity must constantly confront in civil religion. The only way to confront it is through a genuine and authentic preaching of the Law with its call for true repentance.

CHALLENGE NO. 2:
AFFIRMING THE SCANDAL OF PARTICULARITY

The biblical faith affirms the existence of one God and one God alone, who has revealed His name to His people and teaches them to call upon Him by name. Moreover, this one true God has become man in Jesus Christ, who died, was buried, and rose from the dead to become the only way that God has provided for fallen humanity to be saved from eternal death and damnation. This biblical claim to the uniqueness of the true God and the specific ways in which He has worked within history to accomplish our salvation theologians sometimes call the "scandal of particularity." This scandal of particularity is an offense to American civil religion, for the claim that there is only one God, only one way to be reconciled to God, and only one true divine teaching is the essence of the intolerance that Rousseau feared and American civil religion reviles. Yet without it there is no Christianity.

It is the nature of god-talk in civil religion to use words in such a way as to cover over differences between religious teachings for the sake of civic harmony. In civil religion "god" is just the spirit-being and "Jesus" just an especially honored moral teacher. The Christian pastor cannot be a party to the civil promotion of the anonymous God. If we were to use language in such a way as to allow the true God to be confused or identified with other gods, or Jesus to be regarded as simply a moral teacher, we would be breaking the First and Second Commandments and denying Christ as surely as if we were to do so directly and openly. Thus it is incumbent upon us, when we speak in the public square, not to use the term "god" or even the name "Jesus" in such a way that our hearers may easily construe those terms according to their own framework of belief. Instead, we are to fill out our use of those words with the proper biblical confession of who the true God is and what He has done in Jesus Christ.

CHALLENGE NO. 3:
NOT CONFUSING THE KINGDOMS

God has given the church and the state distinctive roles and means. Because it uses religion for the ends of the state, civil religion tends to blur those God-given distinctions in such a way that the state takes on some roles proper to the church and the church may be in danger of becoming an adjunct to the state. American civil religion, with its teaching of manifest destiny, is especially prone to encouraging the blurring of these distinctions. In American churches, where faithful Christians are rightly reminded of God's teaching that we should be good and faithful citizens by the placing of an American flag in the sanctuary, there is a real danger of crossing over this line, especially in times of national crisis.

Pastors should take regular opportunities to promote Christian discipleship by teaching the balanced biblical understanding of the relationship between the church and the state. We should remind Christians of their God-given calling to be good and faithful citizens, to honor our nation, and to pray "for kings and all those in authority, that we may live peaceful and quiet lives in all godliness and holiness" (1 Timothy 2:2). At the same time we must constantly remember that, like the saints described in Hebrews 11, we are citizens of a "city with foundations, whose architect and builder is God" (Hebrews 11:10), who are "longing for a better country—a heavenly one" (Hebrews 11:16).

CHALLENGE NO. 4: UNDERSTANDING THAT CIVIL RELIGION IS NOT ENTIRELY BAD

Despite the challenges described above, civil religion plays a useful and important role in our nation. In the civil sphere it does promote good citizenship and harmony in society. Our quite proper wariness of the dangers of substituting civil righteousness for the righteousness that comes only by grace through faith in Jesus Christ can sometimes blind us to the fact that civil righteousness is a good thing *per se*. Civil religion promotes civil righteousness, and we should welcome that, even while recognizing that civil righteousness does nothing for the soul before God. The valuable social functions of civil religion, by which it contributes to the common good of our land, should not go unrecognized by us.

Beyond that, civil religion can serve the interests of the church as well, even if to a limited degree. It serves the interest of the church when it creates a space in the public square for religious discourse to occur in a way that does not violate the First Amendment of our nation's Constitution. It would be a harmful thing, to us and to society, if all religious speech were banned from the public arena. Civil religion keeps religious issues and religious language before the public. Civil religion also serves the interest of the church by promoting religious freedom, a fact that C. F. W. Walther understood and appreciated, as Cameron MacKenzie's essay reminds us. Finally, even though the god-talk of civil religion does not take a form that Christians can accept, it does provide an opportunity for us to engage others and teach the truth about God and the Gospel of Jesus Christ, much like the altar to the unknown god on the Areopagus in Athens created an opportunity for the apostle Paul to witness to Christ (Acts 17:16ff.). David Liefeld's essay on Athenagoras demonstrated how the Christian apologists of the second century employed the language of their culture to reach out with the Gospel. The civil religion of our day offers us the same opportunity.

Thus while we cannot accept American civil religion as a substitute for orthodox Christian teaching, and we must always be wary of the challenges and temptations to compromise what it presents, we ought not dismiss it as a wholly undesirable thing with no merit whatsoever. It often opens a door for our witness. It is for us to take advantage of the opportunity civil religion presents by proclaiming the full and authentic Gospel of Jesus Christ. When we fail to do so, that failure is ours; it is not the failure of civil religion.

CHALLENGE NO. 5:
MAINTAINING ENGAGEMENT

In the face of the challenges that civil religion poses to biblical Christianity, and in view of the warning that God gave through the apostle Paul that in the last days there would come those who had a "form of piety, but denying its power" and cautioning the faithful to "have nothing to do with these" (2 Timothy 3:5), one might be tempted to withdraw from engagement with the broader culture altogether. This would be a great error. Paul's concern in writing to

Timothy was the danger that the outward appearance of piety might deceive and mislead the faithful (2 Timothy 3:6ff.). The proper form in which "having nothing to do with these" should take is not withdrawal from the world (a course that neither Paul nor the other apostles ever advocated), but an aware and faithful engagement with the world on the basis of the authentic teachings of God's Word.

In sending the church into the world with the mission of making disciples, Jesus thrusts His people into an engagement with cultures and states "to the ends of the earth." In this engagement the church must remain aware that the state will attempt to use it for its own purposes, as Ron Feuerhahn's essay reminds us. Our fear of being used by the world can never become the excuse for our withdrawal from engagement with the world. To proclaim the Gospel to those who do not know the revelation of God in Jesus Christ, the church must be among unbelievers. As I said earlier in one of the essays that make up this volume, the Great Commission obligates the church to be *in* the world without becoming *of* the world to witness *to* the world. The love of Christ for the lost compels us aggressively to seek out every opportunity to bear witness to the truth of God in Jesus Christ. Withdrawal into a safe corner can never be an option for the people of God. What we seek and what we must not compromise is *faithful engagement,* an engagement with the lost and with our society that does not compromise the true and entire teaching of God in His Word but boldly proclaims the whole Gospel in our culture and in every culture to the ends of the earth.

Notes

1. The lecture was delivered on 24 January 2001.

2. *Epistle to Diognetus* 5:1–5.

3. Scripture passages in this essay are taken from the NIV.

4. "This is what the LORD Almighty, the God of Israel, says to all those I carried into exile from Jerusalem to Babylon: 'Build houses and settle down; plant gardens and eat what they produce. Marry and have sons

and daughters; find wives for your sons and give your daughters in marriage, so that they too may have sons and daughters. Increase in number there; do not decrease. Also, seek the peace and prosperity of the city to which I have carried you into exile. Pray to the LORD for it, because if it prospers, you too will prosper' " (Jeremiah 29:4–7).

5. Cf. Matthew 5:11; 23:34; John 15:20.

6. Most often this compromise comes in the form of a willingness on the part of Christians to avoid the public declaration that the God who has revealed Himself in the Old and New Testaments is the only true God.

7. Despite its discomfort with biblical morality, the world would rather have Christians reduce Jesus to just another good moral teacher than hear Him declared to be the only way that a lost humanity can be reconciled to God.

8. Closely connected to the previous point, the world would prefer that Christians emphasize a "gospel" of moral reformation than proclaim the true Gospel of redemption in Jesus Christ alone. The reason for this is that a world that rejects the grace of God in Jesus Christ can still find a kind of comfort in substituting its own civil righteousness (or for that matter, the morality promoted by other religions) for a gospel–as–morality message. When Christians allow the Gospel to be reduced to a morality, they not only deny the import of Christ's redemptive death and resurrection, but also play into the hands of the world by reducing the Christian message to the level of just one of many moral systems. By contrast, the true Gospel leaves the world no "wiggle room." The call to true repentance and to faith in the redeeming death and resurrection of the God-man Jesus Christ as the sole way to be reconciled to God allows the world no easy alternative. This is one reason why the world always prefers to hear the message of the Law and despises the message of the Gospel.

9. The world would have the church compromise on two general aspects of Jesus' teaching. First, it would like us to cease claiming that the Word of God teaches absolute and objective truths in favor of an emphasis on relationships and personal spiritual growth and development The latter can be more easily accomodated with other religions, while the former are a part of Christianity's scandal of particularity. Second, however much the world prefers to hear the message of the Law over the message of the Gospel (see previous note), it nonetheless rejects the absolute moral claims of the Word of God. While any truth-claim of the Bible could become the basis of a conflict with the broader society, such conflicts tend to arise over Christian moral claims, as over slavery in the nineteenth century and the

ongoing conflict over such issues as abortion and homosexuality in our own day illustrate.

10. As the earlier anecdote about the attitude of the congressional staff member toward Christian persecution illustrates, the world would prefer that Christians be content to hold their faith as a private, inner matter and give up the missionary task for which God sent the church into the world.

11. Dietrich Bonhoeffer, *The Cost of Discipleship*, trans. R. H. Fuller (New York: Macmillan, 1963), 45.

12. Bonhoeffer, *Cost of Discipleship*, 47.

APPENDIX

Two-Kingdom Theology, Civil Righteousness, and Civil Religion

MARK E. SELL [1]

A s our country finds herself engaged in a war against terrorism, the phrase "God Bless America" echoes throughout American society. Each of us tends to react somewhat emotionally to the phrase. We want God to bless our country. However, as Christians we need to step back and think about the "god" addressed by this phrase. Who is this "god" whose blessings we desire for America? How are these blessings brought about? Moreover, how does a Christian participate in the community and support it, while at the same time remaining faithful to the confession of the Christian faith?

This essay will address these questions through Luther's theology of God's governance in two realms, often called "two-kingdom" theology. First, it introduces the basic tenets of this theology and identifies the importance of civil righteousness for the Christian. Then it explains why grasping this theology aids us in understanding the Christian life. Finally, the Christian life in two kingdoms will be related to American civil religion.

GOD'S GOVERNANCE IN TWO REALMS

"Two-kingdom" theology is a most helpful teaching. It explains the relationship between Sunday morning and the rest of the week.[2] It helps Christians live out our daily callings (vocations). It speaks to the professional church worker, businessperson, factory worker, or farmer; to a mother or father, a son or daughter. In short, it speaks to all the positions to which the Lord has called His people.

Two-kingdom theology makes Christianity "practical." It touches the daily life of every believer. It is the medicine that cures moralism, yet it identifies the high place of morals in daily Christian life. Two-kingdom theology frees Christians to live in society and become servants to everyone. It frees us to engage fully in our communities as good citizens. Because of two-kingdom theology, we can recognize others, even non-Christians, as good citizens with whom we engage in society. Two-kingdom theology provides the order and justice for which a chaotic world longs, and at the same time it provides the forgiveness and life won by Christ. It helps us understand the yearning for a community to be religious, yet it permits the Christian to be faithful to the one true God.

Two-kingdom theology distinguishes between the realms. Although both of them are given by God and ruled by Him, they are characterized by different purposes, different tools, and different realities. While distinct, the two kingdoms depend on each other.[3] In fact, the wisdom of two-kingdom theology lies in the *distinction* and *dependence* of the two kingdoms. Two-kingdom theology does not confuse order with salvation. It permits civil leadership and patriotism to reign in the sphere of civil order and just government, while it teaches that there is an eternally just God who rules in His church through the submissive Lamb of God sacrificed for human salvation. God and His actions are hidden in our everyday created life in both kingdoms.

GOD'S LEFT-HAND RULE

Biblical Foundation

The primary purpose and function of the kingdom of the left is *civil justice* and *order*. Its secondary purpose and function is compassion and grace, though not in the sense of Christ's forgiveness. In this realm there is more concern with daily kindness, mercy, and service to one's neighbor—or as Lutherans put it, civil righteousness (*iustitia civilis*).[4] See Romans 13:1–7:

> Let every person be subject to the governing authorities. For there is no authority except from God, and those that exist have been instituted by God. Therefore whoever resists the authorities resists what God has appointed, and those who resist will incur judgment. For rulers are not a terror to good conduct, but to bad. Would you have no fear of the one who is in authority? Then do what is good, and you will receive his approval, for he is God's servant for your good. But if you do wrong, be afraid, for he does not bear the sword in vain. For he is the servant of God, an avenger who carries out God's wrath on the wrongdoer. Therefore one must be in subjection, not only to avoid God's wrath but also for the sake of conscience. For the same reason you also pay taxes, for the authorities are ministers of God, attending to this very thing. Pay to all what is owed to them: taxes to whom taxes are owed, revenue to whom revenue is owed, respect to whom respect is owed, honor to whom honor is owed.[5]

Also see Romans 2:14: "For when Gentiles, who do not have the law, by nature do what the law requires, they are a law to themselves, even though they do not have the law."

Everything in this life begins with what God gives. God gives rulers their authority as His ministers or servants (Romans 13:4). Rulers are to bring order and civil peace to society and protect temporal life. Their primary tool in this endeavor is reason, especially as it is manifested in civil law. They do not make use of God's Word as such.[6] When well-reasoned laws are disobeyed, force is employed to maintain order and societal peace. In the sphere of the kingdom of the left, civil righteousness (morality) is the measure of good citizenship. In the kingdom of the left, those in authority keep track of good works as an evaluation of civil righteousness. The kingdom of the left is responsible for rewarding good and punishing evil.[7] It enables the continuance of life in an orderly society.

God works in the kingdom of the left differently from the way He works in the kingdom of the right. In the kingdom of the left, people live with the lesser of two evils for the purpose of order. The goal is to make society decent and good and just for all people, not to make the society Christian. Trying to do so would confuse the message of God's Word. Efforts to "Christianize" society flow from Reformed theology and its cousins, which promote a "one-kingdom" theology that attempts to treat church and state as the same thing. Such efforts lead to theocracy. But a theocracy should not be the desire of Christians.[8] To turn society into a theocracy is as wrong for Christians who desire to "Christianize" the laws of the land and vote only for Christians as it would be for Muslims who seek to govern the community by the Qur'an as interpreted by Muslim clerics. Both are contrary to God's Word and bring injustice to the community.

Justice and order in civil society are important for its own sake but most especially for the sake of the church. Here is where it becomes clear that the two kingdoms depend on each other. The church needs order and civility to be free to proclaim the Gospel.

Here we realize that "the whole 'Left Hand' kingdom is but a vast scaffolding for God's ultimate purpose: the eternal salvation of His church."[9]

The Kingdom of the Left in Luther's Small Catechism

In the Small Catechism the kingdom of the left is founded in creation, which is discussed in the First Article of the Apostles' Creed. The kingdom of the left forms the daily environment for actions governed by the Fourth Commandment.[10] God created all things, including humanity. Humanity and the earth require order to function. All earthly authority flows through those who are second in authority only to God, namely, parents.[11] God calls parents into service to populate the earth. From our parents, we as Christians learn that all good gifts come from our heavenly Father through the means of creation. Parents are to teach children to use these gifts of creation wisely and to God's glory. Our parents teach us the two tables of the Law and how we are to live them. They exemplify ways we are to love our neighbor as we love ourselves.

God governs the world and the universe through power. His power is vested in the means of creation. He gives parents power and authority to rule the earth. Thus civil authority flows from parents. For example, teachers teach on their behalf: "Where a father is unable by himself to bring up his child, he calls upon a schoolmaster to teach him. . . . Thus all who are called masters stand in the place of parents and derive from them their power and authority to govern."[12] Therefore, police officers, rulers, executioners, and soldiers all carry out their functions in society because God has given parents the authority to maintain order, justice, and peace in society. Parents cannot do everything, so they assign the government, teachers, the police, and the military various tasks of ordering society.

In service to the Gospel, the church also uses the unbreakable relationship between parents and an orderly society. Congregations maintain order in Bible studies, Sunday schools, meetings, and the Divine Service. The realities of creation as explained in the First Article allow people to accomplish their tasks inside and outside the church. However, the church uses the power of the kingdom of the left to support her real purpose—proclaiming Law and Gospel, the former to identify sin and the latter to forgive it.

GOD'S RIGHT-HAND RULE

Biblical Foundation

Simply stated, the kingdom of the right is the church.[13] Christ is its Head. This kingdom is discussed in Ephesians 1:22ff.; Romans 8:9ff.; Colossians 1:13; and Ephesians 4:4–6.[14] The primary purpose and function of the kingdom of the right is eternal salvation through the proclamation of sin and grace. Civil justice and order as it affects believers and teaches them to love their neighbor only comes into the picture as a secondary function within the kingdom of the right.

Christ does not rule the right-hand kingdom through power but instead through humility, servitude, and faith created through the means of grace. Correspondingly, the church's power follows the fashion of Jesus' incarnation and subsequent humility. It lies in the hidden glory of the cross—of human words, of water, of bread and wine, all bearing the creative Word of God. God is present everywhere, of course, but only in His power. That is, God's general presence is Law, not Gospel. God is present on earth *for the Gospel's sake* only in the means of grace, which are the right-hand kingdom's only marks. This kingdom is manifested only as the Word of God is properly proclaimed and the sacraments faithfully offered. Through these means of grace come forgiveness, mercy, and Christ's saving presence.

In the kingdom of the right, God's Law exposes sin (*lex semper accusat*) so it may be forgiven. Here sin is sin. There is no place for the "lesser of two evils." Spiritual righteousness is needed, not civil righteousness. Any claim of personal morality, goodness, or "becoming a better Christian" propels the claimant to hell. Punishment for any evil is total and complete. Believers do not find justice by becoming "better" or "more mature" Christians. Eternal justice (justification) is found in Jesus' forsaken punishment for all the world's sin.

Good works are not motivated by force in the kingdom of the right. Christians do them voluntarily. Their "weapon" is the Word of God and sacrificial love for their neighbors, whether or not these neighbors are Christian. The only justice that counts is that of the Father, who brought His wrath to bear on Christ, then declared sinners justified by grace on account of Christ's work for us. The church stands or falls on this justifying verdict. Thus people can participate in the kingdom of the right only by faith.

As faith grows and matures, it trusts all the more in what it has already been given in Baptism. Faith itself is God's gift through the means of grace. It does not result from a believer doing "more" to fulfill God's Law. We can improve in our vocations, yet such improvements are a matter of the left-hand kingdom, not the right-hand kingdom. The Christian improves in civil righteousness. The more we Christians understand God's Law, however, the worse we see that we are when judged by absolute standards of spiritual righteousness. Therefore, we rejoice to be clothed in the righteousness of Christ.

In the kingdom of the right there is no respect of persons. Everyone is knit together as one in the mystical body of Christ. The kingdom of the right is where God works His ultimate purpose (*opus proprium*). Second, the kingdom of the right makes use of creation in an orderly fashion to reflect the will of God for salvation. Overall, though, the church is not to create the civil realm in her image any more than the civil kingdom is to create the church in its image.

The Kingdom of the Right in Luther's Small Catechism

The Small Catechism's teaching on the church may be found especially in the explanation to the Second and Third Articles of the Apostles' Creed. In the Second Article we confess the work of Christ for salvation. The Third Article focuses on the work of the Holy Spirit, who calls, gathers, enlightens, and sanctifies the church through the work of Christ confessed in the Second Article. Sanctified or baptized reason employs the "First Article" gifts as means to love the neighbor.

DISTINCT AND DEPENDENT

Although it may seem that within its own realm neither of the two kingdoms needs the other, this is not so.[15] The kingdom of the right benefits from societal order when it preaches the Gospel and administers the sacraments.[16] The kingdom of the left depends on the goodness that only God's Word can create in the hearts of believers who will go the extra mile, live a holy life, and bring repentance and mercy into the world. Each of the two kingdoms thus depends on gifts that the other brings into this world.

Yet neither kingdom can function well in the other's sphere. In the category of civil righteousness, an unbeliever can be "good"—a good parent, a good governor, a good police officer, a good soldier, and so on. However, none of this makes the unbeliever good in God's sight. His "good" reputation might even make him blind and presumptuous before God. Likewise, the kingdom of the right does not possess the resources to bring outward peace to the world. (See Matthew 10:34!) Order cannot be maintained in the kingdom of the left by governments lavishing forgiveness upon lawbreakers. Chaos would result. Rather, when the kingdom of the right preaches the Word, hearers grow to love and respect authority as God's gift. The kingdom of the right *uses* order. The kingdom of the left *needs* forgiveness.

THE CHRISTIAN LIFE IN THE TWO REALMS

Vocation

The two kingdoms come together in daily Christian life via vocation. Vocation has been called the "spirituality of ordinary life."[17] God functions in daily life through means.

What is important is that *God* is doing the work in vocation. He rules the whole world through vocation.[18] When someone asks, "Where is God when I'm sick?" Lutherans answer: "He is working in the doctor who diagnosed you, the pharmacist who dispensed your medication, and the auto worker who built the car to drive you to the pharmacy." Of course, the list could go on and on, but the point is clear. God provides through many vocations. In the Lord's Prayer we pray, "Give us this day our daily bread." God answers this prayer and gives daily bread through countless vocations in this life. It all begins with mother and father as we understand our relationship with our heavenly Father.

He is our dear Father who has forgiven us and now looks out for us. In *Our Calling*, Einar Billing wrote about vocation as it flows through the forgiveness of sins. Billing indicated that Luther understood a Christian's calling primarily as a gift, and only in the second or third place as a duty.[19] Billing also wrote:

> When I look out over the path guarded by providential acts which "God's fatherly goodness" has prepared for me, I see by the side of the gift of the forgiveness of sins also another gift, the call assigned me. So it still remains more correct to say, as we just stated it, very briefly thus: the call is the forgiveness of sins. Or, more specifically expressed: my call is the form my life takes according as God Himself organizes it for me through His forgiven grace. Life organized around the forgiveness of sins, that is Luther's idea of the call.[20]

Because all callings come to Christians as forgiven sinners, none is higher or lower before God than another. Sometimes the call to be a pastor is misunderstood as somehow more special than other callings. However, the call to be a pastor is no "holier" than God's call to be a parent, an architect, an engineer, a soldier, or a student—all are vocations.[21] The various positions or stations in life are different and distinct. God created each office for service in the appropriate realm. The call to be a Lutheran day school teacher and the call to be a pastor are no better, no closer to God, than the call for a Christian to be a mother or a doctor. The offices are different and are derived from different sources for different purposes; however, they intersect when the teacher teaches theology on behalf of the pastor or the pastor does so on behalf of the parent.

In the first three commandments Christians understand who God is. Hearing the Word of the God, who is our all in all, and calling upon His name, we receive by faith what He has done for us in Christ. This leads us into life with our neighbor in the Second Table. Here no commandment is more basic than the fourth. From it flow commandments five through ten.

Thus Christians move from a forgiven relationship with God in the kingdom of the right into the variety of opportunities for service to the neighbor in the kingdom of the left.[22] In our daily lives the two kingdoms overlap and interpenetrate each other. While distinct, they are never completely separate. Therefore, we understand life in a twofold manner, according to spiritual righteousness and according to civil righteousness. Just as all things in both kingdoms, these are judged differently.

SPIRITUAL AND CIVIL RIGHTEOUSNESS FOR THE CHRISTIAN

Christians sometimes misuse vocations within the church when they start looking for "practical" answers for life situations. Answers can be lifted from pop psychology, with little or no connection to God's Word except a veneer of biblical-sounding language. In their worst forms, these answers twist God's Word, inviting people to feel good about doing "what God wants them to do." Such answers may take the form of "six easy steps to being a better Christian" or "Christian leadership in the Bible." In the case of war, for example, it is tempting to say: "We will fight a Christian war" or "I will pray about going to war and wait for God to lead me into what to do." Slapping a Christian veneer atop the subject of war, however, is not the answer. It loses sight of the two kingdoms.

Ironically, this temptation to be biblically shallow holds particular allure where the Bible is regarded highly as God's Word. The temptation often results in a biblicism that is not Lutheran but rather Reformed. This biblicism can on one hand denigrate legitimate "left-hand" disciplines such as psychology, sociology, medicine, technology, and so on. On the other hand, it can exalt them so they rule God's Word. The answer to this confusion is to understand the difference between spiritual righteousness and civil righteousness.[23]

Our spiritual righteousness (in the kingdom of the right) is totally dependent upon Christ and His work. It is pure Gospel, a gift. Christ's righteousness is given (imputed) to the Christian. It becomes my righteousness as the Holy Spirit works faith in my heart. This righteousness with which I am clothed is holy, perfect, and pure. It is Christ's righteousness, the righteousness of Christ's works. It is not my righteousness resulting from my works. This righteousness is given in Baptism. Therefore, by faith the Christian can declare himself to be holy and perfect because of Jesus. By God's grace I have received His holiness through faith and I am declared by God to be one who measures up. I can look at His Law and still say that I am holy. Why? Because Christ Himself has lived the Law for me and the Holy Spirit gives to me what Jesus earned. Do I look to my neighbor to see how I measure up? No! I look to Christ, trusting that He measured up for me.

Civil righteousness (in the kingdom of the left) is different. God calls us to live holy lives in our vocations. We are called to love our neighbor. In this world we are measured by human and soci-

THE ANONYMOUS GOD

etal standards. Christians are indeed called to civil righteousness. Scripture teaches in Romans 12:17–21:

> Repay no one evil for evil, but give thought to do what is honorable in the sight of all. If possible, so far as it depends on you, live peaceably with all. Beloved, never avenge yourselves, but leave it to the wrath of God, for it is written, "Vengeance is Mine, I will repay, says the Lord." To the contrary, "if your enemy is hungry, feed him; if he is thirsty, give him something to drink; for by so doing you will heap burning coals on his head." Do not be overcome by evil, but overcome evil with good.

This passage helps us to understand that we live according to human reason in this world. Reason can grasp the good things that we do in society. Reason can produce societal good works.[24] Society stands in judgment as to whether or not the deed is good or bad according to civil righteousness. Here, good works make a difference in the Christian life. They have everything to do with loving our neighbor. However, even when society judges a work to be good, the good deeds that we do are still tainted with sin when measured against God's Law.[25] They do not bring us the holiness that God demands for salvation. However, because of Christ, the good works of believers are holy in God's eyes. The crux of the tension between our lives in the two kingdoms lies in this: that the Spirit works good works in us, but the community sees works that can be measured. This crux is understood only when Christians are involved in a daily exercise of applying Law and Gospel. The world sees the good that I do and praises it, but the Christian will still confess his sin and repent.

The Christian lives, as it were, with one foot in the kingdom of the left and one in the kingdom of the right. Standing thus, we Christians live out our vocations in daily life. We live as if everything depends upon us, yet we believe and confess that it all depends upon God. The Christian will never look to his good works and regard them as acceptable to God apart from Christ.

276

They are acceptable only by faith in Christ's work and redemption. Yet by doing the good works wrought by the Holy Spirit the Christian will be judged in the world as civic-minded, obedient, and loyal. It is not moralism to do deeds the community finds morally acceptable. Even when the community judges those deeds by its standards rather than God's standards, the Christian does good works because he is God's workmanship in Christ.[26]

CIVIL RIGHTEOUSNESS FOR THE UNBELIEVER

Civil righteousness is of critical importance in the kingdom of the left. This includes not only the civil righteousness of Christians but also that of unbelievers. For the purpose of the left-hand realm is worldly order and peace. In the kingdom of the left, Christians can acknowledge the good that unbelievers do. The unbeliever who picks up the garbage weekly does good deeds of civil righteousness, as does the unbelieving lawyer who argues cases in court. Their thought and purpose flow from created reason. Their good works are measured by the standards of society and declared to be good or bad. Morality is important here. The Christian can recognize and commend the good that a moral person brings to the community when that person, though an unbeliever, does good things for the community. Christians must not overlook the contributions unbelievers make to the ordering of society in the kingdom of the left.

In fact, Christians can and should evaluate contributions in the kingdom of the left according to their merit. For example, one does not need to be a Christian to be a good architect. In the kingdom of the left, a good architect is one who does good architectural work. However, the Christian alone realizes that the good architect and his great work, even if in designing a church, still is not spiritually good—not good in the kingdom of the right—unless the architect has by faith received the righteousness of Christ. This is the difference between spiritual and civil righteousness.

So when the architect who is a Christian puts forth his best effort, he does so moved by Christ. Still, his architecture is based upon human reason. His accomplishments are measured by reasonable human standards of good architecture, the same standards that apply to the non-Christian architect. By these standards, society will accept or reject architectural work. But the church realizes that God accepts any work only because He accepts the person who did the work by justifying that person by grace for Christ's sake through faith.

It is important to distinguish *good* in the kingdom of the left (civil righteousness) from *good* in the kingdom of the right (spiritual righteousness). This distinction helps us to avoid confusion. It is easy to fall into the trap of thinking that only Christians do "good" things in the world, but God uses the civil righteousness of unbelievers to bring order and peace into the community in the kingdom of the left. Christians can also fall into another trap: thinking that because they are doing something good by civil standards it must be acceptable to God, even though the only righteousness that avails in the kingdom of the right is the spiritual righteousness of Christ that God reckons to the believer.

THE CHRISTIAN LIFE AND AMERICAN CIVIL RELIGION

In this book's first essay, David Adams summarizes American civil religion with the aid of the template provided by Jean-Jacques Rousseau in *The Social Contract*. Rousseau's four essential dogmas of civil religion were:

1. the existence of a powerful, wise, and benevolent Divinity, who foresees and provides for the life to come;

2. the happiness of the just;

3. the punishment of the wicked; and

4. the sanctity of the social contract and the laws.

Adams adds the following two tenets, which are more unique to American civil religion:

5. the notion of America's manifest destiny and

6. the anonymity of God.

I shall use this summary to evaluate American civil religion from the standpoint of two-kingdom theology. Briefly stated, from the kingdom of the right standpoint the entire philosophy is filled with theological problems. On the other hand, from a kingdom of the left perspective American civil religion brings much good to the table.

A Mixed Bag

Let us examine the above six tenets and recognize where Christians can and cannot make use of them.

Tenets 1, 5, and 6

Tenets 1, 5, and 6 can be considered together in the kingdom of the left. They are: (1) the existence of a powerful, wise, and benevolent divinity, who foresees and provides for the life to come; (5) the notion of America's manifest destiny; and (6) the anonymity of God.

Tenets 1 and 6 recognize the existence of a god or divinity. Because the purpose of the civil realm is to bring order and peace into the world, this can be affirmed as good from a kingdom of the left perspective. To acknowledge a wise and benevolent divinity will entail a certain amount of order and morality in the society. If people know that "god is watching" and is a "wise and powerful" god, then they will curtail abhorrent behavior to an extent. Therefore, such general acknowledgment of God is good for society.

Yet—though in the kingdom of the left we Christians can applaud the recognition of a powerful, wise, benevolent, but otherwise unidentified god—in the kingdom of the right we cannot publicly join in the worship of a generic god. For we know the way in which the true God wants to be worshiped, which includes identifying Him by name. We can even give thanks for the order in society promoted by the acknowledgment of a generic god. Yet our thanks must be accompanied by prayers of repentance for any ways in which we have acknowledged false gods. Of course, we should also pray for our fellow citizens to be converted to faith in Christ and join us in God's right-hand kingdom. But Christians ought never participate in ceremonies or public proclamations that would mix worshiping any false god with worshiping the true God, the Father of our Lord Jesus Christ.

These three tenets (1, 5, 6) also speak of the divine being who "foresees and provides for the life to come" and the "notion of America's manifest destiny." In the left-hand kingdom both of these items can serve the cause of order, peace, and morality. Christians can recognize this contribution. On the other hand, we Christians understand that in Scripture God gives no guarantee of America's future, nor does He grant this country "most favored nation" status. While Christians can give thanks for the order that results from optimistic civic philosophies, we work in our daily vocations to proclaim the truth of our citizenship in God's kingdom. "Manifest destiny" is a dubious tenet even in the kingdom of the left. It has no place in the kingdom of the right.

Tenets 2, 3, and 4

Tenets 2, 3, and 4 can also be taken together. They are: (2) the happiness of the just; (3) the punishment of the wicked; and (4) the sanctity of the social contract and the laws. In the left-hand kingdom these three tenets have to do with obedience to civil law and the resulting societal order. Citizens who follow the rules will be happy. Those who do not will be punished.[27] This awareness is good for society, as Christians can agree.

In circumstances small or large, from parking restrictions and speed limits to laws against riots and terrorism, these three tenets assume an understanding of justice and morality. In the left-hand kingdom the Christian acknowledges the important role played by morality. It is easier and safer for everyone to live in a good and moral community than in a bad and immoral one. On the other hand, the Christian recognizes that morality does no good in the right-hand kingdom. No one is sufficiently "moral" in God's sight. His Law requires perfect living, inwardly as well as outwardly.

In the left-hand kingdom morality is measured, then punished or rewarded. Good deeds count for something. However, in the right-hand kingdom the sinner is not capable of perfection, and sin looms as the problem. Its only solution is the forgiveness of sins on account of Jesus Christ.

What about those matters that God calls wrong, but society calls right? One cannot misconstrue the two-kingdom theology to conclude that all things approved by society amount to civil righteousness. For example, society currently approves of abortion, yet God's Word is against it. We obey God rather than man (Acts 5:29). For the Christian, what makes something fall into the category of civil righteousness is the fact that God acknowledges something as good and it is done in the kingdom of the left. God and His Word remain supreme for the Christian. Civil righteousness does not mean what society judges as a good deed is permitted to overrule God's Word for the Christian.

As Christians live in both kingdoms we will see both good and evil. In the left-hand kingdom, living a law-abiding life is good for society. However, in the right-hand kingdom all our righteousnesses are as filthy rags and we live only by God's forgiveness in Christ.

CHRISTIAN CITIZENS LIVE IN TWO KINGDOMS

"God bless America!" How should a Christian understand this phrase? In the kingdom of the left it is good that citizens recognize a divine providence, a god. Thus they realize that there is something and someone more important than themselves, both individually and collectively as a nation. This realization promotes order in the world. It brings morals and, to a certain extent, civil peace, to a society.

On the other hand, the Christian immediately will question: "Which 'god' is supposed to bless America?" The Christian knows that only the true God—the triune God—can bestow blessing. Despite the civic realm's false confession of a generic god, we know that it is the triune God who does bless America and all governments through the means of rulers, His ministers, or servants (Romans 13:4).

The Christian knows that God's Law is written in every man's heart (Romans 2:14–15). What reason sees as common sense is really a reflection of God's Law, which the Christian knows with clarity only through revelation.[28] However, the Christian can build upon the common sense that reflects God's Law for the sake of order, civility, and morality in the community. Christians can participate in civil righteousness. God calls us to participate in the civil realm by doing good for our neighbors within our various vocations.[29] We realize, however, that these good works are wrought *only* by the Holy Spirit. The world will see "good people" whose works it will measure against other works by other people, believers and unbelievers. Yet we know that only what is done in true faith is considered a good work by God (Romans 14:23). We know that even our most admired works in this world are still filled with sin, for which we repent.

How does the Christian live with American civil religion? We Christians straddle both kingdoms, but our words and actions ought never straddle God's truth as revealed in His Word. We are called first and foremost to be faithful to the Law's First Table. We confess the God and Father of our Lord Jesus Christ, acknowledging Him as the true God who alone can bless America. We dare not fall into the trap of confessing or worshiping an unnamed generic god, a god of civic order only. That would be a confusion of societal good and civil righteousness. It is not an act of civil righteousness for the Christian to pray to, confess, or acknowledge a false god. At the same time, in the civil realm we can be supportive of the good that civil religion does for America in facilitating morality, order, and peace.

Life in God's two kingdoms brings common sense, reason, and God's Word together in the Christian's daily experience. Daily we practice distinguishing between:

- promoting morality and identifying sin;
- a bad person and a damned sinner;
- a respected civil servant and a holy child of God;
- civil righteousness and spiritual righteousness; and
- the kingdom of the left and the kingdom of the right.

	Kingdom of the Left	Kingdom of the Right
Scripture	Romans 13:1–7	Ephesians 1:22; Colossians 1:13–14
Catechism	4th Commandment, 1st Article	2nd and 3rd Articles, Baptism, Lord's Supper, Office of the Keys
Purpose	Order, civil peace	Identify sin, forgive it
Means	Reason in civil law; when law is rejected, force is used to maintain order. Lesser of two evils. Reward good, punish evil.	Christ rules through Word and Sacraments. Sin is sin, and spirtual righteousness is by faith.

Notes

1. The Rev. Mark E. Sell is senior editor of Academic, Professional, and Consumer books at Concordia Publishing House. He holds an S.T.M. in New Testament exegesis from Concordia Theological Seminary, Ft. Wayne, Indiana.

2. The following sources are helpful in summarizing two-kingdom theology: Kurt E. Marquart, "The Two Kingdoms or Governments," in *The Church and Her Fellowship, Ministry, and Governance* (Waverly, Iowa: The International Foundation for Lutheran Confessional

Research, 1990), 174–94; Gustav Wingren, *Luther on Vocation* (Evansville, Ind.: Ballast, 1994); and Paul Althaus, "The Two Kingdoms and the Two Governments," in *The Ethics of Martin Luther* (Philadelphia: Fortress, 1972), 43–82. The footnotes in Althaus's book provide a nice entry point to Luther's writings on this subject. For a primary source study, one can explore Luther's writings on "The Christian in Society" in *Luther's Works* (American Edition), vol. 44–47 (Philadelphia: Fortress, 1966, 1962, 1967, 1971). For a summary directed more toward laypeople, see Gene Edward Veith, *Spirituality of the Cross* (St. Louis: Concordia, 1999), 91–106; and *God at Work: Your Christian Vocation in All of Life* (Wheaton: Crossway, 2002). See also the chart at the end of this essay entitled "Two-Kingdom Theology." A thorough discussion of two-kingdom theology, particularly as it relates to church and state, is offered by Hermann Sasse, "Church Government and Secular Authority according to Lutheran Doctrine," in *The Lonely Way: Selected Essays and Letters*, Vol. 1, trans. Matthew Harrison (St. Louis: Concordia, 2001), 173–244.

3. Hermann Sasse wisely notes: "The correct ordering of the relationship between state and church is one of those great problems throughout the history of the church [that] must always be solved anew. . . . Still, no matter what circumstances may obtain, solving the problem of "state and church" is always one of the greatest tasks of an era" (*Lonely Way*, 1:175).

4. To some extent the human will "can achieve civil righteousness or the righteousness of works. It can talk about God and express its worship of him in outward works" (Ap. XVIII, 4 [Tappert, 225]).

5. Scripture quotations in this essay are taken from the ESV.

6. "Reason" must be understood in a precritical perspective. It does not mean something that is "purely instrumental and content-free, namely logic, 'I.Q.,' or the computing function. . . . Rather [it is] a power of judgment deeply embedded in man's irreducibly moral nature (Romans 1:20; 2:14, 15)" (Marquart, "Two Kingdoms or Governments," 176). On the other hand, when reason is objectified, it produces the romantic and naïve conclusions of modernism, which turn science into a deity that will solve all human problems. A modernistic approach to Scripture and creation eventually removes Christ from both. Furthermore, reason embraces the order that God, as creator, has built into the cosmos. Thereby, reason is shaped by what we understand as the first use of the Law.

7. See also 1 Timothy 2:2; 1 Peter 2:13, 14.

8. A desire to avoid theocracy sets Lutheran theology apart from both Reformed and Roman Catholic theology. Roman Catholic and

Reformed churches seek to Christianize society. This confusion of the two kingdoms also confuses believers as they seek to live out their vocations. Although Christians often seek biblical answers to daily decisions, God's Word does not address most situations we face in direct or detailed ways. In these situations Lutherans apply the gift of reason, which is one of God the Father's gifts to His creatures; see Luther's explanation of the First Article of the Apostles' Creed. Sasse wrote: "Over against the ascetic and theocratic errors of the Papal Church and those of fanaticism [*Schwaermertum*], this 'high necessary article' regarding secular authority shows 'what a gloriously great office' the office of secular authority is (Ap XVI 13 [65 German][sic]). It admonishes the spiritual office to be mindful of its limitations and to acknowledge and honor the office of secular authority with its tasks and value" (*Lonely Way*, 1:179, 180).

9. Marquart, "Two Kingdoms or Governments," 176.

10. The Augsburg Confession links two-kingdom theology to authority: "Our teachers have been compelled, for the sake of comforting consciences, to point out the difference between spiritual and temporal power, sword, and authority, and they have taught that, because of God's command, both authorities and powers are to be honored and esteemed with all reverence as the two highest gifts of God on earth" (AC XXVIII, 4 [Tappert, 81]). See also AC XXVIII, 12–14 (Tappert, 83).

11. "To fatherhood and motherhood God has given the special distinction, above all estates that are beneath it, that he commands us not simply to love our parents but also to honor them. . . . Thus he distinguishes father and mother above all other persons on earth, and places them next to himself. . . . Honor includes not only love but also deference, humility, and modesty, directed (so to speak) toward a majesty hidden within them . . . that we respect them very highly and that next to God we give them the very highest place. . . . Therefore, we are not to think of their persons, whatever they are, but of the will of God, who has created and ordained them to be our parents. In other respects, indeed, we are all equal in the sight of God, but among ourselves there must be this sort of inequality and proper distinctions. God therefore commands you to be careful to obey me as your father and to acknowledge my authority" (Large Catechism I, 108–10 [Tappert, 379–80]).

12. Large Catechism I, 141–42 (Tappert, 384).

13. By church, we do not mean the institutionalized church, local or national. Rather, we mean the *Una Sancta* or the kingdom of God.

14. Additional passages could be cited, along with imagery of Christ's

church as bride, body, temple, heavenly company, communion of saints, etc. The Augsburg Confession says that the "one holy church is to continue forever. The church is the congregation of saints, in which the Gospel is rightly taught and the Sacraments are rightly administered" (AC VII, 1 [Tappert, 32]).

15. See Althaus, *Ethics of Martin Luther*, 59–61.

16. Here one can begin to grasp how the order of creation serves the order of salvation. Order serves salvation and thus places creation in the proper context. Without this context, order exists only for the sake of order, a view that might be characterized as more Calvinist than Lutheran. The biblical teaching of Christ's incarnation places creation in service to salvation.

17. See Veith, *Spirituality of the Cross*, 71–90. This "daily divinity" of life helps Christians, especially church workers, appropriately understand their call in the church's life. It provides the biblical structure for understanding the relationship among the auxiliary offices of the church. See also Kenneth A. Cherney Jr., "Hidden in Plain Sight: Luther's Doctrine of Vocation," *Wisconsin Lutheran Quarterly* 78 (Fall 2001): 278–90. Cherney correctly points out that there is "relative silence" among Lutherans on the doctrine of vocation. "A good dose of vocation is the medicine that would cure much of the confusion that exists in the area of church and ministry and what is the role of the layperson in the church. We must get back to elevating other works of love: the binding of wounds, feeding the hungry, clothing the naked. Playing with a child. Giving my employer or my customer his money's worth" (289).

18. Veith, *Spirituality of the Cross*, 73.

19. Einar Billing, *Our Calling* (Rock Island, Ill.: Augustana Press, 1958), 8.

20. Billing, *Our Calling*, 11. Does vocation come through the Law or through the Gospel? There is a difference between Billing's *Our Calling* and Wingren's *Luther on Vocation*, but this is not the place to contrast and compare these two fine works on vocation.

21. See Veith, *God at Work*, 18, for an overview of vocation and the different offices God uses.

22. "God's commandments take on specific form for us in terms of our station and vocation. Our station is the place—although not the only place—where we are to obey God. Our work in this vocation or station is our appropriate service to God. Since God has commanded this work, it certainly pleases him. As a result, Luther rejects any piety that tries to find especially 'holy' works. Luther constantly contrasts the works that God commands us to do in our station and vocation

with the pious works that we choose for ourselves" (Althaus, *Ethics of Martin Luther*, 39).

23. "Therefore we may profitably distinguish between civil righteousness and spiritual righteousness, attributing the former to the free will and the latter to the operation of the Holy Spirit in the regenerate. This safeguards outward discipline, because all men ought to know that God requires this civil righteousness and that, to some extent, we can achieve it" (Ap. XVIII, 9 [Tappert, 226]).

24. "Reason can produce civil works" (Ap. IV, 27 [Tappert, 111]). Again, "Our opponents concentrate on the commandments of the second table, which contain the civil righteousness that reason understands" (Ap. IV, 34 [Tappert, 111]).

25. "If the mind that is set on the flesh is hostile to God, then the flesh sins even when it performs outward civil works. If it cannot submit to God's law, it is certainly sinning even when it produces deeds that are excellent and praiseworthy in human eyes" (Ap. IV, 33 [Tappert, 111]).

26. Ephesians 2:8–10. See Romans 14:23: "For whatever does not proceed from faith is sin."

27. Luther wrote in explaining the Fourth Commandment, "If you are unwilling to obey father and mother or to submit to them, then obey the hangman; and if you will not obey him, then obey the grim reaper, Death! This, in short, is the way God will have it: render him obedience and love and service, and he will reward you abundantly with every blessing; on the other hand, if you provoke him to anger, he will send upon you both death and the hangman" (Large Catechism I, 135, 136 [Tappert, 383]).

28. On the necessity and existence of vocations or stations Althaus writes, "Reason also recognizes that they are necessary and useful for the world—this knowledge is part of the natural law that everyone knows. However, only the Christian knows that these stations have been established by God. They are instituted, presupposed, recognized, and honored by the Scripture and are therefore 'contained and involved in God's word and commandment.' Christians alone know and teach that these are divine ordinances and institutions. Therefore, they alone can truly give thanks and pray for them in their churches" (Althaus, *The Ethics of Martin Luther*, 38–39, quoting WA 26, 505 [LW 37, 365] and WA 31.1:410 [LW 13, 370]).

29. "This commandment of love, valid everywhere and for all people, becomes specific for us as individuals in the context of the station of life in which God has placed us. Through our station in life we are placed into a definite and particular relationship to one another" (Althaus, *The Ethics of Martin Luther*, 36).